502.3 PRI

KW-135-966

CONSERVATION POLICY DIRECTIONS

*An annotated digest of recent papers
by The Royal Society for the Protection of Birds*

WITHDRAWN

WITHDRAWN

CONSERVATION POLICY DIRECTIONS

An annotated digest of recent papers
by The Royal Society for the Protection of Birds

edited by

D. E. Pritchard

Copyright © Cameron May 1996

Published 1996 by Cameron May Ltd., 69 - 71 Bondway, London
SW8 1SQ, Tel: +44 (0)171 582 7567, Fax:+44 (0)171 793 8353

*All rights reserved. Except for the quotation of short passages for the purpose of criticism and
review, no part of this publication may be reproduced, stored in a retrieval system or transmitted,
in any form or by any means, electronic, mechanical, photocopying, recording or otherwise,
without prior permission of the publisher.*

*This book is sold subject to the condition that it shall not by way of trade or be lent, re-sold, hired
out, or otherwise circulated without the publisher's prior consent in any form of binding or cover
other than that which it is published and without a similar condition including this condition
being imposed on the subsequent purchaser.*

ISBN 1874698 76 7

RESOURCE CENTRE, SPARSHOLT COLLEGE, HAMPSHIRE

ACCESSION No: 021960   WITHDRAWN   X

CLASS NUMBER: SL   502.3 PRI

Cover Design: Vivienne Reay

CONTENTS

Chapter 11 WETLANDS AND WATER 162

Chapter 12 AGRICULTURE POLICY 184

Chapter 13 FORESTRY POLICY 210

Chapter 14 TRANSPORT AND ENERGY 221

FOREWORD

Over the past quarter century most people and institutions have become better aware of the environmental dimension in all human affairs.

We may bemoan lack of progress in putting environmental policies into effect and the apparent obtuseness of those in the seats of power, whether in government, industry, business, academe or elsewhere for not seeing the green light. Yet understanding of environmental issues is better and more widely spread than ever before and the burden of proof now rests with those who want to exclude environmental considerations. Such terms as ozone holes and the greenhouse effect have entered the common currency. Even in the five years since the Rio Conference on Environment and Development, advance has been rapid. There is now little excuse for failure to act.

At the Rio Conference and since, nongovernmental organisations have played an increasingly important role. They can often bring people and ideas together in a way beyond the reach of governments or international organizations. Among the nongovernmental organisations the Royal Society for the Protection of Birds has a high and much respected place. The current collection will show what the RSPB has been doing for conservation, what its ideas are and how it insinuates them into the processes of policy formulation. I commend a book which demonstrates how environmental policy has arrived at the centre of the decision-making process.

Sir Crispin Tickell GCMG KCVO.

ACKNOWLEDGEMENTS

This book draws on the work of a huge number of past and present RSPB staff, sometimes aided by consultants, advisors and collaborators. Their painstaking efforts are warmly acknowledged.

Assistance in marshalling material or advising on aspects of this project was also provided by Lloyd Austin, Clifton Bain, Olivia Bina, Barnaby Briggs, Sarah Brennan, Clare Brooke, Paul Buckley, Brian Cleary, Jacqui Cuff, Jonathan Curtoys, Jim Dixon, Andrew Dodd, Margaret Duncan, Euan Dunn, John Faulks, Sarah Fowler, Debbie Fuggles, David Harley, Deborah Harrison, Duncan Huggett, Rob Lake, Ian McCall, Clive Mellon, Lesley Nundy, Daniel Owen, Nathalie Pillow, Matthew Rayment, Phil Rothwell, Steve Sankey, Sara Smith, Mark Southgate, Vicki Swales, John Taylor, Roger Turner, Nicola Watts, Julie Wilbraham, Gwyn Williams, Robin Wynde, Graham Wynne and June Young.

CONSERVATION
POLICY
DIRECTIONS

*An annotated digest of recent papers
by The Royal Society for the Protection of Birds*

Introduction

THE RSPB AND CONSERVATION POLICY

By any measure, there is huge public sympathy for wildlife in the United Kingdom (UK). A significant part of the motive of the thousands who join organisations like The Royal Society for the Protection of Birds is simply a shared celebration of the joy of birds and nature. To some, it may seem wrong to sully this with the less than virginal world of policy or, worse, politics.

In reality there can be little justice done even to sharing a sense of values, much less making those values persist and count for something in the world, without active involvement in policy. The RSPB was in fact a radical campaigning organisation from its inception in the late 19th Century, successfully engaged in the cut and thrust of Parliamentary lobbying for protection of birds against mass killing for their plumes.

Most fields of public policy have some implications for the well-being or otherwise of the natural world. In order for the RSPB to secure its objectives, it must spend time and money influencing the content and implementation of laws, policies and decisions which might help or hinder those objectives. This requires capabilities in analysis, advocacy and tactics. These in turn must be backed up by a clear legitimacy for our claim on decision-makers' attention, which comes from our significant constituency of public support and a record of credible performance. These are not won easily but the RSPB is fortunate to have them in abundance. More is needed, as the pressures the Society faces in doing its job mount inexorably.

This book draws on the efforts of an army of specialised experts working for the RSPB on economics, fisheries, town planning, farming, road traffic and a host of other facets of the administration of modern society. A Parliamentary Unit oversees the interface with the legislature. RSPB policy-thinking influences the attitudes of political leaders and the drafting of new laws, is requested in evidence to Parliamentary Select Committee inquiries and features prominently in (among other things) guidance to decision-makers, land-use frameworks adopted by local councils and the strategies of corporate industry. Examples of all of these are presented here.

The RSPB cannot afford to ignore any of the multitude of policy issues which affect its interests. Equally, no policy-making or policy-implementing entity can afford to ignore environmental factors. Human society may have had phases of believing that, for example through technology, it has been subjugating the natural world. In reality our dependence on natural resources, healthy skies, seas, soils and waters and all the ecosystem functions and values of the earth's life-support systems was always going to lead to realisation of the fundamental concept of environmental sustainability, which is now accepted as a goal for the world's leaders.

Sound environmental choices can be and are sound commercial and developmental choices. Any policy needs to be workable in the light of the environmental constraints which operate and also in terms of what the public is prepared to accept as an environmental price for material gain. The currency of this latter point may be as much a cultural and aesthetic one as a utilitarian one (if indeed such a stark distinction is valid), but is no less important for that. For these reasons, the argued case the RSPB puts forward on any issue deserves close attention.

On this basis, the bird conservation policy agenda might appear to consist of everything and anything. One of the most prominent characteristics of the work of the RSPB and some other conservation bodies in the past decade has been the evolution of methods for systematically prioritising effort so that it is as focused and cost-effective as possible. Good housekeeping should be taken as read for subscription-based charities and the tools of the trade for ensuring this among the larger players have come to resemble those of any corporate business.

The question of effectiveness, however, demands deeper thought when it is measured by the fortunes of wild birds. Deciding which species need more help than others, identifying the critical elements in the nature of that help, quantifying results and attributing results to causes are all fundamental requirements. "Red lists" and action plans for species and habitats now underpin all of the choices the RSPB makes about where to direct its efforts, where to avoid wasting effort and where risks borne of uncertainty are acceptable or unacceptable. These explicit rationales provide a framework for defining targets and accounting for success and failure. Carefully thought-out mid term strategies help to maintain the focus. This businesslike approach marks a certain coming of age of the conservation movement as a whole. The examples of what emerges from this process given in Chapter 1 of this book, which draw on the collaborative efforts of several organisations, help to set the scene for what then follows.

There are a number of characteristics which distinguish the way the RSPB in particular pursues policy and other work. For example, we painstakingly build a scientific research foundation for any stance we adopt. Being able to show with sufficient rigour the biological basis of our views may mean that they cannot be developed overnight; but their resulting greater robustness is more important.

The RSPB's style of operation consciously seeks to be positive and constructive. It is not sufficient to clamour ever more loudly about the threats and woes afflicting wildlife, without at the same time being able to offer realistic and well-researched solutions which meet the other legitimate social and economic needs which exist. Hence we must be technically competent to map out future strategies for farm incomes, urban regeneration and water supply, for example, just as ably as we may define regimes for habitat management. Conflict is often inevitable and embroilment in it may provide a natural short-term crusading gratification: but the end result is the important thing and wherever possible the RSPB will seek first and foremost to build a problem-solving partnership among key players to find the most durable solutions. Chapter 16 shows how even litigation can be used in this way.

The picture presented by this book is very different from the one many people would conjure up to portray what conservation campaigning is about. Painstaking searching-out of opportunities, gradual piece-by-piece building up of a case sometimes over years, waiting to make a move when the time is right, building a sequence of moves, like a chess-game, to manoeuvre into the desired position, diplomatic shadow-boxing and reading between the lines are all truer representations than the tabloid headlines might have us believe. Provocatively polarised disputes can certainly mark watersheds in advancing the cause, either to jolt a necessary awareness of the seriousness of an issue, or as a last resort when other techniques have failed. There is nothing wrong with wildlife conservation being a passionate business: indeed it is too important not to be.

Notwithstanding this, the RSPB has built a certain reputation for being more "behind the scenes" in its method of operation, believing that this tends to be more productive. Some of our influence is obvious. Much of it, however, is won by quietly persuading others to adopt our thinking as their own and promoting it without necessarily revealing the real guiding hand behind it.

It might be thought that the stricter the controls applied by law and policy on those things which harm wildlife, the better it would be for the RSPB's interests. But this is an oversimplified view. A more durable approach is to have an appropriate mix of incentives and controls, giving a balanced set of tools to achieve a wide range of tasks. Relying on compulsion at every turn would make the whole business overly negative, and risk mere minimal grudging compliance with requirements, stifling voluntary initiative and being dependent on labour-intensive enforcement. It would also inevitably be met by pressure for increased rights of redress against perceived disadvantage. This said, aspects of existing regulations are without doubt effectively toothless and considerable improvements are required.

The models which the RSPB advances for decision-making régimes are based on a vision of workable systems which serve the public interest, in which nature conservation objectives are given the importance we believe they deserve. This does not mean providing maximum scope for special pleading or "cheating" so that "birds win" every time, regardless. Rather, we set great store by rational and transparent observance of a due process which pays sufficient regard to testing claimed needs, examining alternative options, honestly reviewing information about environmental impact, setting targets and objectives, making prudent use of natural resources, valuing significance correctly, erring on the side of caution when there are environmental risks, and so on. By these lights, we must accept that birds cannot prevail over all other public interests every time there is a conflict. Sometimes other things must prevail. But there must be rational ways of making sure that this happens only when there is a genuine and proven case, according to standards such as these, for it to do so.

It is also a feature of the RSPB's style of working that, once all of the factors described above are in play and the Society has committed to a cause which it believes is right, it will champion it tenaciously to the end with no half-measures. This is a logical corollary of an approach based on research and targeting and under full sail it represents a formidable force with an impressive record.

All of these ingredients realise their full value when a consistent pattern and a record of performance takes shape over a period of years. The RSPB's influence and credentials draw on this well-known track record and reliability, in addition to the specifics of any one involvement.

Increasing trends of globalisation affect conservation as much as some other fields of policy. Bird conservation objectives have themselves substantially been defined on an international canvas from the start. Migratory birds are the classic example of the nonsense it would be to provide protection in one part of their range of distribution and not in another: hence the need for international legal agreements on the subject. As is pointed out, for example in Chapter 12, for issues like agriculture, the "domestic" policy arena is in effect the European Union (EU) and it is at that level that the RSPB must engage to achieve anything for UK interests. The selection of topics in this book leans primarily towards what the RSPB does in the UK, rather than attempting to do equal justice to our international programmes: but clearly this distinction is of only limited validity.

As explained further in the section on "the approach taken in this book" below, the topics addressed here are a sample which does not attempt to be scientifically representative of the policy work the RSPB does. They do, however, signal some of the most important areas of concern. The issues of species exploitation and persecution, which caused the Society to be formed, led on in time to more habitat-based preoccupations; though as Chapter 16 shows, there are still too many species-protection problems persisting in the present day. Campaigns to save important sites from destruction by development involved the Society in building up expertise in the planning system: Chapters 7 (on development plans) and 8 (on development control) show some of the current issues on this front, while site protection law itself features in Chapter 4. Decision-making frameworks of all sorts can benefit from techniques for environmental appraisal and this is covered in Chapter 5.

Safeguarded sites are indispensable but are only part of the picture and the fortunes of wild birds are perhaps more fundamentally influenced by policies determining the way the generality of the countryside is managed. Chapters on wetlands and water (Chapter 11), agriculture (Chapter 12) and forestry (Chapter 13) explore examples of these. Wise use of natural resources is central to notions of environmental sustainability: as well as featuring in Chapter 11 on water (and in Chapter 10 which is devoted to a range of problems particular to our marine and coastal ecosystems), this subject is prominent in Chapter 9 (minerals and waste) and Chapter 14 (transport and energy).

No policy endeavour is free of knotty debates about institutional structures for delivering action, and while this crops up in several places (including the Chapters on marine and coastal policy and on forestry policy), it is central to Chapter 3 (the Environment Agencies) and Chapter 6 (local government organisation and regional planning). No area of policy can be divorced from the realities of economics either, though as Chapters 2 (rural policy) and 15 (trade, employment and structural funds) both show, there is huge scope for these forces to work with the grain of conservation objectives rather than necessarily against them. Finally, as mentioned earlier, the modern approach to setting objectives for biodiversity conservation is explored in Chapter 1.

This book goes to press at a time the UK is anticipating a General Election. It will be obvious to the reader that the future of wildlife and the environment is inextricably linked with the economic and social issues which traditionally loom large at such times. It is equally obvious to the RSPB that deep public concern on the environment makes it a voting issue which political parties underestimate at their peril. Biodiversity has huge economic value as the basis of our life-support system and millions of people treasure the countryside. The cost of about £40 million per year which has been put on implementing action plans under the UK Biodiversity Action Plan makes wildlife conservation an extremely cost-effective endeavour.

The RSPB has a clear view of the priorities a "greener" Government should set itself. For example, environmental concerns need integrating with economic decisions and the tax system. Doing so creates jobs in areas such as energy efficiency, pollution control and waste management schemes. Nature conservation employs more than 10,000 people in the UK, many in rural areas with currently high unemployment. Money spent on agriculture should switch from subsidy to environmental schemes. Transport spending should focus on public transport, not roads. Responsibility for the environment must be at the heart of all government decisions. All departments and agencies need environmental objectives. We must ensure through the education system that young people are equipped with an understanding of the environment so that they become wise guardians of the Earth's future.

At the time of writing, some 70 Sites of Special Scientific Interest (SSSIs) are threatened by road proposals alone. Changes are urgently needed. New roads, ports and airports should not be built on key UK habitats. New environmental objectives and targets, including new limits on pollution, must be set for transport. Effective action must be taken to counter the threat to our coastal fisheries, communities and wildlife from oil spills and deliberate discharge of oily waste. Water abstraction also damages wildlife sites. More than 50 rivers suffer low flows and 56 SSSIs are being damaged by abstraction. We need a long-term approach to managing water demand if we are to protect the environment and provide supplies for everyone.

Farming has a profound influence on the environment: it is a threat to biodiversity yet can also contribute to conservation. The Common Agricultural Policy needs to be part of a rural and environmental policy for Europe, based on environmental protection, rural development and sustainable agriculture. Farmers should be stewards of the countryside as well as producers of food. At sea, overfishing is driving key fish stocks to a point from which they may be unable to recover. Europe has failed to reduce fishing effort enough to safeguard stocks: the UK has been among the slowest to reduce its fleet. The UK Government must take firmer action to ensure sustainable fisheries.

In relation to energy, the commitment to a 60% reduction of sulphur emissions is a positive step but will leave a quarter of the area of all SSSIs at risk from acidification. Action to reduce energy use throughout the economy is urgently needed. The EU is not on target to meet its commitments and the UK Government should take a lead. Protected areas are in trouble more generally too. UK SSSIs (with SSSIs in Northern Ireland) cover 8% of the land surface. In England about 120 are damaged by development each year. Protecting these is vital if our wildlife is to survive. Finally, environmental improvement could be achieved by a more creative approach to land-use issues. The potential for putting back some of what we have lost is enormous.

The well-developed nature of advocacy agendas such as these among a wide range of nongovernmental organisations (NGOs) in the UK is testament to a relatively long history of such debate in this country and to a tradition of a strong voluntary sector through which public concern on the subject is voiced. By comparison with many countries, UK NGOs are well resourced, articulate and often influential. It is an irony that this sort of situation is most evident in just those countries which are the most industrialised and populated and whose countryside, wildlife and natural resources have already suffered most. The strength of the UK conservation NGO movement certainly represents an awakened popular realisation of the need to plan for an environmentally sustainable future: but this awakening has been more of a reaction to a crisis than prudent forethought. Unfortunately, it seems probable that the same pattern will emerge in many other nations in their turn.

Although appreciation of what needs doing is growing, the strength of NGO efforts is not always matched by the statutory sector's efforts. This is as much a statement about decisions by the Treasury as it is about the actions of the conservation agencies themselves. Splitting a formerly unified Great Britain agency has not helped either. As the RSPB has become an increasingly respected (some might say a rather "establishment") player in the policy-forming and decision-making process, we have noted a growing tendency for the process to rely more and more heavily on what we offer to it. In one sense, this is what we have striven for and we pride ourselves on delivering a crucial rôle effectively and with influence. At the same time, however, there must be some concern that more of a mainstream public responsibility than before may be falling to the voluntary sector. If such work were better funded by the Exchequer instead, NGO resources could be deployed in extra ways so that more is delivered overall. Subscribing RSPB members are also tax paying citizens who expect environmental responsibilities to be properly shouldered by the public authorities acting on their behalf.

The question must be asked, finally, whether all this strenuous activity is producing real progress and benefits. Answering this is not very straightforward. At least the RSPB has the tools, in terms of species and habitat targets, success criteria and performance indicators, to make objective judgements about success or failure in terms of the birds and habitats themselves and to encourage others to measure progress by these "end objectives" rather than simply the amount of activity towards them.

For some of the highest priority species there is positive news. There are signs of encouraging recovery in the corncrake population and stone-curlews are faring better than in recent years. Bittern numbers have shown the beginning of an upswing, following intensive reedbed rehabilitation efforts, while red kites have increased in Wales and are showing successful results from reintroduction projects in England and Scotland. There are sorrier tales to tell as well. Disastrous declines in familiar species on farmland such as grey partridge, skylark and song thrush have been documented and capercaillie and black grouse are suffering in the uplands.

Attributing any of these to particular policy events or attitudes, however, is not easy. Inappropriate building of roads and other developments, inefficient management of water resources and overfishing of the seas might indicate that conservationists' proposals have fallen on deaf ears. Each of these, however, can of course be matched by examples of more enlightened actions and the evolution of a national Action Plan for Biodiversity must represent a particularly significant forward step.

One factor worth pointing to as a positive sign is that in many areas the nature of the discourse has moved on significantly. Initially there may have been uncomprehendingly polarised worldviews which repeatedly clashed, leaving one side victor and the other vanquished. Now (although the picture is not uniform throughout the UK), more often the basic mission of each "side" is better understood by the other, fewer opportunities are missed for both to be accommodated together and there should be fewer simplistic confrontations. This means that the focus of the RSPB's policy dealings with decision-makers and others can increasingly be about adding value for nature conservation to what otherwise would be done and taking positive opportunities. There are numerous examples of this in this book.

The remaining question is whether the overall sum of society's actions is starting to deliver better custodianship of the natural world than it previously did, in net terms. Part of the answer to this may be that however good or bad it happens to be at present, it would have been a lot worse without the persistent pressure on policy matters which has been exerted by the RSPB and like-minded organisations.

The practitioner's point of view would probably be that a certain dynamic tension or equilibrium operates whereby a "gain" to conservation interests (say a strengthening of legal interpretations concerning site protection, in caselaw or in planning guidance) is counteracted (perhaps somewhere quite different in the system) by a "gain" to opposing interests (say a move to reduce the number of sites covered by the provisions at issue). This can make the process feel like taking two steps forward then two steps back. Analysts may see only one side of this and draw mistaken conclusions about how much real progress is being made. The challenge of making progress in net terms is clearly a painstaking business needing long timescales.

This book gives a brief flavour of what is involved in a form which has not been available before. It seems certain that future years will require at least as much if not more considered inputs to policy-making and implementation, in order to continue championing the cause of bird conservation. The RSPB's commitment to this is as strong as it is possible to be.

The approach taken in this book

The structure of this book should allow the reader to focus on individual topics in any order, with the help of the contents list and some cross-references between linked items. The structure is described a little further below, followed by an explanation of the approach which has been taken to the selection of items for inclusion. This includes some important caveats to bear in mind.

Each listed item is a summary of a recent policy paper produced by the RSPB, or sometimes the RSPB together with others. These are presented in a standard format, beginning with the title or citation (including the date), followed by the summary (of varying length, depending on the original document). At the end of each summary a short "comment" is given. This provides a brief up-to-date insight into the political context for the work: perhaps the significance of the issue, the climate of debate at the time and what happened subsequently.

The 80 summarised papers have been grouped into 16 subject-based chapters. It will be readily apparent that there is no ideal breakdown of mutually exclusive topics: many policy initiatives and political opportunities do not fit neatly under a single heading. For example, Strategic Environmental Assessment (SEA) of water resources or transport, or mineral extraction in the marine environment, could each be placed in one of two or more chapters. A pragmatic approach, with cross-references, has been the only possible one to take here. To an extent, the chapters mirror areas of specialist activity in the RSPB and readers wishing to pursue issues in more detail should be able readily to locate staff in relevant work centres.

The items included are a selection of some of the more interesting ones from, in the main, a period from the beginning of 1995 to the summer of 1996. This means that they give a snapshot of one phase of policy activity. While part of the intention has been to indicate the variety of this, this has been done with examples: in no way has it been attempted to make the selection comprehensive or scientifically representative. Unless indicated, no particular point should be inferred about the relative importance or priority of items included.

As a consequence, it may be that a policy paper on an issue which is more significant than the one included here was perhaps produced the preceding year: if reference to this is important to an understanding of what the RSPB was seeking to achieve, or had achieved, then this will generally be given in the "comment" under the included item. The same applies to the implied balance of effort between different topics: a snapshot from a different period might show many more items in some chapters and fewer in others.

Other work of a similar type exists which happens to fall outside the selection given here, such as education policy, or much of the RSPB's international policy work: again a pragmatic and, some might argue, somewhat arbitrary dividing-line has had to be drawn.

The sequence in which items are presented is based mainly on grouping them according to some logic of how they may be most instructively read, perhaps in notional "sub topics". Hence there is not necessarily a chronological ordering within chapters and again no implication as to priority, except that in a sub grouping the most important or most general item may be presented first.

Many of the papers summarised here are technical working documents or submissions which have not previously been distributed to a wide public (although even some of these, by filling a vacuum, have become almost standard reference works among practitioners). The full texts should in almost all cases be available on request from the RSPB. The more major ones may carry a cover charge. Readers wishing to obtain additional sources of information which complement the material here may find it useful to be placed on mailing lists for newsletters, such as *Conservation Planner* which is sent to town and country planners. The Society also publishes the annual *RSPB Conservation Review* containing a wide variety of in-depth papers giving additional insights into aspects of our conservation work.

David E. Pritchard,
RSPB,
The Lodge, Sandy,
Bedfordshire, SG19 2DL
December 1996

Chapter 1

BIODIVERSITY AND SUSTAINABILITY

M aking tangible sense of the concept of environmentally sustainable development is a challenge all environmental
groups and society at large have been attempting to grapple with
for two decades or more. The concept has been given sharper focus
and at the same time more voluminous commentary since the Earth
Summit in Rio de Janeiro in 1992. It pervades the whole conservation policy agenda and is therefore placed first in this collection.
Target- and objective-driven plans of action for prioritised habitat
and species interests constitute one of the milestone achievements
of the conservation movement in recent years; and the papers summarised here emphasise that measures of the fate of biodiversity
based on these are a key test of whether sustainability is being
achieved. Some of the most significant documents on this have been
produced by a broad coalition of conservation interests and are included here as exceptions to the general approach in this book of
presenting only the RSPB's own papers.

Biodiversity Challenge: an agenda for conservation in the UK.
Second edition. **Wynne, G, Avery, M, Campbell, L, Gubbay, S,**
Hawkswell, S, Juniper, T, King, M, Newbery, P, Smart, J, Steel, C,
Stones, T, Stubbs, A, Taylor, J, Tydeman, C and Wynde, R 1995.

Summary

1. *Biodiversity Challenge* makes the case for and sets out a systematic approach to the conservation of biodiversity in the UK. The
first edition was produced in 1993 by a group of six voluntary conservation bodies as a contribution to the production of a UK
Biodiversity Action Plan.

2. In January 1994, the Government published *Biodiversity: the*
UK Action Plan - a tentative though valuable step in the right direc-
tion. One year on, the same six organisations (the "Challenge
Group") have published this enlarged and revised edition of
Biodiversity Challenge as a contribution to the Government's con-
tinuing biodiversity work. It is intended to help take the UK Action
Plan forward and addresses many of the challenges set by the Plan,

drawing on the knowledge of dozens of experts across the conservation spectrum.

3. The Challenge Group argues that planning and action to conserve UK biodiversity should be sharply focused on outcome - what needs to be achieved for individual species in terms of numbers, ranges and habitats in terms of extent and quality. The *Biodiversity Challenge* approach is therefore objective-led.

4. We provide in this document an audit of UK biodiversity, giving particular attention to internationally important and threatened species and habitats. The number and variety of species in serious decline is a cause for very great concern.

5. We propose broad conservation objectives and detailed targets for species and habitats in the UK. Targets are essential to set the direction for conservation action, to monitor progress and to enable actions to be reviewed in the light of their success or failure. We present over 600 species targets and 35 habitat targets to demonstrate the feasibility of the approach. The targets are ambitious but realistic and refer to a period of about the next 10 years.

6. We argue that a priority in the UK must be conservation of those species and habitats for which the UK is internationally important. This is essential if action at the national level is to meet the ultimate goal of conserving global biodiversity. We argue that high priority should also be given to threatened species and habitats; they are not more important than others, they are simply in need of more urgent action. If the needs of these priority groups are comprehensively addressed, biodiversity as a whole will benefit enormously.

7. We propose that conservation action plans should be written as soon as possible for all priority species and habitats. We present here 50 example plans to demonstrate the feasibility of the approach. Both the preparation and implementation of plans will be essential if our conservation targets are to be met. The UK Action Plan calls for targets and action plans to be produced for globally threatened and endemic species. The 44 species action plans we present therefore cover a high proportion of the globally threatened and many of the endemic species which occur in the UK. Summary action plans are provided for six important habitats.

8. We argue that to be successful, conservation objectives and targets must be embedded in all aspects of government policy and action. We believe that the conservation of biodiversity is a key "test" of sustainability; development cannot be regarded as sustainable unless biodiversity is conserved. Responsibility for meeting biodiversity targets must be shared between government departments and not treated as the concern of a single sector of government.

9. We recognise the wide range of threats facing the natural environment and call for an equally wide range of solutions, from a much improved research and monitoring base to fundamental policy shifts in areas such as agriculture, fisheries and forestry. We propose an agenda of the key actions needed to conserve our biodiversity: a synthesis of those identified in our species and habitat plans and of the underlying policy changes required.

10. We address the difficult issue of the resources needed for biodiversity conservation and consider various approaches to costing biodiversity targets. We show that conservation action can often make more economic sense and sometimes be cheaper than implementing schemes which damage the environment.

11. We recognise that both *Biodiversity Challenge* and the UK Action Plan are simply beginnings. We present this document in a spirit of collaboration to the many government departments and agencies, other organisations and individuals who must act urgently if our biodiversity is to be conserved. Some environments, particularly the sea, continue to prove difficult to cover adequately and present a particular challenge to us all. We also freely acknowledge that this document is focused primarily on the biodiversity of the UK and that there is a pressing need to address the wider international impacts of UK policy in a structured and similarly determined fashion.

12. Our remaining biodiversity is vitally important and highly vulnerable. We must reduce the extent to which its continued existence is left to chance. A more systematic approach to conservation must be adopted, focused sharply on the end results. The UK Government now has a superb opportunity to pioneer an objective-led approach to biodiversity conservation and thus to show the way forward to the international community. We offer this document as a visionary but practical contribution to the implementation of the UK Action Plan.

Comment

The UK Government was committed to producing a national Biodiversity Action Plan following its signature of the Convention on Biological Diversity in Rio de Janeiro in 1992. The UK voluntary conservation sector saw this as a key opportunity to press jointly for the best possible product. The production of the *Challenges* was timed to shadow the UK Government's own process. *Biodiversity Challenge I* was produced in December 1993, just prior to the first Government document (*Biodiversity: the UK Action Plan*) which emerged in January 1994. *Biodiversity Challenge II*, summarised here, marked the first anniversary of the publication of the UK Plan and sought to keep the spotlight on the need for continuing progress while expanding the material presented to include a number of worked-up examples of plans and targets. Promotion of this was also pursued through the voluntary organisations' involvements with the UK Biodiversity Steering Group (and its sub-groups) which produced its official report in December 1994.

The UK Government response to the Steering Group report was published as Command paper *Cm 3260* in May 1996. This gave a welcome endorsement to the report of the Steering Group and to the action plans associated with it (116 for species and 14 for habitats); and the process for completing plans for a further 286 species and 24 habitats was approved. The status given to the document, its joint "ownership" by all key Secretaries of State and the setting up of a proper Biodiversity Secretariat were all seen as welcome by the Challenge Group. Important principles such as policy integration, a leadership rôle for Government and the use of biodiversity as a key test of sustainability were accepted by Government, as generally were the targets and costings suggested. The RSPB and others were however critical of the failure to put forward any new resources for biodiversity conservation; and the key challenge for Government will remain in the implementation of these measures across all sectors in an integrated way.

The Challenge Group has also issued summary leaflets for different target readerships, such as *Biodiversity Challenge: a practical guide to conserving biodiversity for local authorities* (1995), *Biodiversity Challenge: a guide to help your organisation conserve biodiversity* (1995), and *Biodiversity Action and the Environment Agency* (1996).

Environmental Measures / indicators for the UK environment.
**Published by the Environment Challenge Group. MacGillivray,
A (Ed) 1994.**

Summary

1. There is a strong case for using indicators to describe and monitor the state of the UK environment. The requirement for indicators has been explicitly recognised by the UK Government in *Sustainable Development: the UK Strategy* (1994). Indicators – measures which can represent and communicate some of the many complex trends in the state of the environment – will be key tools in assessing our progress towards sustainability.

2. This report has been prepared for Environment Challenge, a broad group of environmental organisations. The aim is to move on from the theoretical debate about the "indicators approach" and to begin tackling the practicalities of indicator use. In addition to providing a detailed discussion of possible indicators, the report presents a number of indicators. These highlight some serious concerns about environmental trends in the UK.

3. Numerical data are the vital raw component of indicators. The report shows that there are many gaps in the availability and reliability of the necessary data. The Government and environmental agencies should remedy this rapidly by better and more frequent data collection. This calls for more resources and new priorities but innovative techniques and technologies will ease the task.

4. Indicators are intended to quantify, simplify and communicate complex environmental phenomena. The hard data must be meaningful, statistically robust and representing a trend or situation of importance. Simplifying the state of the environment achieves resonance: the indicators can then become emotive and strike a chord with their audience. There is sometimes a trade-off to be made between these objectives.

5. Achieving the right balance between quantitative rigour and simplicity is the key to communication. The type of indicators presented and the channel of communication need to be closely aligned to the target audience.

6. Two key audiences will be addressed by state of the environment indicators in the UK:

(i)   Decision-makers and policy analysts (in particular in the UK Department of the Environment, the relevant officials at the Welsh, Scottish and Northern Ireland Offices, the statutory agencies and environmental groups). This report makes a positive and timely contribution to the debate about the development of indicators and their value in assessing policy and performance – a debate that is only just beginning to get off the ground in the UK.

(ii)   The "general public" which is bombarded by confusing information on the environment and is often unsure about what exactly is happening. Useful indicators allow the public to gain an understanding of the state the environment is in and to judge the success of the Government and the country as a whole in improving it. Feedback on the resonance of proposed indicators is essential.

7. This document is mainly addressed to the first of these audiences, the decision-makers relatively familiar with the concept of indicators and the environmental issues involved. A number of the indicators discussed in this report are however suitable for a wider public audience. The Environment Challenge group is committed to producing such indicators to promote a broader understanding of key environmental trends in the UK.

8. Indicators can be powerful tools in helping to monitor the state of the environment at high level. However, they are complementary to, rather than substitutes for, more detailed measures to assess what is happening and why, and direct specific action to influence environmental outcomes.

9. This report emphasises the need for indicators of the actual state of the UK environment. Such indicators help to ensure that the effects of human activities and policies on the environment itself are fully taken into account. In general, it is easier to devise indicators for human pressures on and responses to the environment than on the state of the environment itself. This report discusses some "pressure" indicators but stresses the paramount importance of finding good "state" indicators.

10. We have assessed and consulted widely on a large number of possible indicators, selecting them for data availability, meaningfulness and resonance. In each case, important challenges emerge about

the indicators approach itself, the types of information we want, the interpretation of the trends revealed and the need for agreed targets in order to measure performance in achieving improvements in the state of the environment.

11. Despite – indeed because of – these challenges, this report establishes the benefits of using indicators and the urgent need for the UK Government and others to take this forward. The indicators approach can in practice make a useful contribution to public understanding and decision-making. Indicators can galvanise action to improve the state of the environment and progress towards sustainable development.

12. The report contains indicators which are already of sufficient "quality" (a blend of availability, meaning and resonance) to show trends in and allow judgements to be made about many significant aspects of the UK environment. As well as pointing out where further analysis and debate is needed, these indicators suggest that in many areas the UK environment is in poor condition.

13. Three key challenges highlighted by the report are:

(i)   *Lack of clear commitments and policies to reverse deteriorating trends.* Where trends show continued deterioration, or no significant improvement, the immediate priority must be to reverse the direction of the trend. The absence of adequate policy measures suggests that this reversal is not occurring, for example, in the case of continuing loss of hedgerows or generation of certain types of wastes.

(ii) *Lack of Government targets for improving environmental quality and reducing human pressures.* Where trends show a recent improvement, it is difficult to judge the adequacy of progress without reference to clear future targets. There is a rôle for such targets even when they are only currently tentative in nature. Lack of targets is evident in issues such as nitrogen oxide emissions from cars, and in river quality. Targets also help to prevent future backsliding, especially in cases where a recent improvement may be the result of the failure of economic policy rather than the success of environmental policy.

(iii) *Lack of readily available data, suggesting lack of action.* The problem is so severe for some key themes and issues that there must be a strong suspicion that problems are not being adequately addressed. This is especially acute in the issues of biodiversity, quality of life, the marine environment, energy and waste.

14. The Government has made a clear commitment to sustainable development. We fully recognise the need for a full suite of measures for monitoring, assessing and communicating progress towards this goal. This report concentrates on indicators for the state of the UK environment, with reference also to the UK's "footprint" abroad, and identifies key areas for action if the state of the environment is to be improved.

15. We believe this report will make a useful contribution to current debate on environmental measures. It helps show the way forward, both in terms of the indicators needed and some of the policies which will ensure that the trends they reflect start to move in the right direction.

Comment

The same Environment Challenge Group organisations which published this document produced at the same time *Green Gauge*, showing, for ten of the indicators, which were getting worse, staying the same or improving. These included biodiversity and farmland birds (both in decline). This was intended to provide a model for periodic updating publications and the second *Green Gauge* was published in 1996 when selected indicators were organised into six "clusters" including vanishing species, disappearing countryside and coastal and marine.

In 1996 the Government published its own set of indicators of sustainable development for the UK. This acknowledged the contribution of *Environmental Measures* and other reports, but expressed an intention to go beyond the environmental indicators approach and to "link environmental impacts with socio-economic activity". A danger of this is that it focuses attention on intensity of resource use (e.g. energy use per unit of GDP) rather than measuring actual impacts on the environment (e.g. concentration of pollution emissions).

Environmental Challenge: an agenda for local government. **RSPB. 1995.**

Summary

Every day, politicians and planners make decisions which affect wildlife and ultimately the quality of all our lives. Nature conservation cannot be achieved in isolation from other social and economic activities. It has to be an integral part of all policies and decisions at national and local level. Local authorities can play a major part in this process by producing their own Local Agenda 21. The RSPB encourages local authorities to:

1. Biodiversity: set measurable targets for the conservation of species and habitats and publish action plans to achieve these targets.

2. International: produce your own Local Agenda 21 by 1996.

3. Town and country planning: conserve and enhance the natural environment in all planning policies and decisions.

4. Environmental audit: conduct a regular environmental audit to assess wildlife value and develop policies to reverse declines in environmental quality.

5. Forestry: produce forestry strategies which promote multi-purpose forestry for timber production, recreation and wildlife.

6. Energy: develop energy conservation plans.

7. Marine and coastal conservation: produce Coastal Zone Management Plans and support the designation of Marine Protected Areas.

8. Transport: promote public transport and ensure that transport proposals avoid damage to SSSIs and other wildlife sites.

9. Education and awareness: designate Local Nature Reserves and encourage schools to use them as education facilities and train local government staff in environmental matters.

10. Peatland conservation: use peat-free products.

Comment

The RSPB seeks to influence local authorities throughout the UK. Our relations at officer level and with certain individual Councillors are usually excellent. Establishing contact with the majority of Councillors who are very busy and who may only be elected for a limited time has been more difficult. This short pamphlet was therefore designed to provide an accessible introduction to our aims and objectives for this audience. We originally produced it prior to local government elections in spring 1994 and issued an updated edition one year later. In both cases the guide included endorsements from senior figures in the local government associations.

The pamphlet has helped to raise interest in our work among Councillors. This has provided an opportunity to provide them with more information on issues of particular local concern. It has also led to a number of debates at council meetings and recommendations for additional steps to further authorities' environmental work. The text includes a summary of the RSPB's broad agenda which we would like to see authorities follow in their work to fulfil Local Agenda 21.

Sustainable Development / the importance of biodiversity. RSPB. 1996.

Summary

1. Biodiversity simply refers to the variety of life on earth.

2. Biodiversity is a key test of sustainability. Sustainable development must conserve and where possible enhance biodiversity while meeting economic and social goals.

3. We are losing biodiversity. Half of all species of birds and mammals could be extinct within the next 300 years. We have lost over 100 species in the UK this century.

4. Biodiversity matters because:

-       biodiversity supports life itself;

-       ecosystems can be harvested for economic benefit like food and raw materials;

- biodiversity can provide indirect economic benefits like flood control or waste water systems;

- biodiversity has an economic and social value for recreation;

- biodiversity has aesthetic and spiritual value;

- people value the existence of biodiversity and care whether or not it is conserved.

5. Biodiversity conservation need not block economic development. Society needs development but development which is sustainable.

6. We must take a precautionary approach, avoiding development if it threatens serious or irreversible damage to biodiversity.

7. We must be especially careful to protect certain minimum levels of biodiversity, especially where a species or habitat is close to extinction.

8. Sustainable development must avoid individual and cumulative actions which threaten biodiversity.

9. We must look for warning signals showing that biodiversity is under threat. Rates of species and habitat decline and environmental indicators can play a useful rôle.

10. The UK Steering Group report on biodiversity is an excellent step towards the conservation of many priority UK species and habitats. To succeed, the Steering Group's plan needs support across government departments - from Transport to Treasury.

11. To achieve sustainable development the conservation and enhancement of biodiversity must be integrated into all our decision-making - from industry to individuals.

12. The UK can achieve development which is sustainable. Government should identify policies and actions that will achieve economic, social and biodiversity conservation objectives.

Comment

In some of the documents summarised in this book, in its representation on the UK Sustainable Development Round Table and the UK Biodiversity Steering Group, and in other ways, the RSPB has stressed the fundamental message that "biodiversity is a key test of sustainability". The document summarised here (strictly speaking a leaflet rather than a policy report) was intended to provide a concise explanation of why this should be the case, to aid in dialogue with decision-makers. It was intended for a broad readership, but the references to ways in which biodiversity can provide significant economic benefits perhaps make it of particular interest to the world of industry and commerce. The RSPB has made wide use of it in stimulating progress with Local Biodiversity Action Plans and Local Agenda 21 initiatives around the country.

Chapter 2

RURAL POLICY

Gone are the days when serious conservation bodies' efforts were dominated by explaining how various human activities impacted adversely on wildlife interests and by clamouring simply for tougher restrictions. Following the models of sustainability which underlie the material in Chapter 1, much of the RSPB's policy effort has to be in articulating alternative strategies which will not only deliver the wildlife benefits we seek but will also offer realistic and well-researched solutions for the whole range of other legitimate social and economic aspirations which must be addressed. These rural policy papers seek to map this out, for some of the main issues relating to the countryside as a whole and for the communities who live in and depend upon it. The joint initiatives with Scottish crofting interests show a particularly significant example of the kind of integrated vision which is possible.

Comments to the Department of the Environment and the Ministry of Agriculture, Fisheries and Food on the *Rural White Paper for England*. RSPB. January 1995.

Summary

1. The countryside is changing rapidly in terms of its economy and its environmental character. In respect of the environment, at least, many of the changes are for the worse. We welcome this opportunity to comment on the possible scope and content of the *Rural White Paper [see page 41]*, the challenge for which is to set a policy framework to tackle the problems arising from the scale and pace of transition. To do so, it will have to take account of the complexity of the countryside in a visionary yet realistic way.

2. Rural policy will have failed unless steps are taken to reverse the decline in the UK's biodiversity. There are many other pressing claims for attention but the scale of habitat destruction and species loss in recent decades has been so great as to demand urgent, concerted action. The *Rural White Paper* must be a key vehicle to ensure that such action is now delivered.

3. Many of the "special" elements of UK Biodiversity the rare, vulnerable and threatened species, and the habitats on which they depend continue to decline. The best sites continue to be degraded, both in terms of area and quality. Such damage is further detracting from an already severely depleted wildlife resource.

4. So-called common and widespread species are also experiencing dramatic population falls. As land use becomes more intensive and specialised, the quality of the environment for wildlife deteriorates. Skylark populations, for example, have fallen by 54% in a little over 20 years. The grey partridge could become a rare species.

5. These environmental declines are not just a cause of concern to experts and enthusiasts: the general public, whether they live in town or country, are increasingly worried, as is shown by large and growing support for conservation organisations.

6. The *Rural White Paper* comes at a time when both the approach of government to rural areas and the traditional economy that created the countryside are changing rapidly. The rural economy is becoming more like the wider economy but is subject to special pressures and demands from users of rural goods, services and space. This has produced new pressures and problems for wildlife and for the whole rural environment and these have come in a period of retreat in public spending and in regulation.

7. Perversely, however, much of the public spending that has fuelled environmental problems has been retained (particularly in farming, forestry, trunk road building and regional development). Policies in these areas have seen some reforms but not so as to replace damaging "subsidies" by environmental payments.

8. Any further deregulation of rural activity and development could increase the risks to rural biodiversity.

9. The *Rural White Paper* comes, therefore, at an opportune moment to review these issues and will make a substantial contribution to better rural policy if it:

    -    is visionary and acts as a catalyst for change, addressing policy over at least the next 15 years;

- develops a comprehensive rural policy for all relevant parts of government;

- treats rural issues as inseparable from wider social, economic and environmental processes;

- sets out how the components of rural policy will implement the UK Biodiversity Action Plan and the National Sustainable Development Strategy; and

- clarifies the rôles and responsibilities of the various tiers of government, from central policy-making to local delivery.

10. Biodiversity conservation is a particular "service" that rural areas provide and it should become a core objective of all rural policy. The rôle of government in the countryside should increasingly be to ensure that such "services" are provided when the marketplace fails to do so.

11. The White Paper should set out clearly the policy measures to be taken across all parts of government to support production of such "public goods", specifically meeting the targets defined in the UK Biodiversity Action Plan. Resources need to be redistributed to the biodiversity and other environmental priorities which the Action Plan identifies.

12. The *Rural White Paper* must set out a comprehensive, government-wide "vision" and policy for the future of rural areas. If rural policy is to succeed, it is vital that government as a whole shares such a vision. Measures on transport, energy, industry and commerce, education and social policy in rural areas need to be directed towards clear, shared objectives in which protection and enhancement of the environment feature prominently.

13. Regional and local government have key rôles in rural areas, including the delivery of nature conservation: they need the resources and authority to fulfil this national service.

14. The *Rural White Paper* should make clear that biodiversity conservation will be a central objective of sectors which exploit (or regulate the exploitation of) natural resources such as water, energy, fish stocks and minerals.

15. The *Rural White Paper* should set out how the components of rural policy will implement the UK Biodiversity Action Plan. Measures to conserve biodiversity in the countryside are needed at five levels:

- in sustainable development as part of the whole economy;

- in measures that apply across the whole countryside;

- in special measures to protect areas of particular wildlife conservation value;

- in an expanded area of nature reserves;

- in recovery programmes for particular species.

16. Wildlife and the countryside matter to the public, and economically. They are major national assets and the *Rural White Paper* must make clear that development must not be at the expense of the best components of them.

17. Development must be guided by a strong and effective planning system (taking both local and national interests into account). The hierarchical framework of planning guidance, strategic plans and local plans provides for accountable decisions: the planning system must be retained as the principal means of resolving land-use conflicts in rural areas, as elsewhere.

18. Planning policy should however be more innovative. The use of Environmental Impact Assessment and Strategic Environmental Assessment needs to be further developed, as do demand-management techniques. Housing development should be subject to full economic and environmental scrutiny, with housing demand and need questioned much more rigorously than at present. Transport and natural resource use need similar scrutiny. When development is permitted, it should be undertaken to the highest standards of design and environmental quality and be sited where it will not affect locations of high nature conservation value. The interaction between forestry, agriculture and the planning system should be re-examined.

19. The *Rural White Paper* should make it clear that each of the countryside designations, for special areas of one sort or another,

fulfils a specific rôle: they need to be defended and not treated as a homogenous barrier to development. The *Rural White Paper* needs to stress government's commitment to safeguarding protected areas from development and from neglect and to set out how this will be achieved.

20. The area of land under conservation ownership and management by both voluntary and statutory agencies should be extended. Just over 2.8% (6,800km²) of the UK land area is currently under sympathetic conservation ownership and/or under "assured" sympathetic management. With the current rate of acquisition, this could rise to 3.2% (an additional 980km²) by 2000. A reasonable target for the year 2010 would be 4% (a total of 9,760km², or nearly 1 million hectares), which would mean an increase in resources for land purchase by both state and private organisations. The *Rural White Paper* should endorse this target and commit government (including funds from the National Lottery) to part-financing its achievement.

21. The *Rural White Paper* and the Minister of Agriculture's think tank should include a clear statement of the need for and direction of CAP reform. The imperative of "food production at all cost" has been superseded by policies to reduce the costs of support to agriculture, broaden the economic base of the countryside and protect the environment. However, the measurable impact of new policies and instruments have been very limited. A consensus on CAP reform is needed, based on an analysis of reforms to date and of the new international political scene (especially EU enlargement). The CAP needs to become a system in which the market determines farmers' returns from food production, while government secures the "non-market" benefits that farming should supply.

22. Management agreements, based on the existing "agri-environment" regulation, need to become more central to agricultural support régimes and play a larger rôle in the rural economy. They should account for a greater proportion of UK spending: by the year 2000 at least 30% of the UK farmland area deserves to be designated as Environmentally Sensitive Areas, or to have similar schemes available to farmers. An objective of agriculture policy must be to expand this form of support to the whole countryside by the year 2010.

23. Forestry policy in the past decade has changed in favour of "multi purpose" forestry, leading to better design and location of new planting and an expanded area of broadleaved woodland.

Current reviews of forestry institutions should be used to make specific environmental performance targets part of future policy. However, progress could be jeopardised unless forestry operates in a policy framework that integrates it with other land uses and other relevant policies. The *Rural White Paper* should provide such a framework.

24. The *Rural White Paper* should set out how the recommendations of the Royal Commission on Environmental Pollution report on transport should be implemented in rural areas. Rural areas face special problems of accessibility and high transport costs: indeed, better transport infrastructure has been a cornerstone of modern rural development. This means that rural areas are incurring high environmental costs from transport and must not be "exempted" from the urgent national need to reduce these impacts.

25. Policies for the leisure industry which reflect its environmental costs should be developed. While visiting the countryside helps people to understand and appreciate nature, leisure "infrastructure" (such as riding stables, theme parks or marinas) and disturbance effects (from water-skiing, power-boating, etc) can pose major problems for wildlife.

26. The planning system cannot control demand for leisure, as it can its location. The lack of information on disturbance effects suggests that the precautionary principle should apply in many cases of leisure development: the *Rural White Paper* should make this clear and call for more attention to the management of quiet, informal access.

Comment

The RSPB was one of 400 organisations to submit comments to the DoE in early-1995 on the content of the proposed *Rural White Paper*. Government held exhaustive discussions internally on the subject and a series of regional and topic-based seminars and bilateral meetings (including with the RSPB). The *White Paper "Rural England: A Nation Committed to a Living Countryside"* was published in October 1995 (similar papers were subsequently published for Wales and Scotland [see page 44]). *"Rural England"* set out a strategy for the countryside under the headings of "Government and People", "Working in the Countryside", "Living in the Countryside" and "A Green and Pleasant Land". The latter covered nature conservation, environmental protection, agriculture and transport.

"Rural England", whilst short on specific and ambitious targets, set some important principles for the protection of the environment. It set out as an objective of government policy to reverse the declines in wildlife; it recognised that high environmental values were generally an economic asset to the countryside; and it outlined the expansion of the remit of nature conservation from protected areas to the countryside as a whole. These principles reflected the RSPB's concerns. The White Paper says little about demand management for housing, transport and leisure; and went no further on CAP reform, biodiversity and rural development than other government papers. More positively, it did not signal the radical weakening of the planning system, site designations and the statutory agencies that had been feared. Proposals to reduce the protection given to grade 3a land, to backtrack on common land legislation and to increase arbitrarily the UK area of forest cover have raised concerns. A follow-up paper is expected from government in autumn of 1996.

Submission to the House of Commons Environment Select Committee inquiry on the *Rural White Paper for England*. RSPB. January 1996.

Summary

1. The RSPB welcomes the opportunity to contribute to the Committee's inquiry into the White Paper *"Rural England: A Nation Committed to a Living Countryside"*. Rural policies matter considerably to the conservation of the countryside because they provide the framework of laws and incentives which guide commercial land uses. These land uses are, in turn, the greatest influence over wildlife, landscape and the rural environment. Most of our countryside has to serve several functions of conservation and economic significance. If the nation requires rural land management to be sustainable, then rural policies must encourage it to be so.

2. An increasing proportion of the rural and urban population values the countryside's natural and aesthetic attributes. As we demonstrated in our submission to the Government on the preparation of the White Paper, environmental quality is a distinguishing feature of rural areas and is crucial to their economic success. Environmental protection must therefore be integrated fully into rural economic development policies.

3. We believe that the White Paper has set out clear principles for future rural policy. We recommend that it would be very helpful to all involved in the rural debate were the Committee to focus on the

Government's plans and initiatives to implement the directions "sign posted" in the White Paper.

4. The Government's response to the UK Biodiversity Steering Group report will be crucially important to rural England and to the issues in the Committee's terms of reference. We recommend that the Groups' report and the Government's response receive careful examination by the Committee.

5. Action to address such issues as the budgets of the countryside agencies and the expansion of the Countryside Stewardship scheme to provide incentives for arable extensification are crucial to turning the spirit of the White Paper into reality. We recommend that the Government be urged to resource adequately the wider countryside work of the agencies and of MAFF.

6. The Government's commitments to protecting the environment will need to be fully reflected in the draft revision of *Planning Policy Guidance note 7 ("The Countryside and the Rural Economy")*. The DoE research report *"Planning for Rural Diversification"* indicates that PPG7 has facilitated rural diversification. Calls for further deregulation of planning controls should be resisted if these will damage biodiversity and other elements of the rural environment.

7. The issue of managing demand for transport, housing, leisure, etc needs to be tackled. Strategic Environmental Assessment needs to be developed, particularly in respect of housing allocations in Regional Planning Guidance and development plans.

8. Where development must be accommodated, PPG7 needs to indicate that sometimes grade 1 - 3a agricultural land may need to be developed in order to protect the environmental importance of poorer grade land. This would go further than the commitment on grade 3a land contained on page 132 of the White Paper.

9. We believe that the failure of the White Paper to set in motion the development of a national forestry strategy is a missed opportunity. We hope the Committee will restate its earlier commitment to such a strategy and urge Government to reconsider.

10. We recommend that the Government should request the Countryside Commission to convene a meeting of interested parties, with a view to revisiting the Common Land Forum's recommendations

to establish what progress can be made, now that all concerned are in no doubt as to what the absence of action on this means in both legal and management terms.

Comment

This inquiry was set up in response to the publication of the Government's *Rural White Paper*. The Committee ranged across a wide spectrum of topics and found it difficult to focus down on a few issues. The Committee endorsed concerns about reducing the protection of grade 3a land (mainly a concern of landscape conservation interests) and endorsed demands for more targets to be set for rural policy. A government response to the inquiry which followed had little of a controversial nature to defend.

Comments to the Scottish Office Environment Department on the Scottish White Paper on Rural Policy. RSPB. June 1995.

Summary

1. The RSPB warmly welcomes this opportunity to offer views and ideas for consideration by the Scottish Office in their review of rural policies and the machinery for their delivery. Scotland's natural environment is outstanding. Its spectacular scenic beauty and abundant wildlife are among the most important of any area in Europe. As well as being of great conservation importance these features can offer significant economic, social and cultural benefits, provided they are wisely managed. However, many areas are environmentally degraded and in need of restoration and many species and habitats are not in "favourable conservation status". Much of the rich natural heritage which remains and the opportunities for restoration depend on the maintenance of traditional land uses, which may be under threat from changes in the rural economy.

2. The White Paper should recognise that rural prosperity should be measured in terms of quality of life, encompassing economic, social, cultural and environmental factors, specifically embracing and adopting the following general principles:

-   Biodiversity conservation should become a core objective of all rural policy. This will help strengthen the rural economy. The White Paper should set out how the components of rural policy will implement the UK Biodiversity Action Plan.

-   The White Paper should set out a comprehensive, government-wide "vision" and policy for rural areas.

-   Wildlife and the countryside matter to the public for their own sake, as well as economically. They are major national assets and the White Paper must make clear that development must not be at their expense.

-   Special areas need to be given better protection through positive management incentives, such as those under the Agri-environment Regulation.

-   Sporting land use must be pursued in a manner which enhances the management of special habitats and is consistent with EU Directives and biodiversity commitments.

3. Agriculture and forestry policy has a key rôle in determining the fate of Scotland's important wildlife. The *Rural White Paper* presents an opportunity to review the effectiveness of these policies in conserving biodiversity and providing associated economic benefit to rural areas.

4. The White Paper should recognise that further reforming of the Common Agricultural Policy (CAP) and expanding and improving the agri-environment programme can bring economic, employment and environmental benefits. This could be achieved through:

-   the Scottish Office adopting a proactive and leading rôle in pressing for further reforms of the CAP to conserve and enhance Europe's environment;

-   the Scottish Office seizing this opportunity to review and plot the future course of agri-environment policy in Scotland - this should include planning for the full implementation of the Agri-environment Regulation in Scotland;

-   the Scottish Office setting clear environmental objectives and priorities appropriate to Scotland, a process that would be aided by establishing an interdepartmental panel with representatives of the Agriculture and Fisheries Department, the Environment Department, Scottish Natural Heritage and non governmental organisations;

- the Scottish Office abolishing or significantly raising the financial limits applied to Environmentally Sensitive Area (ESA) payments in Scotland - these penalise Scottish farmers and crofters compared to those elsewhere in the UK.

5. The expansion of Scotland's agri-environment programme, which will strengthen the farming and crofting economies, should include at least the following elements:

- Further ESA designation - Orkney should be designated as an ESA immediately. The Machair ESA should be extended immediately to cover the whole of the Western Isles.

- A "Countryside Management Scheme" should be established by the Scottish Office to provide support for the sensitive management of habitats and countryside features.

- The Scottish Office should introduce an improved extensification scheme for sheep, including shepherding support, with specific environmental objectives. In specific areas, a similar extensification scheme for cattle should be introduced.

6. The White Paper should commit the Scottish Office/Forestry Commission to integrate further environmental objectives into forestry policy, especially those relating to the conservation of Caledonian pinewoods, by for example:

- restoring and substantially expanding the area of native pinewoods, particularly within the core pinewood areas of Deeside, Strathspey and the Beauly catchment;

- establishing an interdepartmental group, responsible for developing integrated policies, plans and actions, to secure the future of Scotland's pinewoods;

- encouraging the control of deer in and around pinewoods, to secure natural regeneration, through improved differentials in Woodland Grant Scheme grant levels;

7. The Forestry Authority and Enterprise Development organisations should encourage local forestry and timber marketing initiatives

and ensure that they promote timber use from native pinewoods. This should include assistance to pine timber processors and wood users in the Highlands and the establishment of an eco-labelling scheme for native Scots pine timber.

Comment

The RSPB viewed this White Paper as potentially an extremely important top-level policy steer from government on issues affecting biodiversity interests of great importance. The Government is keen to stimulate economic growth in rural areas, particularly because European funding is available for this throughout most of Scotland. The RSPB in partnership with other bodies such as the Scottish Crofters Union (SCU) has emphasised the need for this economic growth not to damage the environment and to help restore degraded habitats and species. We have also emphasised that better integration of biodiversity commitments across all sectors of rural policy such as agriculture, forestry and tourism could bring economic benefits to rural areas. Agriculture policy has the most significant impact on priority biodiversity interests in Scotland and the Society's submission on the White Paper emphasised the need for agri-environment policy changes to be made to address problems affecting birds.

The White Paper turned out to be less of a strategy and more of a vision with no identified objectives, mechanisms or properly ensured integration of policies. It did however display a major policy shift, with nature conservation being made a cornerstone of Scottish Office rural policy and sustainable development a guiding principle. The paper also announced welcome proposals for the expansion of the agri-environment programme. A new Rural Partnership was established to help fund and direct economic improvements but the voluntary conservation bodies were excluded from direct participation despite being experienced in the economic benefits of sound environmental policy.

*Rural Development and the Environment: Opportunities in the Highlands and Islands. **RSPB and Scottish Crofters Union. 1995.***

Summary

1. In *"Crofting and the Environment"* in 1992 the RSPB and the Scottish Crofters Union called for a revitalised future for the crofting

areas. In the same year, at the Earth Summit in Rio de Janeiro, the world's leaders agreed on the need for sustainable development. Since the summit, the UK Government has launched the UK Strategy for Sustainable Development and published its own Biodiversity Action Plan.

2. Meanwhile, the reform of the Common Agricultural Policy and the Common Fisheries Policy and the completion of the Single European Market have brought new economic challenges to rural areas such as the Highlands and Islands. The granting by the European Union (EU) of Objective 1 status to the area provides new development opportunities and environmental challenges. This document continues the co-operation between the SCU and the RSPB , drawing on the two organisations' broad experience of the various sectors that comprise rural development.

3. We aim to protect the area's communities and biodiversity by ensuring that crofting survives and all sectors of the economy affecting the environment are appropriately managed.

4. The natural environment of the Highlands and Islands is outstanding. It is among the most important of any region in Europe. The area has spectacular scenic beauty and wildlife in abundance. The appendix to this document lists many of the important species.

5. But not all is necessarily well with the environment. The rich landscape and wildlife depends on the maintenance of traditional patterns of land use (e.g. crofting and woodland management). These are under threat from changes in the rural economy and the support systems which have traditionally sustained them. In places, past policies have encouraged the destruction of native woodland or the overgrazing of heather moorland.

6. The Highlands and Islands area is the stronghold of crofting, with its small-scale, low-intensity farming systems. It has a rich cultural heritage incorporating Gaelic and Norse influences and language. But the remote and very rural nature of the Highlands and Islands also results in social and economic problems. Remoteness, higher costs and a reliance on traditional industries are among the factors contributing to the economy "lagging behind" that of the rest of the UK and the European Union. Yet policies to address these social and economic difficulties have to date largely failed to reverse the trend.

7. We set out in this document nine guiding principles which the RSPB and the SCU believe should be followed in promoting rural development. While this document concentrates on the Highlands and Islands, these principles should be applied to all rural development schemes. They are:

- Development must be both environmentally and economically sustainable: the conservation of biodiversity (the variety of life) is a fundamental test of sustainable development.

- The maintenance of rural communities and biodiversity is a "public good" which cannot be sustained by market forces alone. In the Highlands and Islands, the environmental, social and cultural interests are significant enough to justify continued public support.

- The market should be helped to work more effectively to support the activities that help sustain biodiversity and rural communities.

- A strategic, environmentally-based approach to planning development in rural areas is needed to identify environmental priorities, assess the implications of planned development programmes and select the most environmentally attractive options. This approach is sometimes referred to as Strategic Environmental Assessment.

- Development funds should be conditional on ensuring that the environment is appropriately conserved. Support should be available to fund measures which enhance the natural environment.

- Employment not directly linked to the environment should also support biodiversity conservation. Support should be available to expand such opportunities.

- Local control of resources and development, within a nationally and internationally agreed conservation framework, could yield significant environmental benefits, as local people would have a vested interest in managing them sustainably.

- Adequate public funding should be provided to supply and maintain the range of social and cultural amenities and services on which thriving local communities depend.

- Training, awareness and education are essential to support environmentally sensitive and sustainable development.

8. These principles should be applied to all aspects of the rural economy. We make specific proposals for the sectors most directly related to the environment: agriculture, forestry, fisheries, tourism, conservation itself, transport and energy; and other suggestions for action on housing, cultural activities and local amenities and training. Key recommendations are that through the implementation of the Single Programming Document for the Objective 1 programme for the Highlands and Islands, or by other means, the Government should ensure that effective support is available to encourage:

- low-intensity, environmentally sensitive agriculture;

- establishing and managing native woodland;

- developing sustainable fishing practices and environmentally sensitive fish farming, as well as local processing and marketing initiatives;

- developing "green" tourism;

- expanding conservation as an "industry";

- the Strategic Environmental Assessment of new transport and energy developments and support for environmentally and socially beneficial renewable energy schemes; and

- greater resources for housing, cultural and leisure facilities, training, environmental awareness and education.

9. Little has been done to date to explore and exploit the potential for biodiversity conservation to be linked to business opportunities and local economic benefit. We discuss in this document local processing and marketing of crofting lamb and native pine as just two examples. Far more work is needed in this area.

10. The SCU and the RSPB challenge everyone involved in rural development and the environment in the Highlands and Islands to embrace the principles we have set out wholeheartedly. If the actions proposed are taken forward, together with other ideas consistent with our principles, the Highlands and Islands should support prosperous rural populations and develop thriving economies, while retaining and enhancing their outstanding environments.

Comment

This publication, produced jointly with the Scottish Crofters Union, followed our earlier joint publication *"Crofting and the Environment: A New Approach"* in 1992. The Rural Development and the Environment document summarised here represented a broadening of this partnership with the SCU. It looks beyond agricultural landuse to all aspects of economic and community life in the Highlands and Islands, and the ways in which this interacts with the environment. It was a topical publication, being launched as the Highlands and Islands were about to receive new European funds (Objective 1) to support rural development initiatives.

Since publication, liaison between the RSPB and SCU on a range of issues has continued and both bodies have been involved in debates over the use of Objective 1 funds (which are still implicated in environmentally damaging projects). An emerging dimension is the handing over of land from the Scottish Office to crofting trusts. The Society has also begun to broaden its work in this area, with work on nature conservation and local economies and an assessment of a Local Enterprise Company's environmental impact.

Chapter 3

THE ENVIRONMENT AGENCIES

A substantial reorganisation of statutory environmental protection responsibilities was ushered in by the Environment Act 1995, which created a new Environment Agency for England and Wales and an Environment Protection Agency for Scotland. These have taken over functions of the former National Rivers Authority, HM Inspectorate of Pollution and other waste regulation authorities, and river purification authorities. Draft guidance on the Agencies' responsibilities towards sustainable development offered an opportunity for influencing their rôle in nature conservation.

Comments to the Department of the Environment on *Draft Guidance on the Environment Agency and sustainable development.* RSPB. December 1995.

Summary

1. The RSPB welcomes the opportunity to comment on this draft guidance to the Environment Agency. We recommend that the draft text that is to form the statutory guidance to the Agency should be improved in several respects.

2. Firstly, specific statutory guidance to the Agency under section 4 of the Environment Act 1995 should be prepared and issued on targets for the conservation and enhancement of biodiversity. Targets should include those on action to protect particular sites of importance for nature conservation and those derived from the species and habitat action plans recommended by the Biodiversity Steering Group and accepted by Government for implementation.

3. Paragraph 11(i) should have a section added which includes reference to project environmental assessment and strategic environmental assessment as key tools for taking a holistic approach to the protection and enhancement of the environment.

4. Paragraph 11(iii) should be redrafted to recognise that the Agency can make a significant contribution through its actions to the enhancement of biodiversity.

5. Finally, wherever guidance is given on consultation and working relationships, reference must be made to environmental bodies (both statutory and voluntary). Such contacts should be at the national level on policies, objectives and strategies as well as the local level on site-based actions.

Comment

The Environment Act 1995 includes, in its definition of the aims of the Environment Agency, contributing to the achievement of sustainable development. The RSPB saw this submission as a key opportunity to strengthen the guidance under which the new Agency was to implement this requirement, by adding biodiversity targets. Such targets in the Society's view offer a key test of sustainability, which we argued should feature in all the Agency's policies and operations, alongside economic and social objectives.

Sustainable development: comments to the Scottish Office Environment Department on draft Guidance to the Scottish Environment Protection Agency (SEPA) on sustainable development. RSPB. August 1995.

Summary

1. The RSPB considers that this guidance must put more emphasis on the Scottish Environment Protection Agency's rôle in meeting the needs of European conservation priorities and the targets set out in the Government's Biodiversity Action Plan. Guidance should be given on the "ends" objectives and standards that SEPA is expected to achieve. This should be distinguished from the "means" by which it will do so.

2. The guidance should contain a framework for environmental targets, including biodiversity targets. Relegating such targets to future Agency corporate plans will not ensure sufficient public accountability.

3. The draft guidance is heavily laden with text on processes which SEPA is expected to follow in the exercise of its functions, but with one major omission, namely processes for defining the environmental effect of its decisions. Text on strategic and project Environmental Assessment (EA) should be added to remedy this. These tools are of equal if not greater relevance to SEPA than the assessment of

costs and benefits to which so much prominence is given. EA is a statutory requirement in many cases in respect of projects and this should be referred to. EA of plans and programmes is also highly desirable and is a requirement under Directive 92/43 on Habitats & Species in cases where there are likely to be significant effects on a Special Protection Area (SPA) or Special Area of Conservation (SAC).

4. Relegation of nature conservation duties to Part B of Annexe A is not acceptable to the RSPB. It sends an unfortunate signal about the priority being given to this issue which should feature instead in the main body of the guidance.

5. The guidance should include specific reference to the obligations which SEPA has towards SPAs and SACs, including the new statutory duties under the Habitats Regulations.

6. The guidance was always intended to give detail on the requirements for analysis of costs and benefits. The current draft does not in our view do this adequately. In particular it should explain the circumstances in which the cost and benefits duty does not apply. It will be important to highlight the deficiencies currently displayed by techniques for valuing the environment.

7. The RSPB has gained the impression, from the tone of the language used in the draft guidance, that the interests of industry will be given special treatment by SEPA. The RSPB wishes this to be changed to give a clear indication that the Agency is being established with a function of championing the interests of the environment. Obviously SEPA will work closely with industry but the guidance must make clear that it has specific environmental targets to achieve over defined timescales and has a regulatory and enforcement rôle to play in doing so.

Comment

A further RSPB submission was made in January 1996 on a further draft of the guidance. In this we asked for specific guidance to be provided on biodiversity targets derived from national action plans. We asked again for references to EA/SEA, for recognition of the contribution SEPA could make to the enhancement of biodiversity and for reference to statutory and voluntary environmental bodies in sections on consultation and working relationships. A very brief comment was sent in March 1996 on a separate consultation on draft guidance on the composition of the Agency's Regional Boards, in which we simply emphasised the need for enough of their members to have conservation expertise.

SEPA was created on 1st April, 1996. The final draft of the *Guidance* (at the time of writing still not formally published) includes a section which emphasises that the conservation and enhancement of biodiversity is an essential element of sustainable development. RSPB staff have been meeting SEPA staff and Board members to promote biodiversity conservation through the work of the Agency. The Regional Boards were duly appointed, with a membership including representatives of environmental NGOs.

Chapter 4

THE HABITATS & SPECIES DIRECTIVE AND SITE PROTECTION

Protected areas legislation has long been a central part of the RSPB's agenda and the operation of relevant systems in the UK depends heavily on the non government sector as providers of scientific data, as "eyes and ears" to assess whether protection is working and as direct managers of many nature reserve sites. The RSPB has been closely involved in assisting with the crafting of relevant statutory provisions, an experience which informs our critical reviews, such as those covered here, of implementation in practice. Major changes to the system have included the Wildlife and Countryside Act (WLCA) in 1981 which created the modern Sites of Special Scientific Interest provisions, and in 1992 the adoption of the European Directive on the conservation of natural habitats and of wild flora and fauna, the "Habitats & Species" Directive. The designated sites provisions of the latter are the subject of the first two items in this Chapter.

Comments to the Department of the Environment on *"Possible Special Areas of Conservation in the UK"*. RSPB. May 1995.

Summary

1. The RSPB contributes a distinct perspective on the consultation on Special Areas of Conservation (SACs), including a long history of involvement in the gestation and implementation of the EU Habitats Directive. Some of our nature reserves are proposed as SACs.

2. The RSPB welcomes the opportunity to comment on the proposed SACs. We regret the delay and excessive secrecy involved in the processes leading up to this.

3. Recognition of the UK's special responsibility for some habitats and species is welcomed. Our concern is the inadequate representation of this special responsibility in the proposed list of SACs.

4. The RSPB regrets the lack of integration of the SAC consultation with the review of Special Protection Areas (SPAs) and their selection

criteria. There is no clear picture of the coherence or otherwise of the "Natura 2000" network until this review is complete.

5. The RSPB welcomes the combined publication of proposals for England, Wales, Scotland and Northern Ireland. We also welcome the inclusion of marine and terrestrial sites and selection criteria. We regret that prior consultation did not take place on the selection criteria as we had asked.

6. Inconsistencies exist between the treatment of SACs and SPAs designated under the Wild Birds Directive. This applies particularly where SACs and SPAs overlap. We believe it is valid to retain both designation "labels". However, confusion may exist in the interpretation of priority species under the two Directives.

7. The Habitats Directive requires the achievement of "favourable conservation status" for relevant habitats and species. The correct understanding of favourable conservation status is fundamental to the correct selection of SACs.

8. The list of proposed SACs fails fully to recognise the need for inclusion of sites capable of restoration to a favourable conservation status. This concern is reflected in our detailed comments on specific sites. The Government should programme future actions for all the measures needed to meet the favourable conservation status objective.

9. We have made a number of comments on the site selection criteria contained in section 3 of the SAC consultation document. We are concerned that the interpretation of the Directive's requirements does not give sufficient weight to the objective of restoration.

10. We are concerned that for some multiple- and single-interest sites, identification of other features which justify the site's qualification have been omitted. This could cause problems when future management decisions are being made. Habitats and species listed in the Directive and occurring on an SAC must receive full appropriate conservation measures.

11. We have commented on the extent of proposed SAC coverage in the UK. The RSPB does not object to the inclusion of any of the sites chosen, subject to our detailed comments. We have particular concerns in respect of marine areas, native pinewoods, peat bogs

and heathlands. We have suggested a number of additional sites we believe should be SACs. The Government is urged to include these sites in the final SAC list.

12. The Habitats Directive offers a major opportunity to provide meaningful protection for the marine environment. The RSPB encourages the Government to seek an early review of the annexes and the definitions in the Directive, to include consideration of offshore habitats.

13. In the meantime the exclusion of certain UK estuaries and other important marine sites as SACs should be rectified.

14. It is crucial that conservation objectives are set, monitoring begun and integrated management schemes implemented for SACs below the low water mark. Sections 36 and 37 of the Wildlife and Countryside Act 1981 require urgent review to give due protection to the marine environment.

15. Caledonian forest is a priority habitat under the Directive. The RSPB is concerned that proposed SAC coverage of native pinewoods is inadequate. We recommend that all native pinewoods be designated as SACs, including those with restoration potential.

16. We have other concerns regarding the treatment of SAC boundaries for native pinewoods and on the implications of SAC designation for future management and resourcing.

17. Peat bogs are recognised throughout Europe as one of our rarest and most threatened habitats. We are disappointed with the proposed SAC coverage of these habitats. We urge the designation of all active raised bogs as SACs and also of other sites identified as capable of restoration to a favourable conservation status, or where protection is required to maintain the integrity of active bog sites. Peat bogs omitted from the list of proposed SACs because of lack of SSSI/ASSI designation should be added as quickly as possible.

18. The extent of some of the proposed peat bog SACs is inadequate. We are particularly concerned that sites may have been wrongly excluded because of the existence of planning permissions.

19. Important heathland sites (such as parts of the Wealden Heaths and all of the Thames Basin Heaths) have been excluded from the

list of proposed SACs. These exclusions should be rectified as soon as possible.

20. The list of proposed SACs is acknowledged to be incomplete. The Government is asked to clarify whether subsequent proposals will be announced and consulted on as they are brought forward, or whether they will appear as a second finalised "tranche".

21. When the final list of proposed SACs is published, an account of reasons, site by site, should be given for any changes from the consultation proposals.

22. The work of designating SACs and their future management will require considerable resources. These must be provided to the statutory agencies and government departments concerned. There should be no diversion or dilution of resources from other priority work such as the SPA programme.

23. Designation of sites as SACs will have implications for additions to the list of existing and candidate Ramsar sites. The Government is asked to state what plans are in hand to act on this.

24. The Government has announced its intention to review nature conservation designations in England and Scotland. We request details of the terms of reference for this review.

Comment

The RSPB has placed importance on satisfactory implementation of the SAC provisions of the Habitats & Species Directive, in addition to its obvious interest in seeing good implementation of Special Protection Area provisions under the Wild Birds Directive. Our principal concerns lie with ensuring sufficient representation of habitats of EU interest in the UK. The process of identifying SACs is also an important focus for reinforcing the requirement in the Directive to give attention to the restoration potential of degraded habitat, which is critical to the underlying "favourable conservation status" objective.

The submission summarised here was a response to a single central government consultation but our comments were copied to each of the territorial Departments of State, with some additional remarks. They contained, in an appendix, the summary of the main RSPB response to consultation proposals in 1993 on the implementation of the Habitats & Species Directive in the UK, on which subject a range of RSPB papers (e.g. contributions to conferences) has been produced. A marine and coastal site supplement was submitted in June 1995, consisting mainly of comments on individual sites. In this context it is also worth referring to the submission made to the European Commission in July 1996 by BirdLife International, and co-authored by RSPB, on proposals for a Commission Communication on the Implementation and Enforcement of EC Environmental Law. Implementation of the Directive generally continues to exhibit problems, and at the time of writing a House of Lords Select Committee is planning an inquiry into the wider implementation and enforcement question, to coincide with debate on the Commission Communication.

SACs complement SPAs and together they form the Natura 2000 network: progress with both types of designation is thus interlinked, and there are overlaps on the ground. Criteria for designating SPAs are at the time of writing under review, and a less than complete picture of what the Government sees as their eventual contribution to the overall network therefore has so far been made public.

There is concern about the ability of the UK Government to ensure that adequate resources are available for the statutory agencies to progress designations within the timescales required by the Directives (SPAs are already seriously delayed). The spectre of potential exclusions or omissions of sites for reasons which are not legitimate also remains. Whilst the UK Government has submitted lists of suggested SACs to the EC, the decision has yet to be taken on many other controversial sites, such as those to which objections have been made or additional sites proposed by NGOs. There is also still some debate about selection criteria.

Comments to the Department of the Environment on *European Marine Sites in England / a guide to the Conservation (Natural Habitats, etc) Regulations 1994 and to the preparation and application of schemes of management*. RSPB. August 1995.

Summary

1. The RSPB welcomes this Department of the Environment initiative. Guidance on how the Habitats Directive will apply in the marine environment, and more particularly how Special Protection

Area (SPA)/Special Area of Conservation (SAC) schemes of management should be set up, is badly needed. Having said this, we have a number of general concerns about the draft.

2. The Society is dismayed to see that yet again a potentially useful initiative is limited to England. As a Coastal Forum initiative, this can be understood. However, we would like some indication as to how and when such guidance will be extended to the rest of the UK. Since the guidance is currently restricted to England, the Department must make quite sure that any references to "GB", or whatever, do not mislead the reader.

3. The Department will note from our detailed comments that many of them are directed towards interpretation of the Habitats Directive, rather than towards the guidance as such. Having said this, the draft guidance goes little further than restating what is contained in the Regulations. This in itself is not wrong. However, the usefulness of the guidance could be greatly increased if Government were to provide a greater body of policy and policy interpretation, as is common for example with Planning Policy Guidance notes.

4. We are concerned that, throughout the draft guidance, the implication is that SPA and SAC schemes of management should be set up for sites classified/designated since the Habitats Directive came into force. This should not be the case. There are a significant number of "marine" SPAs (in that they include intertidal areas) which should also have schemes of management developed for them.

5. The draft guidance also gives the impression that implementation of the Habitats Directive in the marine environment will make little difference to the way sites are currently managed. This is most misleading. The Directive provides, for the first time, a legal mechanism to manage marine sites for nature conservation purposes. The emphasis on maintaining the status quo must be changed to an emphasis on proactive management. The Society supports the principle of management by consensus and voluntary agreement. However, the draft guidance fails to indicate that there are now legal requirements to make sure management within SPAs/SACs does not have detrimental impacts and to ensure that this is fully enforceable in UK and European law.

Comment

As part of its response to the 1992 House of Commons Environment Select Committee inquiry into coastal zone protection and planning, the Government published two important discussion papers. *"Development below low water mark"* reviewed the mechanisms regulating all kinds of development in the marine environment, concluding that there was no evidence that the prevailing "sectoral" approach was a problem. *"Managing the coast"* reviewed the coastal management planning system and in particular the powers available to coastal planners. This concluded that there were limitations in existing powers to zone and regulate the use of the seashore and coastal waters.

In 1994, the Government was once again criticised by the Select Committee for its lack of positive action in the coastal zone. This time, it responded with four initiatives. One was to establish a national Coastal Forum for England, to bring together coastal planners, managers and representatives from Government Departments. The Forum facilitated the setting up of short-lived "topic groups" to draw together a small number of specialists on particular issues. The first of these groups was convened to assist DoE in the development of guidance on the production of management plans for marine SACs.

The RSPB was invited to participate in the Topic Group, contributing to and commenting on three early drafts before the final draft was circulated widely for consultation. At the time of writing, the guide has not been published. With the Society's assistance, numerous changes, particularly relating to matters of factual accuracy, were made between drafts. The scope of the guidance was extended to cover both England and Wales. However, in other areas, improvements are still required, such as the provision of specific "how to" guidance for relevant authorities such as ports (legal advice suggests that legislation would not allow ports to gain powers to manage activities on nature conservation grounds) and a more balanced approach to what constitutes "plans and projects" in the marine environment.

The guide is significant in that for the first time integrated management plans for marine areas whose primary objective should be nature conservation will be produced. Three trial plans are being developed, for the Severn Estuary, Morecambe Bay and

Flamborough Head. Moreover, Government has stated here probably for the first time that the jurisdiction of some local planning authorities extends below the mean low water mark. It is implied that where this is the case, SSSIs too may extend below low water; an approach which the RSPB supports. A separate consultation paper was subsequently issued by the Scottish Office.

Safe and Sound? **A health check of Northern Ireland's Areas of Special Scientific Interest. Davidson, LE and Mellon, C. 1996.**

Summary

1. The RSPB attaches great importance to the need to protect and manage Northern Ireland's best wildlife sites through the statutory network of Areas of Special Scientific Interest. However, a 1991 report for Wildlife Link, "*SSSIs: A health check*", found that SSSIs were failing to protect Britain's most important areas and that many of these had been seriously damaged.

2. That exercise did not extend to Northern Ireland where the Department of the Environment was at an early stage in its designation programme. After the production of DoE's "*Target 2001*" document in 1993, the rate of designation increased, and by 1995 the RSPB considered that enough progress had been made to allow a detailed review of the process.

3. "*Safe and Sound?*" is, therefore, a review of site safeguard in Northern Ireland. Compiled with the co-operation of staff from the former Environment Service of the DoE(NI), now the Environment and Heritage Service, this report assesses the effectiveness of existing legislation and government policies in protecting sites of nature conservation importance.

4. Each stage in the ASSI process has been analysed, from habitat surveys to the declaration, management and monitoring of sites. In each case, the strengths and weaknesses of the relevant legislation and of government policies and procedures are identified and recommendations made for improvements to the system.

5. A number of key areas of concern are identified in the report:

- Site selection criteria have not, as yet, been fully developed or published.

- There is no clear expression of priority or any published objectives for the protected site network.

- The present system has yet to address the protection of more difficult and mobile species such as dispersed bird species.

- A site monitoring programme has not yet been devised. A pilot study to consider monitoring requirements has just been completed.

- Most of the sites surveyed in the pilot study had been damaged – some seriously. This leads to concern that many other ASSIs may have sustained significant damage since their designation.

- Procedural and legislative changes are needed to enable site management and enforcement to be carried out effectively.

6. Many of the current shortcomings of the system can be attributed to the paucity of resources which are available to the Department to carry out all aspects of the ASSI programme. The report does not set out to answer all of the questions which are posed but seeks to highlight those issues which are most important to ensure that ASSIs are protected effectively. We provide 43 recommendations for the statutory bodies involved in protecting our best wildlife sites and believe that, in the light of the damage some ASSIs have sustained, these must be acted on without delay.

7. This report finds that many of our ASSIs appear to be in a state of poor health similar to that affecting the SSSIs analysed in the Wildlife Link report. It may also be some time before enough monitoring has been carried out for the full extent of the problem to be known. Urgent action must be taken now, so that our most important sites receive the protection they need, to conserve them for future generations.

Comment

This document fulfilled an intention, held for some years by the RSPB, to do full justice to reviewing the ASSI system following the Wildlife Link "Health Check" exercise which had not covered Northern Ireland. It also followed a separate RSPB *"Health Check"* of the UK's Important Bird Areas, published in 1992, which complemented the Link review by, for example, covering site threats as well as damage. Close collaboration with the NI Department of Environment was maintained throughout the *"Safe and Sound?"* review, and the project was viewed as a constructive independent commentary on their site safeguard programme.

The Department welcomed the report's conclusions publicly at its launch and undertook to deliver a considered response. Aspects have since been discussed with the NI Environment Minister, in particular the question of resourcing the Environment and Heritage Service. Following this the Minister has asked that the Department investigate the comparative staffing levels of the Service in relation to the statutory agencies in Great Britain. (The RSPB was involved in a previous investigation of this question in the 1980s which showed the GB agencies to be proportionately better off: it is believed that this may still be the case.)

The SSSI system: priorities for improvements to the law. **Pritchard, D E. 1996.**

Summary

1. This paper is not a comprehensive review of the rôle of Sites of Special Scientific Interest (SSSIs), nor a full analysis of the system's performance and options for the future. Much has been written on this elsewhere. Instead this paper focuses on some targeted specific proposals for improvements to SSSI legislation which are judged by the RSPB to be top priorities for urgent action.

2. A summary of previous reviews of this subject, by statutory and non governmental interests, is presented. The 1981 Wildlife and Countryside Act (WLCA) was itself a response to the perceived weakness of the 1949 SSSI system. Originally this just required notification of SSSIs to the local planning authority and later laws provided for management agreements on the initiative of the Nature Conservancy (though no obligation to notify owners generally about the existence of sites) and consultation by planning authorities over applications affecting sites.

3. Commentaries just before and after adoption of the WLCA were critical of the new provisions based on notification to and consultation by owners and occupiers, as the trigger where necessary for management agreements. Initially concern focused on the likely

expense and the danger of unnecessary payments in response to spurious threats. It became apparent also that loss and damage to sites, which had been unacceptably frequent before, continued at alarming rates post-WLCA. Management agreements had some beneficial effect in relation to agricultural and forestry cases, but losses due to built development became more important.

4. The RSPB made submissions to statutory agency reviews and to inquiries by two Select Committees and amendments were enacted in 1985 and 1990 which tightened up some of the provisions. Discussion on the subject stimulated improved central collation of damage and enforcement information and many of the legislative reform suggestions which were generated remain in current "shopping lists" of desirable amendments kept alive since. Several publications were issued by the RSPB and others.

5. Transposition of the 1992 Habitats & Species Directive offered a further occasion for amendments to the WLCA to be promoted. As it turned out, the Directive was transposed by secondary legislation. However, the RSPB paper drawn up at the time remains the most detailed set of specific in-house suggestions for legislative change in relation to SSSIs. One or two of these have been acted on administratively, or in the Habitats Regulations.

6. Our paper then reviews what it is that SSSI legislation is trying to achieve. The objective of the SSSI network has been described as being to form a national network of those areas of the country in which the features of nature are most highly concentrated or of highest quality. Each site is seen as a significant fragment of a much-depleted resource and the total network is to be safeguarded in order to guarantee the survival of a "necessary minimum" of Great Britain's wildlife and physical features.

7. The component parts of this objective embodied in the legislation include:

-       decisions about where sites are located and the nature of their interest;

-       notification of these decisions to those responsible for the sites;

-       mechanisms whereby changes on or to the land which might harm its interest can be considered in advance by the conservation agencies, giving the opportunity for restrictions to be agreed; and

-   in the event of a failure to agree, some (conditional) provisions for restrictions to be imposed.

8. The fate of sites is often governed by statutes other than the WLCA, such as planning or water law. As well as providing for various processes, the legislation is also trying to achieve the upholding of some principles. One is the "purity" of the scientific basis for site selection. Decisions about land-use rights and how they may be affected are supposed not to enter into consideration until later. Another is the so-called "voluntary principle".

9. Whatever part compulsory methods may have to play, one might expect to look particularly to the "basic minimum" resource represented by the SSSI series as the place where they might feature most. Going too far in this direction of course would risk the undesirable result for conservation of mere minimal grudging compliance with the letter of the law, dependent on labour-intensive enforcement: but good fallback guarantees and availability of sanctions are nevertheless important.

10. SSSI law, like any law, is trying to strike a number of balances. For example, there is an inevitable tension between the precautionary approach required towards the uncertain risks of irreversible damage to sites and the convention of erring on the side of strict literal interpretation of laws which risk any interference with property rights.

11. The voluntary principle is characterised by some as necessary to offset the unchallengeability of the scientific decision about where sites are. However, to take this approach is to weigh against each other two unalikes with different currencies: a factual "labelling" of existing importance on the one hand and a political arbitration of competing land-use aspirations on the other. The Act tries to separate these into consecutive phases but the view that one overall "balance" should be sought (wrongly) intertwines and confuses them. Paradoxically, the more that conservationists are successful in "raising the stakes" over what SSSI status represents, the worse this confusion becomes.

12. The correct way to assess the balance which the system should be striving for is, instead, to compare the strength of the voluntary principle (ie the amount of owner/occupier discretion) with the

actual restrictions on future use which may be imposed. The question is whether the compulsion applied is commensurate with the rights of redress available to those aggrieved by it. The more democratic safeguards which the system provides, the more restrictions it can justifiably impose.

13. Conspicuously absent from the component parts of the Act's régime is any statutory conservation objective to be achieved by the SSSI network as a whole. This contrasts for example with the EU Wild Birds Directive and the Habitats & Species Directive in respect of Special Protection Areas/Special Areas of Conservation (which nevertheless depend on SSSIs for their delivery: this could therefore even be viewed as a transposition deficiency). This may yet explain the piecemeal, rearguard nature of the SSSI system's operation which is so often highlighted in criticism of it. There are also no statutory standards defining tests to be used for deciding the balance of the public interest in disputed cases.

14. On any analysis of how well the system is performing, the crude conclusion is "not well enough": SSSIs suffer too much damage, deterioration and disregard. In the context of looking at the Act, however, it is vital to distinguish which problems arise from its design and which from poor application of it. Reviews rightly point to resourcing and political will, etc, as problem areas; but the present exercise is concerned only with deficiencies in the legislation itself.

15. A basic legal weakness of the system is that, in all but exceptional cases, it does not give any certainty of protection. The thrust of the Act's processes is instead to buy time for negotiation, in an expectation that agreement will be reached. Often, of course, it is (and it is important to retain encouragement for this). Too often, however, it is not, and the law does not cope well with such cases. The available "fall-back" powers can only be invoked with difficulty, once some stringent tests are met, and subject to scarce resources and political resolve.

16. Continued damage to sites may increase public demand for strict controls. This is a difficult area, as suggestions for tightening the law are routinely met by counter suggestions for extra appeals, etc. Evidence suggests that inappropriate management is the most significant problem affecting SSSIs. The legal system is based on reacting to intentional damage, rather than guiding or initiating management. Good workable remedies where agreement cannot

be reached are not generally available. Provisions for restoration of degraded habitats and for access by statutory agencies to land are also seen as a high priority.

17. This paper sets out a detailed description of the functional changes to the legislation required to provide for a statutory purpose for the SSSI system; a test for deciding the public interest; enhanced provisions for restoring degraded sites; enhanced powers of entry for agencies and mechanisms for ensuring the right management of sites. The latter is in three parts. Firstly, it is proposed to retain the existing procedures for notification of intent to carry out a Potentially Damaging Operation and for progression to a management agreement, for the (hopefully frequent) occasions where arrangements to secure the interests of the owner or occupier, and all the measures deemed necessary to secure the conservation of the site, can be satisfactorily agreed between the parties.

18. Secondly, a new provision for "management notices" is proposed as a "half-way house" between management measures secured as above and Section 29 Nature Conservation Orders. A notice would be triggered in one of three ways, including breakdown of an agreement or attempts to reach one. The provisions for notices would include a requirement where appropriate to carry out specified works, provisions for resolving disputes and steps to take where requirements are breached. Crucially, also, the issuing of a notice would be accompanied by an offer of an agreement, so that this option remained available. Any agreement reached would then override the notice.

19. Thirdly, Nature Conservation Orders would remain available as an alternative mechanism but amended in some respects, including a provision for specifying positive works.

20. The paper then presents worked-up draft clauses for a Bill which would enact these changes and gives example scenarios and descriptive flow charts of the procedures proposed.

21. In considering how to take such proposals forward, a number of factors which need to be taken into account are discussed. The political importance of the "voluntary principle" is one. Views will differ on whether and how it is affected by any of the proposals in this paper; because views differ on what it is.

22. In general, the RSPB will work hard towards a situation where the right result for conservation comes about because the perceived value of doing so is shared by all concerned and things are arranged so that it is also in each player's interests (economic, social, etc) to work hard so that society can therefore rely on hard work being volunteered.

23. In the meantime, the SSSI system cannot rely on this. The voluntary principle in this context needs more specific definition. It is suggested that the principle should be "a presumption that voluntary action and agreement are possible and will be sought before mandatory requirements are invoked and an emphasis in the legislation on facilitating such an approach".

24. Public expenditure implications (if there are any) are not analysed here, though this will need to be considered. A more effective SSSI system could produce savings, for example through reduced litigation and less need to make up for shortcomings by nature reserve purchase.

25. In conclusion, there is a need and the time is right for a focused and practical change to SSSI law. There are, however, important pitfalls to avoid. Having taken these into account, this paper offers a set of reasoned proposals which the RSPB views as the top priorities. They are commended as a basis for the concerted action with others which will be required to progress an initiative on this front.

Comment

As this summary mentions, numerous reviews of the workings of the SSSI system have been carried out in the past, information about site loss and damage has been published and some changes to the law and procedures for implementing the system have been made. The RSPB chaired and edited a seminal review by Wildlife Link which resulted in the report *"SSSIs: A Health Check"* in 1991, and we published our own review of how these issues affected Important Bird Areas in 1992. An RSPB "health check" of the equivalent ASSI system in Northern Ireland was published in 1996 and is described elsewhere in this Chapter. Extensive proposals for reform have been canvassed with Select Committees, in briefings on Parliamentary Bills, and in submissions to Government on, for example, implementation of European nature conservation law.

While the system has serious failings and certainly needs improvement, organised landowning interests understandably look particularly closely at any proposals which may give an appearance of imposing new restrictions on landuse rights. Workable solutions therefore have to be found which are pitched in such a way as not to bring down on the SSSI system, in Parliament or elsewhere, the kind of attack which would undermine the gains being sought. Advancing proposals for change is thus a delicate business.

In 1994 and 1995 Friends of the Earth put forward proposals for a 12-clause Private Member's Bill which in 1995-96 progressed through the House of Commons but then ran out of time. The Bill did not deal with our main concern about management where agreement cannot be reached; and amendments were tabled by some MPs which threatened to weaken the system rather than strengthen it. The RSPB researched and produced the paper summarised here as a suggested way forward, in discussion with voluntary bodies, agencies and Government, for possible renewed attempts at tabling draft legislation in late-1996 or thereafter.

Chapter 5

ENVIRONMENTAL APPRAISAL

Democratically accountable decision-making in the UK can not be expected always and automatically to find in favour of environmental interests. This places a considerable onus on processes for examining and providing information about the environmental implications of a decision in a way that persuasively shows what the wisest course of action should be. A huge industry has grown up around techniques and regulations for environmental impact assessment and the papers here deal with some of the still-evolving aspects of this, including a comprehensive RSPB review of how the régime's implementation affects nature conservation in the UK. The Society has also pioneered ways to expand this thinking into plan and policy appraisal and examples of this are included here, too. The same theme is picked up under other topic headings, in the papers on appraisal of Trans-European Networks in Chapter 14, and on European-funded water management in Chapter 15.

Wildlife Impact: the treatment of nature conservation in environmental assessment. **RSPB. 1995.**

Summary

1. The RSPB commissioned a research project, carried out by David Tyldesley and Associates in 1994–95, to review the treatment of nature conservation in the Environmental Assessment (EA) process. This report aims to stimulate further improvements in the treatment of nature conservation in project EA and to help to ensure that developers, decision-makers, statutory and non-statutory environmental organisations and others involved contribute effectively to the process.

2. Thirty-seven Environmental Statements (ESs) were reviewed in depth using a standard form. They were selected to ensure a range of project types, geographical locations and publication dates. From the reviews and subsequent discussion with those involved, conclusions about current practice and recommendations for future improvement were developed.

3. The RSPB considers the essence of good EA should be:

-       a rigorous, scientific, objective and impartial assessment.

-       a clearly expressed analysis of the way in which adverse effects may be avoided, reduced or compensated and beneficial effects secured where possible.

-       an open, publicly accountable process involving extensive consultation.

-       a positive contribution to decision-making with clear commitments to comply with conditions and obligations on which any consent would rely.

-       a process with integrity, credibility and reliability, capable of supporting the decision on whether projects should proceed.

4. In particular, it should be clear to the decision-maker what the effects may be, how serious they may be, how they will be avoided or reduced and how measures to mitigate such effects can be guaranteed in the implementation and monitoring of the project, if it proceeds. There should be a clear indication of and a precautionary approach to any uncertainties which exist. It should also be clear that a valid assessment of alternative options and/or locations has preceded the application and how the project fits in with relevant national and local policies.

5. We provide 30 recommendations for all who participate in the EA process. All of the recommendations are important. The key messages is: all ESs should follow good practice guidance and the standard of all statements should meet those of the best statements produced in the past two years.

Comment

Environmental Assessment has been an integral part of the decision-making process for larger projects since the European Environmental Assessment (EA) Directive came into force in 1988. The RSPB has been active at EU and national levels influencing draft legislation and policy, as well as having direct involvement in some 200 specific cases. In 1994 we made substantive comment on the DoE's draft *"Preparation of Environmental Statements for projects that require*

EA: A good practice guide". We are also involved, at the time of writing, in influencing proposed amendments to the parent Directive 85/337.

Many reviews have looked at the quality of EA but prior to *"Wildlife Impact"* none had looked in depth at how the process treats nature conservation. Although ecology frequently forms a large component of Environmental Statements, the data presented are not always the most relevant, nor are the findings always adequately followed through in respect of final design and mitigation. The report therefore sought to influence both EA policy and day-to-day good practice.

Indications are that the report is being widely used as an authoritative work on nature conservation in the EA process. It was widely distributed to about 1,200 recipients, including all local planning authorities, and publicised in the planning press. It has been used in subsequent studies such as that by DoE reviewing the implementation of mitigation measures. Some of the recommendations will be partly delivered by changes to the EA Directive, whilst careful note of our findings by those preparing and reviewing Environmental Statements should improve their quality.

Comments to the Department of the Environment on *Environmental Statements for planning enforcement appeals*. RSPB. April 1995.

Summary

1. The RSPB recognises the loophole in respect of enforcement appeals which currently exists in the implementation of the Environmental Impact Assessment (EIA) Directive. We welcome the principle of these proposals which seek to ensure that any breaches are prevented in the future. We recognise that such cases may well be infrequent.

2. Whilst the requirement for EA within the enforcement appeal process is rather different from the process adopted in normal application procedures, it is important that the mechanisms used are as consistent as possible. In this context, the proposals in the draft Regulations raise a number of issues which may need to be considered further.

3. An impression is given by the consultation paper that the whole process will be undertaken in an unduly hasty manner.

4. The current proposals refer only to environmental statements rather than to environmental assessment. We consider that the production

of an ES is only one, albeit an important, element of the EA process. We comment on some of the others.

5. Overall, we strongly support the proposed introduction of these Regulations. Our concerns relate to the ability of the system proposed to ensure that a rigorous, objective environmental assessment process is undertaken. In particular, we consider that there is a need for a more explicit involvement by statutory and non statutory consultees, for adequate time for ES preparation and for consultations to take place. There should be support for the use of procedures to ensure that any continuing damage can be stopped or mitigated whilst the appeal process is being completed.

Comment

Prior to the Regulations which were the subject of this consultation, the provisions of the EA Directive did not apply to appeals against planning enforcement notices. A successful appeal could therefore result in planning consent being granted for a project without the application being subject to an EA, even if it should have required one. In practice, such cases may be rare but nonetheless this represented a loophole in the implementation of Directive 85/337.

The DoE issued a series of draft Regulations in April 1995, and invited comment.

The Regulations came into force in October 1995. In spite of our concerns, they were issued much as in their draft form. They focus on the procedures for obtaining and considering an ES. We believe that the content of an ES, in a situation where damage to habitats may already have occurred, may need to be rather different from the normal situation. We shall continue to flag up the need for guidance on this, and an opportunity may arise in a promised future revision of the 1988 *"Guide to the procedures"*.

Comments to the Essex Development Control Forum (and for use by the National Planning Forum) on the EDCF report *Environmental Assessment: the way forward*. RSPB. September 1995.

Summary

1. The RSPB strongly supports this initiative by the Essex Development Control Forum (EDCF). The original Essex guide to EA

produced in 1992 was one of the earliest county-based EA guides. Our experience in EA, at both policy and casework levels, would lead us to support most of the conclusions of the EDCF. The report focuses on just some of the main options for improving the operation of EA. We believe that others warrant equal attention. In particular we would like to see the National Planning Forum (NPF) playing a strong rôle in the advocacy of strategic environmental assessment (SEA).

2. The report should make clear whether it relates just to EA as it applies to the planning system, or more widely. Aspects relating to procedural and financial problems faced by local authorities in implementing the Regulations should be distinguished from comments on the need to amend the Regulations themselves.

3. We support the recommendation for mandatory scoping of EA. We agree with the proposed method for recording the scoping and consultation processes that are employed in compiling the Environmental Statement.

4. We support in principle the idea of establishing a process or organisation to provide an independent review of Environmental Statements. If this were to extend to "approval" of the ES, a number of additional questions would arise.

5. We would support the addition of new settlements to the development types requiring EA under the Regulations where they are likely to have significant effects. There are likely to be other development types which NPF members would wish to see added, such as golf courses.

6. We support the proposals regarding consideration of alternatives. A proper system of SEA would reduce the need for broad consideration of alternatives at project level in some cases.

7. We broadly agree with the recommendation to allow more time for completion of consultation and review. We also agree that the price of ESs should not be too high.

8. In addition to a consideration of other project types which should be added to Annexe II of the Directive, there are two other main issues of principle which we believe should com-

mand wide support within the NPF and on which we would urge the NPF to express a firm view:

(i)   Probably the most fundamental criticism of EA is that it comes too late to have an adequate influence on the choice of project type or location. The real determinant of these matters often lies with policies, plans and programmes which are what would be addressed by the concept of Strategic EA. The RSPB has for some time been actively supporting moves towards a European Directive on SEA.

(ii) Provision for post-project monitoring is seen as crucial, too: to ensure that techniques identified to mitigate damage or to provide compensation are actually carried out and that their success or otherwise is measured; to enable actual impacts to be compared with predictions and for remedial measures to be taken if necessary; and thereby to improve the accuracy of other predictions in future.

Comment

The NPF is a group representing a range of key players in the UK planning process. It aims to promote dialogue between different interest groups and to encourage the efficient and effective operation of the planning system, to promote high-quality development.

The EA initiative covered here arose from concern within the planning profession that the EA process was not meeting its full potential and that improvements could be made through a series of technical and procedural amendments. The proposals advanced could be implemented in the UK irrespective of any changes to the EU Directive, although the concurrent discussions on amending the Directive also provided a chance to promote improvements in the system.

The DoE responded in detail to the Forum. The DoE was sympathetic to a number of points. Arising from this initiative, the Forum decided to instigate a study of strategic EA, for which the RSPB has agreed to provide secretariat services.

Comments to consultants for Gordon District Council, the Scottish Office Environment Department and Scottish Natural Heritage (SNH) on their draft methodology for environmental appraisal of Scottish development plans. RSPB. January 1995.

Summary

1. The RSPB is pleased to comment on this pilot study for the application of environmental appraisal to development plans in Scotland. We are keen to see the techniques in due course applied throughout Scotland, as recommended in our report *"Planscan Scotland"* in 1992. There are many aspects of the document, referred to in our detailed comments, which we strongly support.

2. The appraisal process must be carried out by planning authority staff, rather than consultants, as the former know the plan area best. This will also prevent staff being distanced from the process and enable them to get a much better understanding of how their plan relates to sustainability. An important caveat to this is that third-parties, such as the SNH and the RSPB, should be used to provide advice on issues of which authority staff have little or no knowledge.

3. Independent validation of the plan environmental appraisal should be considered. More generally, the crucial point is that the presentation of the appraisal should be done in a transparent way and that all consultees have confidence in its findings and its effect on the plan.

4. The methodology concentrates on its application to local plans. This is understandable given that it is to be applied to the Gordon Local Plan. However, the final methodology should be applicable to both structure and local plans, as the project brief required. Careful distinction will be needed between those elements applicable only to one plan type and those relevant to both.

5. Rather than point out the perceived or actual shortcomings of the DoE guide, it would be more positive to put forward the proposed Scottish methodology as a "stand-alone" initiative. Only where there is significant disagreement with the DoE guide would cross-references be useful.

6. The proposed scoping process is seriously hampered by the

lack of government guidance on key issues. This, however should not be used as a reason not to carry out an appraisal. It does emphasise the need to make use of all available advice from statutory and voluntary sectors.

7. There is no mention in the proposed methodology of using plan appraisal to identify significant indirect impacts of policies/ proposals. This would be difficult to achieve with a matrix but is one of the very important contributions that the appraisal process can make to ensuring that plans become more sustainable. Indirect impacts are too often ignored at plan level.

8. A summary diagram illustrating the whole process would be helpful, to explain the connections between stages.

9. A list of possible consultees should be provided in the final document. This would emphasise the partnership approach that is essential to plan-making in general and which can benefit the appraisal process in particular.

Comment

The use of environmental appraisal in development plan preparation in the UK is largely confined to England, where the DoE published good practice guidance in 1993. This was aimed mainly at structure plans rather than local plans. In Scotland, take-up of such thinking has been very slow, partly due to lack of expressed government support. The pilot project summarised here represented the first real indication of Scottish Office (SO) support for plan appraisal. The SO indicated that, if successful, it would publish the methodology as a Planning Advice Note (PAN) to Scottish local authorities. The methodology broke new ground in applying environmental appraisal to local as opposed to structure plans.

At the time of writing the SO has yet to publish the methodology as a PAN and has given no formal indication of its intent to do so. Some Scottish local authorities are showing interest in using environmental appraisal in their development plan preparation. Since the *Gordon* exercise, only after Central Region (before reorganisation) and Perth and Kinross (post reorganisation) have so far attempted an SEA of development plans. Lack of the mooted PAN is hindering better development of the process.

A Step-by-step Guide to Environmental Appraisal. **Bedfordshire County Council/RSPB. 1996.**

Summary

1. Environmental appraisal of policies, plans and programmes, or SEA is an important decision-making tool which helps planners and others with decision-making affecting the environment. It helps ensure that potential environmental effects are considered coherently during the preparation of a plan or programme and that the resulting framework influences subsequent projects and actions to be more sensitive in their effects on the environment.

2. Environmental appraisal is becoming established practice in the development plan process in the UK. Publication of the *Step-by-Step Guide* marks the culmination of an important collaborative partnership between Bedfordshire County Council (BCC) and the RSPB, drawing on their respective pioneering experiences in this field. Applicable to more than development plans, it is intended that the Guide will encourage the wider use of appraisal by local authorities and other organisations.

3. Some local authorities still regard the idea of appraisal as too complicated and time-consuming. This Guide shows that it can in fact be straightforward, ultimately time-saving and, better still, cost-saving. It gives practical advice on what to do at each stage.

4. The benefits of an appraisal include:

-      helping to formulate and select options for meeting a plan's aims and objectives;

-      allowing alternative policy options to be compared in a consistent way;

-      ensuring policies are comprehensive;

-      showing clearly the specific likely environmental effects of policies;

-      helping to establish monitoring systems; and

-      raising the environmental awareness of all those involved;

- making explicit the justification for the choice of options and policies.

5. Relevant techniques are now fairly well tested but they will need to adapt and evolve further to meet the varied demands of those implementing the Government's commitments to sustainable development. They can be flexibly applied to different types of document.

6. Appraisal should be carried out on any document which includes policies and/or programmes which potentially have an impact on the environment. It should be an integral part of plan preparation from the earliest stage and carried out by the team preparing the plan or programme, aided by an independent assessor.

7. The appraisal process can be broken down into nine steps:

- deciding whether the appraisal can be integral to plan preparation or would need adding later in the process.

- deciding who will carry out the appraisal.

- scoping the factors and criteria for the appraisal.

- appraising the plan's aims and objectives, revising where necessary.

- identifying and assessing different strategic options for meeting the plan's aims.

- appraising the plan's policies, revising where necessary.

- appraising the plan's proposals, revising where necessary.

- presenting the results of the appraisal.

- setting up monitoring procedures for future plan reviews.

8. Early consultation with outside bodies is an important part of both plan preparation and the appraisal process. Getting the scoping stage correct is critical to a successful appraisal.

9. The effects of each policy or proposal on key environmental factors can be presented in a matrix. This will also serve as a framework

for monitoring and reviewing plan performance. Environmental factors would include:

Global environment:	Global footprint
	Transport emissions
	Industrial and other
	emissions
	Energy/fossil fuels
	Global biodiversity
Use of natural resources:	Air
	Water quantity and quality
	Mineral extraction
	Land and soil
	Waste
Quality of the local environment:	Landscape character and
	open countryside
	Quality of life in towns and
	villages
	Cultural heritage
	Open space and public
	access
	Quality of townscapes and
	buildings

10. Appraisal techniques will continue to develop further in future. Emerging areas for this include: exploring the linkages and interactions between policies; social and economic appraisals, leading to a full sustainability appraisal; and more work on specific issues such as environmental carrying capacity.

Comment

The RSPB puts extremely high importance on development plans produced by local authorities as a determinant of the approach taken to land-use policy and decision-making (see Chapter 7). Several publications in the past by the Society have reviewed practice in plan-making and made comprehensive recommendations. A study of non statutory local authority nature conservation strategies was also published in 1993.

Environmental appraisal is becoming established as good practice in the preparation of development plans in England. However, it has failed to penetrate far into district council level in England

and is little used elsewhere in the United Kingdom, at any level of plan preparation. Appraisal of this sort has had even more limited application outside the development plan field. A key reason for this is the perception by strategic planners that the process is complicated and time-consuming. The RSPB is concerned that many appraisals have little effect on the environmental sustainability of the actual plans, leading to criticism of the value of plan appraisal itself. The purpose of the Step-by-Step Guide is to promote best practice and to make appraisal both practical and accessible to strategic planners. At the time of writing it is too early to assess meaningfully the influence of the guide on the quality and range of appraisals being carried out. There has, however, been high demand for the guide which indicates that it is at least meeting a need.

Comments to the European Commission on the *"Proposal for a Directive on Strategic Environmental Assessment (the assessment of plans and programmes)"*. RSPB. (on behalf of BirdLife International) June 1995.

Summary

1. BirdLife International strongly supports the development of a system of Strategic Environmental Assessment (SEA) throughout the EU. We welcome the opportunity to comment on this draft Directive prior to adoption by the Commission. We agree that a system of SEA is an essential and logical progression of the project EA Directive 85/337/EEC. We are confident that it is feasible and practical. It will benefit the decision-making process throughout the EU. The draft Directive is clear and well constructed.

2. We are disappointed that the Directive does not address the full range of policy, plan and programme formulation. We make a series of proposals for ensuring that policy appraisal and the principle of a hierarchy of decision-making are not entirely lost from the Directive. In particular, Annexe II information should include the repercussions of higher levels of assessment for consideration of lower ones, and of those for lower levels still.

3. In the absence of provision for policies, the assessment of programmes and plans must be thorough. We propose some more precise definitions to ensure that some programmes and sub programmes do not "fall between" this Directive and the project Directive 85/337.

4. We also propose a number of additional sectors that should be added to the provisions in Annexe II. In particular, these include plans relating to regional development and to wetland, coastal and marine environments.

5. The Directive as a whole must be more explicit in identifying SEA as a mechanism for exploring a range of strategic options, rather than as a post hoc assessment of a chosen strategy. This can be achieved by modifying the objective of the Directive and by adding to Annexe II.

6. The provisions on exemptions must be tightened to place greater onus, in relevant circumstances, on Member States consciously to "opt out" from certain provisions and to explain clearly their reasons for doing so.

7. Adequate information is the basis of good SEA. We believe that the Directive could support the development of systematic information collation at national, regional and local levels which could then act as a baseline for assessment, and thus ensure consistent and adequate information is available whilst preventing unnecessary repetition and expense in data provision.

8. We believe that most of the information in Annexe II should normally be included within the SEA unless there are good reasons for not doing so. The analysis of effects must explicitly include secondary and cumulative effects.

9. We believe that monitoring of plans and programmes is essential for testing predictions and ensuring a consistent improvement in policy and prediction at subsequent cycles.

10. It is essential that strategic environmental assessment is integrated also into EU programmes and plans. Although the Directive itself is directed to Member States, parallel steps must be taken within EU institutions.

Comment

BirdLife International (BI) is a global partnership of over 100 bird and habitat conservation organisations. The RSPB is the UK partner. Many partners are influential in decisions made about land-use changes which will affect birds or their habitats. We have found environmental assessment to be indispensable in improving understanding and highlighting the environmental implications of these landuse changes. However, like others, we find that the EA process has limitations: not least the fact that many project options are foreclosed as a result of decisions made prior to the project stage. It is this gap that we seek to close through the development of systems of SEA. SEA can also address cumulative and synergistic impacts of multiple developments, as well as the impacts of measures which are not implemented by specific projects.

Research commissioned by the RSPB from Oxford Brookes University was published by Earthscan Publications in 1992. That book set out in detail the need for SEA, reviewed experience to date and considered the rôle of SEA in decision-making in the energy sector, in coastal zones and on lowland heathlands. BirdLife International activity on SEA since that time has focused both on advocacy of a Directive and on research to show that SEA is a practical tool capable of assisting in decision-making, as with the study on hydrological management in the Tajo Basin, Spain, covered next in this Chapter.

Several papers on proposed EU legislation on SEA have been issued by the Commission since 1991. Since the RSPB submission to the Commission in 1995 described here, we have discussed specific issues further both with them and with the UK Government. At the time of writing, it seems likely that the Commission will publish a proposal for a Directive in autumn 1996. Their scope to strengthen its provisions is currently limited by reservations held by a number of Member State governments. BirdLife and other non government organisations will need to try to win support from these governments if an effective SEA process is to develop throughout the EU.

Strategic Environmental Assessment and hydrological planning in the Tajo Basin, Spain. **Summary report of a study by Lola Manteiga and Rodrigo Jiliberto. RSPB/SEO BirdLife España. 1995.**

Summary

1. A review of hydrological planning in the Tajo river basin, Western Spain, was commissioned by the RSPB and undertaken in 1994 by consultants and the Sociedad Española de Ornitología (SEO/ BirdLife España). The core aim of the study was to assess whether

the existing hydrological planning process exhibits, or could exhibit, the principles of Strategic Environment Assessment (SEA). Primary methods were analysis of the three major relevant instruments of planning: the national Water Law, Ley de Aguas (LA), the National Hydrological Plan, Plan Hidrólogico Nacional (PHN) and the Tajo Catchment Plan, Plan Hidrólogico de la Cuenca del Tajo (PHT).

2. SEA describes a means by which the environmental implications of decision-making processes (within policies, plans or programmes) can be analysed. It could play a key rôle in the integration of environmental policies in the European Union (EU). Based on this study, we sought to make recommendations for the development of SEA, both in Spain and elsewhere in Europe.

3. Although elements of strategic appraisal are apparent in the Tajo system, the study concluded that this system fails to deliver a comprehensive analysis of the environmental impacts of water resource developments. There is inadequate attention to the prioritisation and resolution of conflicting objectives. There is a failure properly to assign responsibilities for environmental protection, poor data on existing resources, no consideration of alternative options and inadequate analysis of impacts or adherence to national or EU legislation.

4. Hydrological planning continues to be driven by the need to meet demand, especially for irrigation, although these demands are not always properly estimated. Environmental protection is a secondary consideration. Seventeen areas of international importance for birds are threatened by water-related projects in the Tajo basin. This threatened environmental damage is especially serious in the light of the substantial funds from the EU which are invested here.

5. Events since the study was completed offer hope that elements of a more strategic approach may yet develop. The Spanish Parliament did not approve the PHN in autumn 1994 as anticipated, because of the lack of information on irrigation. Consequently the Ministry of Agriculture has been asked to draw up a national irrigation plan. This is now underway and appears at least to have included better information on the threats to environmentally sensitive zones.

6. SEA would identify the substantial environmental impacts of the current plans and would help to highlight the gaps in environmental protection which exist in the system at present. SEA could

ensure that revisions to each of the items of legislation and planning built in environmental safeguards in a comprehensive and effective way, without undue overlap. It would assess a range of alternative strategies and options for water resources management and provide consistent information upon which to base choices. End projects could thus be developed within a more environmentally sustainable framework.

7. SEA will not, of itself, achieve necessary policy changes. Policies, plans and programmes themselves must have corresponding environmental protection objectives if assessment is to facilitate this process. Indeed, environmental sustainability could be a core objective of all associated planning régimes. Change is urgently required before EU funds are invested in programmes which have adverse environmental impacts.

8. The study demonstrates that SEA could be achieved within existing policy frameworks and that it could achieve positive environmental benefits. Whilst methods will differ, we believe that an EU Directive will provide the best foundation for its consistent development.

9. The report suggests a basic method for developing SEA, based on a matrix showing the implications of each policy or option for a range of environmental parameters. It also considers the level of detail required in each tier of SEA from national plan through to individual project.

10. To be effective, SEA will also need to cover policy sectors, will need to be undertaken throughout the process of policy formation and will need to be capable of influencing subsequent tiers of assessment. It must be based on sound baseline information which is publicly accessible, alternative strategies must be fully considered and the implementation of the policies must be monitored.

11. In the long term, the objective will be for fuller integration of SEA and decision-making processes. However, even with a full SEA system, there will continue to be an important rôle for a thorough assessment of individual projects, albeit that those projects should have emerged from a more effective and rigorous analysis of options.

12. Fuller consideration of the structure of hydrological planning in the Tajo basin, of the impacts of current proposals on the environment

and on recommendations for improved procedures can be found in the full report *"Strategic Environmental Assessment and hydrological planning in Spain"* by Lola Manteiga and Rodrigo Jiliberto for SEO/BirdLife España and RSPB.

Comment

Following the publication of research commissioned by RSPB from Oxford Brookes University in 1992, we wished to pursue practical examples of how SEA could be made to work. The Tajo study produced, in October 1995, the first of a series of reports investigating the feasibility of SEA in Europe. Other work has addressed Trans-European (transport) Networks and Important Bird Areas, the "environmental profile" in the Structural Funds process and the transport plan for Castilla Y Leon (Castile and Leon), Spain.

Spain continues to make substantial investments in new water resources infrastructure, assisted by funding from the EU. At the outset of this study, the system appeared to be regulated in a way which had good potential to integrate SEA but with serious problems in practice caused by the respective rôles of national and regional government. The Tajo basin was chosen for the study because it contains a good representation of ecosystem types and Important Bird Areas at risk from proposals for irrigation and dams. In addition, the Tajo plan was considered among the most advanced in Spain and a wide range of planned developments were represented in the basin, each with substantial water demands.

The report was commissioned from consultants in Madrid, and the contract managed by SEO, BirdLife's Spanish partner organisation. The final report was produced in both Spanish and English, and an additional summary report in English explored the implications for SEA a little further. The findings have been used extensively in our work on water resources, SEA and the Structural Funds at EU level. In Spain, SEO have used the report to press for better integration of water resource planning activities and to seek reductions in the impacts of proposals in the Tajo itself. They also launched a national campaign, Rivers of Life, to promote the conservation of Spanish riversides.

Chapter 6

LOCAL GOVERNMENT ORGANISATION AND REGIONAL PLANNING

L ocal government determines much of what happens to species and habitats and hence defines a major area of work for the RSPB in interacting, for example, with the formal land-use planning system. Reforms to the structure of local government have therefore demanded a considered input of views on the relative merits of alternative ways forward, in terms of how they might affect the delivery of functions affecting conservation. In the case of consultations over future options in England, the summary presented here is a distillation of a large number of separate area-by-area submissions which nevertheless each promoted similar issues of principle. This Chapter has also been chosen as the place to cover planning policy consultations which deal with systems operating between the UK level and the local authority level; hence the inclusion of items on planning guidance in Wales, Northern Ireland and Scotland. RSPB research on planning policy for the English regions is underway, but at the time of writing is too incomplete for inclusion.

Comments to the Local Government Commission for England (LGC) on *Draft recommendations on the future local government of England*. **RSPB. Various submissions, July 1994 - August 1995.**

Summary

1. It is disappointing that the Local Government Commission's remit does not permit it to examine the functions of local government. It is our view that the present review is incomplete because it is restricted to examining local government structure. It is therefore not allowing local people to express their opinion on what they want their local government to deliver.

2. The review is founded on a belief that current service provision is confused and that the establishment of unitary authorities will reduce this perceived confusion. The reasons for this are far from clear, for example whether it is a function of the two-tier system itself or simply a lack of public information about the functions

that each tier of local government performs. The "no change" option should not be overlooked.

3. The RSPB considers that any change to local government structure will have implications for nature conservation. Any new form of local government administration must be able to deliver effective nature conservation services throughout its service range.

4. Although the Secretary of State's direction to the LGC to "reflect the identities and interests of local communities" is important, in reaching its conclusions on local government structure the LGC must also address what structures are necessary to deliver sound local government in the 21st Century. It must not place undue emphasis on identity with past historical structures (often created to govern communities in the 19th Century) where these are no longer appropriate.

5. Above all, the RSPB is keen to ensure that any future system of local government will enable effective delivery of local authority planning at both the strategic and local levels and of environmental/conservation functions.

6. Planning is a key element of local government reform but only one element of the current review. Planning provides strategic land-use guidance and represents the "bottom-line" for safeguarding sites of importance for nature conservation. It is imperative that planning does not become an "accidental victim" of local government reform. The RSPB therefore wishes to see the retention of a two-tier development plans system (although not necessarily a two-tier local government administration) with strong and separate structure plans and local plans. Strategic plans provide an important overview as they operate over long time-horizons and large geographical areas and can ensure an integrated approach to landuse decisions. Local plans provide the necessary means to examine local needs and to translate strategic issues to the detailed level.

7. The Society is therefore pleased that the LGC generally rejects the unitary development plan approach in its report *"Renewing Local Government in the English Shires - A Progress Report"* (1993) (para. 60). The tension between development plan tiers is an integral part of the planning process. Local preferences must sometimes be outweighed by strategic concerns for the benefit of society as a whole. The two-tier system helps in establishing where the greater public interest lies.

8. Any new structure must be capable of adequately dealing with cross-boundary/cross-border issues, such as river catchment basins and large habitat blocks.

9. Should a system of unitary authorities smaller than present counties emerge anywhere from this review, then statutory joint working will be essential to enable the preparation of a structure plan for the "county area".

10. A number of non planning local authority activities which are important for conservation are likely to be affected by structural reform. These include nature conservation strategies, "state of the environment" reports, provision of specialist advice by in-house ecologists, habitat creation and management on local authority land, designation of Local Nature Reserves and environmental education. The review process must specifically consider these.

11. The Regional Planning Guidance (RPG) system will require careful examination as reform will affect the composition of regional groupings, associations and conferences of local authorities. The content of RPG in any case needs considerable expansion but not as a replacement for structure plans.

Comment

This summary gives the RSPB's principal concerns expressed in submissions on county-by-county reviews by the LGC between September 1993 and November 1994. The LGC had been established to evaluate the most appropriate form of local government structure for all the shire counties of England. This was the first reorganisation of these county areas since 1974. Metropolitan counties were reorganised in 1986, changing from two tiers to unitary councils. We made submissions in respect of all counties except Cornwall, Devon, Dorset, Northumberland and Wiltshire. We sought, among other things, to ensure that important local government environmental and planning functions were not "sacrificed" in the wide-ranging review.

Submissions in 1991 on initial proposals and in 1992 on the draft guidance to the LGC highlighted strategic planning as an important issue. The LGC were subsequently specifically instructed to make recommendations on this area in their reviews.

In 1995 the LGC re-examined 9 county areas - Cheshire, Devon, Gloucestershire, Kent, Lancashire, Surrey, Northamptonshire, Nottinghamshire and Shropshire. The RSPB made additional submissions on these.

The final picture of revised authority areas is an assortment of two-tier, unitary and "hybrid" council areas. From an initial government position of favouring unitary authorities, 15 counties are now to be two-tier, 19 predominantly two-tier with one or two unitary authorities (all bar two nevertheless retaining two-tier planning) and only six counties are to be abolished in favour of unitary authorities. A total of 46 unitary authorities have been created and the last of these will assume power on 1 April 1998.

In Wales and Scotland, reorganisation was achieved in one round, without recourse to an independent commission. Our submissions on initial proposals in 1991 and detailed proposals in 1992 (Wales) and 1993 (Scotland) echoed the broad concerns expressed in England. In Wales, 8 county councils and 37 districts were replaced by 22 unitary councils on 1 April 1996. A unitary approach to planning, too, has been adopted here. In Scotland, on the same day, 9 regional councils and 53 districts were replaced by 29 unitary authorities. The three existing unitary island councils of Orkney, Shetland and the Western Isles were unaffected. Councils are expected to co-operate to prepare structure plans for specified joint areas (an issue dealt with next in this Chapter).

Structure Plan Areas: **comments to Scottish Office Environment Department on "Local Government etc (Scotland) Act 1994: structure plan areas". RSPB. July 1995.**

Summary

1. We warmly welcome the Government's continued commitment to strategic planning and the retention of structure plans.

2. Ideally, we believe that structure planning should take place with biogeographic boundaries which do not artificially divide important ecological systems.

3. With the constraints of the new local government structure, a number of the proposed Structure Plan Areas (SPAs) cause the Society some concern. Specifically, we are concerned that strategic planning

in the Forth and Clyde estuaries, and across the Cairngorms, may not be as effective as it could be. Some suggestions are made for improvement.

4. New and updated guidance on structure planning should be issued, addressing the issues of co-operation and implementation and incorporating up-to-date advice on environmental sustainability.

5. The Secretary of State should indicate his willingness to intervene to appoint Joint Boards wherever this is necessary to ensure the requisite collaboration between Councils. The Scottish Office should also closely monitor development control activities and be prepared to intervene decisively, eg in cases of significant inconsistency.

Comment

This Scottish Office consultation paper followed the passing of the Local Government etc (Scotland) Act 1994 which reorganised local authorities in Scotland into 29 unitary Councils. The Act abolished many of the Councils that had previously been responsible for Structure Plans but the Government remained committed to the maintenance of strategic planning. Structure Plans are thus to be retained and will be produced for areas designated by the Secretary of State as SPAs. This context is the reason for inclusion of this item in the local government organisation Chapter; though obviously it is relevant also to Chapter 7 on development plans.

The 17 proposed SPAs were published for consultation, and the submission summarised here set out the RSPB's views on the proposed areas. In essence, our comments reflected our view on local government reorganisation in general: that is, that good strategic planning should not be the accidental victim of administrative reorganisation. The proposed SPAs were confirmed by the Secretary of State without alteration in December 1995.

A topical controversy at the time of writing, in the shape of the proposed Cairn Gorm funicular railway, neatly illustrates many of our concerns. The Cairngorms are undoubtedly a single (and exceptionally important) biogeographic unit but are divided between three planning authorities. One (Highland Council, in whose area the planning application falls) is strongly in favour of the funicular proposal, while the other two (Aberdeenshire and Moray) oppose the proposal which is sited just 400 yards from the Moray boundary.

Despite this, the Secretary of State has, to date, shown great reluctance to become involved by "calling in" the application.

Submission to House of Commons Northern Ireland Affairs Select Committee inquiry on *Planning in Northern Ireland*. RSPB. September 1995.

Summary

1. The RSPB welcomes this inquiry. At the core of the Society's interest in planning is the statutory site safeguard system. In Northern Ireland [NI], 17 sites have been identified as internationally Important Bird Areas. Many other sites are of national importance and qualify for designation as Areas of Special Scientific Interest (ASSIs). Northern Ireland possesses a rich wildlife heritage.

2. Although the NI countryside is relatively unspoilt when compared to parts of Great Britain [GB], it has still undergone considerable change. The RSPB wishes to ensure that the planning system delivers relevant international conservation commitments and duties.

3. Nature conservation needs to be considered over large geographical areas and long timescales. Development plans are, therefore, crucial tools as they identify sensitive sites and can help to steer potentially damaging development to more appropriate locations. Our report *"RSPB Planscan Northern Ireland - a Study of Development Plans in Northern Ireland"* makes a series of recommendations on this subject.

4. It is a matter of concern that the Northern Ireland Office [NIO] has yet to find the legislative time to introduce the "plan-led" system in NI as it has now existed in GB since 1991.

5. The volume of potentially damaging development applications is expected to rise sharply in NI as a result of the more stable political climate in the Province.

6. The RSPB believes that planning in NI is at present best served by a relatively well-resourced centralised government body. We are not convinced that there would be any advantage in shifting powers and functions currently held by the Department of the Environment Planning Service (DoEPS), for example, to local authorities.

7. The RSPB would ask that the Committee considers preparing a set of requirements or standards which must be met by the system in relation to environmental objectives, whoever is charged with administering it. These should include:

-   a "strategic cascade" of planning guidance;

-   recognition of the need to protect internationally and nationally important nature conservation sites;

-   comprehensive and up-to-date Area Plan coverage of the Province;

-   environmental appraisal of development plans;

-   Area Plans to follow the DoE good practice guidance;

-   introduction of the plan-led system in NI;

-   development proposals to be subject to tests of environmental acceptability based on sustainability principles;

-   a criteria-based approach to determining applications likely adversely to affect sites of nature conservation importance, including examination of need, alternatives, etc;

-   applications affecting ASSIs to be referred to the most senior decision-making authority;

-   adequate public participation;

-   good enforcement;

-   urgent establishment in NI legislation of various provisions already introduced in GB relating to minerals planning, review of old consents and new enforcement procedures, etc;

-   a coastal zone strategy; and

-   replication in NI of a number of environmental functions that rest with local authorities in GB.

8. The precise impact of the proposed restructuring of the Planning Service as a "next-steps" agency is difficult to predict, because information on the reorganisation has not been readily available. It is assumed that while many procedural functions would be adopted by the new agency, the policy-making aspects would be retained by the DoE. We view this as essential. We are concerned that there was no official public consultation on this issue. We are very concerned that the replacement of many sections of leading government Departments by agencies may compromise the integration of policies and objectives. At the same time, opportunities presented by the reorganisation are in our view being missed.

9. Another concern is that the new planning agency will be governed by a series of targets and objectives relating to cost control and efficiency. Financial targets must not be so restrictive that they preclude the achievement of certain biodiversity and sustainability-related targets and objectives which are in themselves government policy.

10. In our view, a new Planning Policy Guidance note series is required, following more closely both the style and content of the PPG series in GB. In particular, this should address minerals, general policies and principles, the countryside and the rural economy, nature conservation, development plans, transport, tourism and recreation, enforcement of planning control and use of conditions. This would help with a necessary improvement in consistency of decision-making, particularly between DoE Divisional Offices.

11. The existing *"Planning Strategy for Rural Northern Ireland"* should be replaced by a NI Planning Strategy, which would highlight the current situation in relation to development in the Province and examine possible future trends and scenarios.

12. The RSPB is concerned that development control decisions are often made without an up-to-date Area Plan being in place. Issues of prematurity may arise and we would advocate the issuing of guidance on this along the lines of GB's PPG1.

13. The RSPB is concerned that enforcement of development control by DoEPS lacks consistency. The Department also has insufficient statutory powers and resources in this area. Recent enhancements of GB enforcement legislation would be worth emulating.

14. We suggest that the Committee might consider whether there are limited grounds that could be established for third-party rights of appeal in certain circumstances.

15. The system could be made more transparent than it is. It is often difficult to obtain detailed information relating to particular planning decisions, even as a formal objector.

16. The Society is concerned that management of the NI coast currently lacks co-ordination. A lead organisation is required to co-ordinate and integrate the activities of all relevant bodies. Planning issues on both land and sea should be integrated, and this would be assisted by extension of planning control jurisdiction beyond the low water mark. Better guidance on coastal planning is required and we also recommend production of a Coastal Zone Local Plan.

17. The RSPB is concerned at the standard of environmental information being provided in Environmental Assessments [EAs], although this is improving in places. Published guidance is out of date. Statutory consultation procedures should be amended so that all main commentators and objectors are notified directly about any key additional information in an EA submitted at the planning authority's request. We commend to the Committee a range of other recommendations in a soon-to-be-published RSPB study of EA.

18. Critical views have been published elsewhere on the NI Rural Planning Strategy and the process by which it was produced, and we draw the Committee's attention to these. We are particularly concerned by its claimed rôle in determining policy content of Area Plans without consultation.

19. The RSPB welcomes the move by Planning Service towards earlier consultation in the development plan process. The use of environmental information in the making of many plans is still poor. We are also concerned at the scant policy detail which is available in most preliminary proposal documents. The distinction between policy and supporting text is often not clear.

20. EA of development plans is now gaining wide acceptance in GB as a valuable tool in the preparation of development plans. This is a form of Strategic Environmental Assessment (SEA) which aims to assess the effects of a plan's policies and proposals on the environment of the plan area. The RSPB applauds the Fermanagh Area

Plan team for adopting this technique in the preparation of their plan and we wish to see it more widely used.

21. The RSPB is concerned at the lack of opportunity for both objectors and supporters of an Area Plan to comment on the Planning Service's proposed modifications to the plan at the adoption stage. Equally, there is no opportunity for third-parties to comment on the Commissioner's interpretation of arguments at Inquiry, or the Planning Service's response. This contrasts markedly with the statutory system in GB, which the RSPB would prefer to see followed.

22. Rural development issues are clearly increasing in importance in NI. This can provide opportunities for nature conservation benefits, for example through environmentally sensitive farming and "green tourism". There is also scope for conflict, so it is particularly important that environmental issues are integrated with economic and social considerations, perhaps through input to groups such as Area Based Strategy Action Groups (ABSAGs).

23. Environmental pressures are already manifest in Fermanagh as a result of tourism schemes. Much has been permitted on a haphazard and piecemeal basis and the true cumulative impact of these developments will not be immediately apparent. The Northern Ireland Tourist Board (NITB) accepts that long-term development is dependent on a high-quality environment and planning decisions need to take account of this.

24. There is much talk of a "democratic deficit" in the context of the planning system in NI. This submission outlines a number of areas where the situation could be improved.

Comment

Following this submission, the RSPB gave oral evidence to the Committee, and provided supplementary written evidence in December 1995. The Committee's report adopted a number of key recommendations from the Society's submissions. These included the need for increased resourcing of the Planning Service, the need for more qualified and expert staff, and the need to adopt a plan-led system in NI. The report described the management of the Service as "dangerously complacent" on the issue of staff workloads and efficiency of the Service. The Government's response to the Committee is due in October 1996.

Planning and Nature Conservation **Comments to Department of the Environment (Northern Ireland) on draft "Planning Policy Statement 2: planning and nature conservation". RSPB. March 1996.**

Summary

1. The Planning Policy Statement (PPS) should have the status of guidance to Divisional Planning Offices and others involved in the planning system, rather than being binding unchallengeable policy.

2. The RSPB supports the use of Countryside Assessments in the preparation of development plans. We recommend the adoption of a common standard for the preparation of such assessments, including the identification of local sites. Proper resourcing must be provided to Divisional Offices.

3. We welcome the Department's support for the use of environmental appraisal in development plan preparation and urge the Department to prepare its own guidance on this topic.

4. Development plans should include maps identifying all designated areas.

5. The RSPB supports the commitment to the use of criteria-led site protection policies for local sites. We recommend that criteria be applied to all nature conservation policies.

6. The PPS should state that all development plans should contain policies for the protection of landscape features of major importance for wildlife.

7. Policies CON 1- CON 3 of the Rural Planning Strategy are not robust enough for development control purposes. We suggest new policies to be used in future development plans as a minimum of good practice.

8. The PPS should not contain reference to the use of habitat translocation as compensation.

9. All Areas of Special Scientific Interest (ASSIs) are nationally important: the PPS should state this clearly.

10. Reference to the potential impact on designated sites of developments outside their boundaries should be amended to include all potentially adverse effects arising from outside the site.

11. A clear commitment to provide adequate resources for planning enforcement work is required.

12. The RSPB welcomes the publication of the draft PPS as it represents a key step in the implementation of the EU Habitats & Species Directive in Northern Ireland (NI). It also presents a major opportunity to ensure that international nature conservation commitments, as well as national legislation and policy, are fully implemented in NI. The international context for species protection provided by the Wild Birds Directive and the Habitats & Species Directive should be clearly set out.

13. It should be made clear that the potential exists for more Special Areas of Conservation (SACs) to be identified as more survey work is carried out.

14. Improved versions of the flow diagrams for decision-making in the context of the Directives should be used in Annexes 4 and 5, as per the draft PPG for Wales.

15. The full text of the Wild Birds Directive, the Habitats & Species Directive, the Ramsar Convention and the Wildlife Orders should be included as Annexes.

16. We consider that the failure of the PPS to include a specific section on the impact of mineral extraction on peatlands is a very serious omission. The Department's existing policy statement on peatland conservation should be reflected in the text and placed in context with other nature conservation issues.

17. Emphasis must be given to the rôle of the Planning Service and other government departments in implementing the targets and objectives of the UK Biodiversity Action Plan.

18. Reference should be made to the need to conserve the "wider countryside".

19. Policy guidance should be provided in relation to NI's coastline.

20. A clear statement is required on the fact that in some cases economic growth cannot be accommodated without harm to the environment and in such cases it should not proceed.

21. The final document must contain a section which sets out the relationship and consultation arrangements that will operate between the Planning Service (PS) and the Environment and Heritage Service (EHS), PS and the Council for Nature Conservation and the Countryside (CNCC) and PS and other relevant Next Steps Agencies (NSAs).

22. Legislative time must be found to update Northern Ireland's planning legislation to bring it into line with that in Great Britain, in particular by the introduction of a "plan-led" system.

23. Policy SP14 of the Rural Planning Strategy (concerning nature conservation) should be updated.

Comment

The RSPB's approach to this consultation included a comparison of the draft PPS with Planning Policy Guidance note 9 in England. Existing planning guidance on nature conservation in the Province dated from 1990 and had become inadequate in important respects. The final version of the PPS appears, at the time of writing, unlikely to be issued before March 1997. In the meantime, the Department of Environment (NI) are believed to be considering the Society's suggestions carefully.

Comments to the Welsh Office on *Draft Planning Policy Guidance (Wales)*. RSPB. September 1995.

Summary

1. The RSPB is deeply concerned by the draft *Planning Policy Guidance (Wales)*. In our view the PPG is too generalised to be of help to many of those involved in the planning process. It represents a backward step by comparison with the English PPG series which, in general, we welcome as a user-friendly framework of policy advice. The Wales draft fails to provide planners, the public, developers and landowners with sufficient guidance to help them interpret the Government's key land use planning policies.

2. Consequently, it is our view that the draft Wales PPG should not be issued, that extant PPGs such as PPG20 ("Coastal Planning") should be retained and not cancelled, while those PPGs that have recently been issued in England but which have yet to emerge in Wales, such as PPG9 ("Nature Conservation") and PPG13 ("Transport"), should be issued in Wales without delay.

3. Our comments on the consultation paper *"Planning Guidance (Wales): Unitary Development Plans"* are contained in a separate submission.

4. The RSPB supports the need for planning guidance in Wales to reflect institutional and administrative differences from other parts of the country. However, we do not support attempts to vary or omit planning advice previously released in England where such advice reflects UK Government policy commitments.

5. There are some potential attractions in adopting the single PPG. It might, for instance, reduce duplication, help with consistency and integration of policies and facilitate environmental appraisal of the PPG. However, the size of the resulting single PPG, if it were to reflect the full range of advice that we consider it ought to, might make it unwieldy.

6. The draft PPG also has significant disadvantages. Its brevity and lack of detailed advice on important planning issues is our foremost concern. In particular, important background and technical material, and statements of general government policy which appear in equivalent English guidance, are missing.

7. Lack of explanatory material in the PPG is likely to lead to confusion and uncertainty on the part of applicants, local authorities, decision-makers and the general public. The brevity of this "all-encompassing" draft PPG is likely to lead to more rather than less debate and doubt over development plans and planning applications and at Public Inquiries.

8. It is essential that comprehensive Strategic Planning Guidance in Wales (SPGW) is issued to provide the necessary framework for planning decisions. It is a matter of great concern that the "slimline" PPG is said to incorporate SPGW. We do not regard the PPG as an adequate replacement for SPGW, particularly with the new Unitary Development Plan system being introduced throughout Wales.

9. The RSPB fundamentally objects to the proposed cancellation of the existing detailed coastal guidance contained in PPG20. The advice contained in the single paragraph of the draft PPG is greatly inferior to the advice on coastal planning that has hitherto applied in Wales.

10. Planning guidance on nature conservation should be consistent throughout the UK to reflect UK Government commitments to biodiversity and sustainability. The nature conservation content of the draft PPG needs to be greatly expanded.

11. There is a significant difference in the guidance relating to consultation and advice, etc, in respect of the Countryside Council for Wales (CCW) by comparison with equivalent parts of PPG9 relating to English Nature (EN). It is imperative that the guidance indicate that CCW should be consulted whenever there is any doubt about whether a development is likely to have an effect on an SSSI.

12. "Minerals Planning Guidance (Wales)" should not cancel extant MPGs in Wales unless there are genuine and legitimate policy differences which apply to Wales. It should reproduce the full breadth of minerals guidance contained in MPGs which have not yet been published in Wales.

13. The map of areas of growth and restraint towards the end of the PPG should show individual designated and candidate Ramsar sites and Special Protection Areas (SPAs).

14. The two flow diagrams relating to (a) the consideration of development proposals affecting SPAs and Special Areas of Conservation and (b) permitted development rights and SPAs and SACs, are an improvement on those in PPG9.

15. Although Technical Advice Notes (TANs) may be helpful for local authority planners, depending on their content, the absence of detail in the draft PPG is likely to cause more doubt and debate for developers, the general public, etc. We do not see the role of TANs as replacing important technical information and background material in the PPG series.

Comment

The redrafting of planning guidance for Wales was requested by the then Secretary of State John Redwood. Despite his subsequent departure, and strong opposition to the Welsh Office's proposals being voiced by the RSPB and others (including discussions at follow-up meetings between RSPB and the Welsh Office), the single condensed guidance note was issued in May 1996, under a revised title *"Planning Guidance (Wales): Planning Policy" (PG[W])*. It contained few changes from the draft, one being the deletion of the two flow diagrams which we specifically praised. The RSPB heavily criticised PG(W) in the planning press.

The first set of 10 Technical Advice Notes (TANs) were issued for consultation in June 1996. These included TAN 9 on "Nature Conservation and Planning". Although this contains some guidance on nature conservation which was missing from PG(W), when compared with the equivalent in England, crucial advice on areas such as protection of species and nature conservation outside designated sites is still seen to be absent. The RSPB submitted detailed comments on this draft TAN. At the time of writing a further 10 TANs were due to be issued for consultation in October 1996.

Chapter 7

DEVELOPMENT PLANS

Development plans are fundamental in guiding planning strategies and individual decisions and have long been a high priority in the RSPB's planning and local government work. Government policy over the past decade has swung from proposals to abolish structure plans to a position, welcomed by the Society, where the plan is now a primary consideration in the planning process. Prior to the papers summarised here, the RSPB published a series of three well-known landmark reports reviewing development plan practice in Scotland, Northern Ireland, and England and Wales, and similarly reviewed local authority non statutory nature conservation strategies. Also relevant are the items on environmental appraisal for Scottish development plans and the Step-by-Step Guide to environmental appraisal (of plans) in Chapter 5, and on Scottish structure planning areas in Chapter 6.

Comments to Welsh Office on *Draft Planning Guidance (Wales): Unitary Development Plans in Wales*. RSPB. September 1995.

Summary

1. The draft Planning Guidance (PG) fails to set out the rôle of development plans in delivering sustainable development. The rôle of development plans in meeting the Government's sustainability commitments must be addressed in the final Guidance.

2. The RSPB supports collaboration by local authorities on strategic objectives and policies. However, guidance must be provided on how such objectives and policies should be agreed, implemented and reviewed.

3. A modified version of Annexe A of Planning Policy Guidance note 12 (Code of Practice on Plan Preparation) should be included as an annexe to the final PG.

4. Guidance should be provided on the use of policy performance indicators in environmental appraisal and in plan monitoring and review.

5. The RSPB fully endorses the use of environmental appraisal in plan preparation. Additional points should be added on the benefits which this technique brings to plan preparation.

6. The use of targets in plans should be extended to cover all issues relevant to the implementation of sustainable development through the planning system.

7. The RSPB does not consider that the draft PPG (Wales) can be relied upon for general policy guidance for Wales. Our separate submission on that draft PPG makes clear our serious concerns about its inadequacy which are such that we have urged that it should not be issued.

8. Full Strategic Planning Guidance for Wales should be published to provide a proper context for "Part I" of the Unitary Development Plans.

9. More specific guidance should be given on the issues to be addressed at the plan survey stage. Assessment of nature conservation issues should be a prerequisite.

10. The RSPB welcomes the continued support given to predeposit consultation on draft plans.

11. We are concerned that the enforceability of the Secretary of State's call-in powers for plans judged not to be consistent with national guidance will be compromised by the very general nature of that guidance (see separate submission on draft PPG Wales).

12. Further guidance should be provided on the mechanisms for the preparation, adoption and implementation of joint plans.

Comment

Local government in Wales was reorganised to a unitary structure in 1996. The Welsh Office published the draft Guidance considered here, with the intention that it would replace Planning Policy Guidance Note 12 with "Development Plans and Regional Planning Guidance". A weakness of the unitary structure is the lack of a strategic approach to key land-use planning issues, including nature conservation. Strategic planning in Wales now relies on voluntary joint working and agreement of joint planning objectives between neighbouring authorities. Both the draft Guidance note and the final version, issued in April 1996, avoid anything more than a general reference to this issue. In other respects the new Guidance is a mixed blessing. It lacks PPG 12's Code of Practice on the preparation of development plans and fails to set out the rôle of Unitary Development Plans in implementing the Government's policy on sustainable development. On the positive side, it promotes the use of environmental appraisal (dealt with in Chapter 5 of this volume) and of targets and policy performance indicators, to give direction to a plan and to measure how well it has achieved its aims and objectives.

Town & County Planning; **Comments to the Department of the Environment on proposed amendments to the Town and Country Planning (Development Plans) Regulations 1991 and the Code of Practice on Development Plans. RSPB. April 1996.**

Summary

1. The RSPB supports the proposal to require local authorities to serve notice of proposed modifications on "such other persons as (they) think fit", in addition to those who have made objections/representations and have not withdrawn them.

2. We do not object to the proposed clarification of a local authority's existing discretion over whether to hold an inquiry/hearing/Examination-in-Public into certain types of objection. If this leads to fewer secondary or re-opened inquiries/EIPs it will be important to ensure that objectors are provided with full and proper documentation of the local authority's response to their objections.

3. The RSPB objects to the proposed amendment to the Code of Practice which would refer only to making the adopted plan available at a reasonable charge, since we believe the current interpretation intends the deposit draft plan to be available too.

4. The RSPB supports the clarification that written and oral objections carry the same weight.

5. The RSPB supports the move to encourage local authorities to produce one set of pre-inquiry changes at least six weeks before the Pre-Inquiry Meeting, and we recommend that all objectors and supporters be formally notified of pre-inquiry changes.

6. The RSPB supports the use of summaries for long proofs of evidence. In addition, we support the move to ensure local authorities provide topic papers and core proofs earlier in the process.

7. We recommend that the Code of Practice be amended to make it clear to local authorities that they should send a copy of the statement required under Regulation 17 to all relevant objectors.

Comment

These consultation proposals were aimed at improving the speed of local plan preparation which has been a cause for concern among those involved in plan preparation and development control. They followed an earlier DoE consultation with more radical proposals on this issue. The DoE decided not to proceed with its more radical suggestions. Instead, it put forward the relatively minor and non-controversial changes commented on here, in an effort to encourage speedier consultation, inquiries and adoption of plans. Many of the measures proposed were of no great concern to the RSPB. Of those commented upon, the RSPB supported the majority as sensible and pragmatic measures which aimed to ensure that objectors to plans are made aware of their rôles and responsibilities during the complicated processes of plan consultation and plan inquiries.

Chapter 8

DEVELOPMENT CONTROL

Development control generally refers to the myriad individual planning decisions taken by local authorities and is thus distinguished from development planning. It is the arena in which much of the RSPB's daily interaction with councils and developers takes place, with professional staff of the Society in regional offices throughout the UK being involved in a total of several hundred cases each year. The Society's policy staff includes chartered town planners formerly employed by local authorities. Some celebrated cases make the headlines: many others are the more straightforward but indispensable currency of influence over decision-making. The cumulative experience generated from this, in terms of perceptions of trends, occasional failings in the system, good practice worth promoting more widely and intelligence about the strengths and weaknesses of the RSPB's own performance, is fed directly into central policy work. The items presented in this Chapter show some examples of the way this is used.

Natural Conditions: a review of planning conditions and nature conservation. **Brooke, C. 1996.**

Summary

1. The RSPB is involved in town and country planning both in the policy arena and in responding to specific planning applications which affect sites of importance for bird conservation. Planning conditions are increasingly seen as a means of overcoming nature conservation objections to proposals. The Society therefore conducted research to examine how effective planning conditions were in securing nature conservation objectives.

2. This research is particularly timely, given the recent updating in England and Wales of government guidance on the use of planning conditions (PCs). It is the first review specifically to relate PCs to nature conservation. As such, it should be an essential reference for all planning officers (PO) and developers involved in relevant development proposals.

3. The report explains good practice in the use of PCs through a wide range of case studies and also examines problems encountered. It has been designed as a practical tool for POs and developers. In particular, 10 "good practice principles" have been drawn up to provide a key checklist when considering development proposals (DPs) with nature conservation implications.

4. This report examines the use of PCs to achieve a wide range of nature conservation objectives. Research has focused on PCs, although some nature conservation measures may instead require planning agreements and these are also discussed.

5. From the year 1990-95, 560 cases were drawn from all parts of the UK where PCs or PAs had been used for nature conservation purposes. These were examined and divided into four groups according to their objectives, *viz* measures to:

-      protect habitats or species;

-      provide environmental enhancement;

-      mitigate potentially adverse impacts; and

-      provide compensation for losses or impacts which can not be mitigated.

6. Government guidance advises that PCs should be used to prevent adverse impacts and to protect important habitats and species. Guidance on nature conservation also encourages better management of sites and care of the countryside in general, citing PCs or PAs as a means of achieving this.

7. Our research found that this is not happening in many cases. Only 12% of the cases studied involved conditions to protect nature conservation interests or to avoid potential adverse impacts. Moreover, only 0.7% directly sought to provide genuine enhancement for habitats, species or features of interest. Of the cases, 8% involved positive nature conservation measures but these were as compensation for loss of habitats or adverse impacts caused by the development.

8. The majority of the cases examined used PCs to provide mitigation, in other words accepting that some impact will still occur. This included measures to be taken before commencement of the

development, during construction works, after completion of the development, or during operation of the permission. PCs used to control the design and layout of built development to reduce impacts on vegetation or protected species, to minimise damage during construction works and to require replanting or reseeding of affected areas. In addition, controls were imposed on the storage and disposal of materials, and on the use of chemicals, fertilizers and pesticides. Mitigation measures were also put in place to reduce the impacts of changes of use, for example to minimise disturbance. Most of these measures involved restrictive, or negatively worded conditions, although some positive works were required, for example the provision of a buffer area between the development and a sensitive habitat.

9. The RSPB wishes to see more use of PCs or PAs to provide genuine enhancement for wildlife. Enhancement could be achieved by improving existing features, for example through planting gaps in hedgerows with indigenous species to enhance a wildlife corridor, or by creating new habitats for example where the current nature conservation interest is low. This requires the will and commitment of developers to seek opportunities to include enhancement in their development proposals. It also requires POs to identify possible enhancement when considering applications.

10. Great care has to be taken over habitat creation, as in many cases the scientific basis for the successful establishment of a particular community of plants and animals is not well developed. This is particularly important if the habitat creation measures are intended to compensate for losses resulting from the development. Of the cases where such measures were provided through PCs or PAs, 11% involved sites of national importance - SSSIs/ASSIs. The creation of new habitats will usually require a PA since commitment over a long period will be needed to ensure that the flora and fauna are successfully established and to secure the necessary finance. These arrangements cannot be imposed as a requirement by PCs.

11. The research highlighted problems in the practical application of conditions and in the procedures followed by planning authorities. The key points which emerged are summarised below. A total of 32 recommendations are made in the report for addressing these issues.

12. The first problem for local planning authorities (LPAs) is identifying the nature conservation interest of a site and deciding what

measures are required to make the development proposal acceptable, or whether permission should be refused. This is a matter of obtaining relevant, up-to-date information on the habitats or species concerned from existing sources where these are available, and/or by conducting a survey of the site. Environmental Assessment (EA) provides a useful tool for assessing the likely impacts of a proposal.

13. EAs are not required for every application, although some developers do submit Environmental Statements (ESs) voluntarily. The RSPB encourages the use of surveys and EAs to provide information to help the planning authority determine applications. The provision of clear and comprehensive ESs by developers can assist in speedy decision-making.

14. LPAs provide an obvious centre for holding information on nature conservation resources within their area and greater emphasis should be given to this. Often it will be necessary to consult specialists such as ecologists, statutory agencies (SAs) and voluntary conservation groups (VCGs). Potential applicants should search through information sources and, where necessary, consult specialists at an early stage in project development and certainly before they submit applications. This will enable any sensitive sites or species in the application area to be identified and, where possible, impacts to be avoided. This reduces the need for LPAs to impose restrictive PCs at a later stage. POs should also consult widely when considering applications, to get advice on the nature conservation implications of the development. (In the case of some applications there will be a statutory duty to consult certain bodies.) This helps the planning officers to decide whether PCs or PAs can be used to make the proposal acceptable in nature conservation terms, or whether this cannot be done and they should recommend refusal.

15. A second major problem identified during the research was the way POs decide whether it is PCs or PAs that are required. Government advice is that PCs should be used in preference to PAs where possible but in practice there still appears to be some confusion. Both fulfil the same function of overcoming a planning objection to the granting of planning permission. Both can be used to secure benefits for nature conservation. Both impose obligations on the applicant which must be honoured if the permission is implemented. Nevertheless, they are separate mechanisms and agreements should not be used where a condition could be imposed. The Courts have

interpreted narrowly the powers to use PCs and so they are limited in what they can achieve. PCs are mostly used as restrictive measures, although in some cases positive measures can be required. PAs will generally be needed for positive requirements such as management of land or financial commitments, for example to fund the establishment of a nature reserve.

16. Our research found examples where conditions had been duplicated by agreements, or where the measures contained in the agreement should, in our opinion, have been imposed as a condition. This report tries to distinguish where each mechanism should be used.

17. A third problem arises in the actual imposition of PCs. Government guidance provides six tests for PCs: that they must be necessary, relevant to planning, relevant to the permission, clear and precise, enforceable and reasonable. In many cases examined, conditions did not meet one or more of the six tests or were unlawful (*ultra vires*). In particular, PCs should not be vague: poor examples include expressions such as "minimise disturbance to wildlife", or "safeguard the interest of", or "during the breeding season". The RSPB believes that good practice should be for all planning decision notices (PDNs) to state exactly what is required for compliance, including:

-       what is required;

-       when it should be done;

-       what processes need to be used to achieve it; and

-       what part of the site or process it relates to.

This must be in language which is unambiguous and readily understood by the lay person.

18. Following good practice such as this avoids problems at a later stage if the LPA wishes to take enforcement action. The introduction of the Breach of Condition Notice (BCN) as a new enforcement tool in England, Wales and Scotland (by the Planning and Compensation Act 1991) has highlighted the importance of setting good PCs. This is because BCNs require conditions to be complied with within a specified period. POs have found that many conditions imposed are not enforceable because they have not been worded sufficiently carefully.

19. The research has raised considerable concern over a general lack of monitoring and enforcement of conditions. Once planning permission has been granted, many LPAs do not systematically monitor the consents. In 38% of the cases studied it was not known whether the permission had been implemented, let alone whether the conditions or agreements had been complied with. The effectiveness of PCs and PAs in benefiting nature conservation depends upon the willingness and/or the ability of LPAs to monitor and enforce them.

20. The RSPB believes that it is essential for planning authorities to monitor developments to ensure that conditions are complied with. LPAs should set priorities for monitoring, with cases potentially impacting on nature conservation interests being a high priority. They should ensure that the responsibility for monitoring is clearly allocated and, where possible, have a nominated officer specifically to monitor compliance with conditions. In addition, they must establish procedures for quickly responding to any breaches found, particularly if irreparable damage to flora or fauna may be done. Monitoring also helps future decision-making by illustrating uses of PCs which have or have not been effective in the past.

21. Training is important to provide POs with a general knowledge of the wildlife in their area. This may also be required for enforcement officers (EOs), if they are expected to check breaches of planning control involving nature conservation interests. In addition, it is vital that POs are aware of any relevant site designations (DSs) and understand the purpose of each designation. This type of awareness would also benefit applicants so that they could avoid designated areas and incorporate measures in their applications to protect, enhance or mitigate in relation to the nature conservation interests affected by the proposal.

Comment

POs can make the difference between a planning proposal which is acceptable and one which is unacceptable and hence between refusal and approval. Nature conservation presents special problems. The successful regulation of development to protect or enhance the natural environment is not easy. It requires a good understanding of the subject, an appreciation of what practically can or cannot be achieved and a will to enforce the result. Our research revealed that these basic requirements are not being met. Further RSPB work is planned which will pick up on particular inadequacies in relation to follow-up of decisions and enforcement.

Much more practical guidance on how to deal with nature conservation in planning decision-making has emerged in recent years. The need to be able to insist on modifications or restrictions to make development more environmentally acceptable also carries more legal weight, for example through the requirements of the EU Habitats & Species Directive. The RSPB's conditions project has been welcomed by the planning profession as a valuable practical tool in the decision-making process. The timing of the project was opportune, because the Government was at the time reviewing its *Circular* on conditions. This review however was more in the nature of an update than a radical rethink. The next review will have the full benefit of our research and recommendations.

Leisure activities: **submission to the House of Commons Environment Select Committee inquiry on the environmental impact of leisure activities. RSPB. March 1995.**

Summary

1. The RSPB is generally in favour of increasing access opportunities in the countryside. We believe it is an important part of nature conservation that people should experience wildlife in natural surroundings whenever possible but not in ways which may cause harm.

2. Increasing leisure activity brings both threats and opportunities for wildlife. Pressure is put on the countryside by the development of recreational facilities and by the general promotion of access. Areas of high nature conservation value are targeted for such development because of their attractiveness to visitors. Greater powers need to be given to local authorities and other tiers of government to manage the demand for leisure rather than simply controlling development in certain areas. Benefits for rural communities from leisure and tourism development will not be sustainable (in economic or environmental terms) if they are carried out at the expense of the very assets which attract visitors.

3. Government planning policy and guidance must:

-    protect designated areas from the direct and indirect effects of tourism and leisure development;

-    assess adequately the likely environmental effects of
     proposed development and guide it to locations where it
     does not result in adverse environmental impacts;

-    where leisure or tourism development is appropriate,
     encourage design plans for facilities, which include environ-
     mental conservation measures such as access by public
     transport, efficient use of energy and water and habitat
     creation; and

-    encourage low-impact tourism requiring minimal development
     and promoting understanding of the countryside.

4. Strategic Environmental Assessment (SEA) should be carried out on all government policies, plans and programmes, and Government should support an EU Directive on SEA.

5. The powers and jurisdiction of local authorities in the coastal zone should be enhanced. This should include the extension of planning powers over the seabed to a seaward distance of 12 nautical miles, and regulatory powers over recreational uses of the water surface.

6. Planning Policy Guidance note 17 (Sport and Recreation) should be revised to make reference to PPG 9 (Nature Conservation) and to the requirements of the EU Habitats & Species Directive.

7. The Sandford Principle (conservation should be given greater weight where it irreconcilably conflicts with recreation) should be extended to areas of nature conservation value outside National Parks (NPs), and should be included in Regional Planning Guidance (RPG) and in the policies of all types of development plan.

8. The Government should revisit its review of permitted development rights and consider removal of these rights in respect of activities such as water sports, orienteering, take off and landing of microlight aircraft, parachute drop zones and hang gliding, within or near SSSIs.

9. Coastal areas illustrate particularly well the range of issues which need to be addressed and the importance of an integrated approach. They also contain 60% of the UK's internationally Important Bird Areas (IBAs). A National Coastal Strategy is needed to

guide and integrate the whole range of uses of the coast. Production of management plans for estuaries and the coast should be mandatory and resourcing and manpower issues must be addressed to enable their implementation and updating. Consideration must be given to extending the powers of management agencies to implement management plans where inadequacies are identified. The RSPB welcomes the review of byelaw powers relating to coastal management.

10. The rôle of the Crown Estate Commissioners (CECs) should be reviewed, and their quasi planning functions transferred to a more appropriate authority. Control of shooting rights over intertidal areas should be transferred from the CECs to local authorities.

11. The RSPB commends to others the principles it follows for visitor management on its own reserves, namely:

-   Where there is conflict between management for wildlife and management for visitors, management for wildlife takes precedence.

-   Improvements to visitor facilities will be in proportion to the likely demonstrable gains for conservation from, e.g., environmental education.

-   Provision of structures such as visitor centres, paths and signs should be the minimum necessary to meet management objectives. Such provision should respect the character of the countryside, with structures which are in harmony with their surroundings.

-   Visitor facilities should, wherever possible, be useable by visitors with disabilities.

12. Nature reserves must have management plans which address visitor management as well as conservation management. Where visiting may conflict with nature conservation, conservation should take precedence and measures should be taken to reduce or manage visitor pressure.

Comment

The House of Commons Environment Committee reported on this inquiry in July 1995. It concluded that "according to the balance of evidence we received, compared to other activities, leisure and tourism do not cause significant widespread ecological damage to the countryside" whilst noting that "there is no need for complacency". The Committee called for a revision of Planning Policy Guidance note 17 to incorporate the concept of sustainability, criticised the slow progress on coastal zone matters and indicated that "there is a need to address the issue of permitted development rights again both in terms of noise nuisance and possible environmental damage". It had little to say on Strategic Environmental Assessment, extension of the Sandford principle beyond National Parks or the rôle of the Crown Estate Commissioners.

Comments to the Scottish Office Environment Department on *Draft National Planning Policy Guideline (NPPG) on planning and flooding.* **RSPB May 1995.**

Summary

1. Lack of regard to development in areas at risk from flooding could adversely affect sites of nature conservation importance.

2. The draft guidance does not adequately address areas of nature conservation importance and the conservation value of areas at risk from flooding. Wetlands support threatened species and habitats and development in such areas can cause direct or indirect impacts.

3. More detailed advice on important nature conservation sites, clearly setting out legal requirements and responsibilities, must be included in the guidance.

4. The RSPB advocates the development of a system of integrated catchment management to achieve strategic co-ordination of the work of local authorities and the other bodies with responsibilities within catchments. The Society has recommended that the Scottish Environment Protection Agency (SEPA) should have a key rôle in this but clearly any such system would have to be very closely tied into the development plan process.

5. The RSPB supports the concept of managed retreat from existing coastal defences where appropriate. The guidance should advise how this principle could be incorporated into the development plan process in Scotland.

Comment

The final NPPG was published in September 1995. The issued guidance does not differ greatly from the draft, although there is greater emphasis on the implications which flood prevention measures can have for the natural environment, and the legal requirements applying to designated sites (DSs) such as SSSIs, SPAs and SACs.

The Guidance states that planning authorities should first seek to avoid increasing the flood risk by refusing permission where appropriate, and secondly, seek to manage the threat of flooding only in cases where other reasons for granting permission take precedence over flood risk. There has been no attempt to address the issue of catchment management with relation to flood defence, or to integrate rural flood management with urban flood management (see the item on flooding legislation in Chapter 11 below).

Comments to the Scottish Office Development Department on *Draft National Planning Policy Guideline on skiing developments.* **RSPB. April 1996.**

Summary

1. We welcome this replacement of the 1984 guidelines, and the acknowledgement of the quality of Scotland's natural environment and obligations to conserve it.

2. Skiing developments only occur or are only proposed in Scotland's highest mountain regions. These are some of our most fragile and valuable areas for wildlife, much of which is covered by national and international conservation obligations.

3. The NPPG tends to over emphasise the importance and size of the skiing industry, and fails to distinguish between the downhill and cross-country sectors. Indications that demand for downhill skiing remains high lack supporting evidence. A full assessment of likely demand should be undertaken before the Guideline is finalised. This should address what level of demand should actually be planned for, on the basis of environmental constraints and other factors.

4. Skiing developments must be fully consistent with the principles of sustainable development, which include the conservation of biodiversity. We support the NPPG's precautionary approach to

the further development of skiing in Scotland and its abandonment of the distinction between primary and secondary areas, as well as the "strict environmental tests" to be applied to proposed new areas for skiing development.

5. Possible new sites, such as Ben Wyvis and Drumochter, are now recognised as being of exceptional environmental interest. We do not oppose the development of new ski centres *per se* but the Guideline should identify those few undeveloped but potential sites proposed for European conservation designations where new developments will not be granted except for reasons of overriding public interest.

6. We welcome the advice regarding consolidation of existing centres and the recognition that growth and expansion in existing ski centres will be dependent on a number of factors, including an area's nature conservation characteristics. These factors should also include the potentially adverse economic effects of skiing developments on other local activities.

7. The inclusion of a section on the conservation of natural heritage is welcome but the NPPG should include a paragraph referring to the proposed nomination of the Cairngorms as a World Heritage Site.

8. The guidance on developments likely to affect Special Protection Areas or Special Areas of Conservation, and sites proposed for such designations, fails accurately to set out the tests necessary for determining planning applications affecting such sites. Skiing developments likely to affect proposed or designated SPAs or SACs should not be permitted unless it can be demonstrated that the proposals will not have a significant adverse impact. Potentially damaging development may only be approved if it has been demonstrated that there are no alternative solutions and, in the case of sites hosting priority species and habitats, it is necessary for reasons of human health or safety (or in the case of other sites, imperative reasons of overriding public interest).

9. Areas designated under national environmental legislation are also very important for nature conservation. SSSIs should benefit from a similar approach to that set out above for international sites. They require a similar demonstration that there will be no significant adverse impact, or that no alternative solutions are available and the development is of overriding national interest.

10. We welcome the inclusion of the section on use of skiing developments for purposes other than downhill skiing. Such non-skiing use can have serious environmental consequences. In most Scottish centres, skiing developments would be wholly uneconomic without associated non-skiing uses, yet it is these latter which in many cases leads to the possibility of conflict between the development and the environment. The consideration of any proposed non damaging complementary development, where the skiing development itself is acceptable, must be undertaken by the developer and planning authority as early as possible in the project design/planning process.

11. We recommend that the word "summer" is replaced throughout paragraphs 38, 39 and 40 with "non-skiing". We consider that skiing developments should not carry any automatic "presumption in favour" of allied (non skiing) use.

12. The section on monitoring and management should be amended to indicate that monitoring and management will be employed to keep damage to within pre determined acceptable limits.

13. The Society strongly supports the use of Environmental Assessment as a tool to help foster well-informed and sound decision-making. We have concerns about a number of the statements in this section and consider that some paragraphs require re-drafting to reflect the EA Regulations properly.

14. The draft does not provide adequate justification for the total expansion provided for in the "area guidelines", which amounts roughly to a 50% increase in capacity over the next five years. It is unclear whether this increase is envisaged as a target, a limit, or whether there are further targets or higher limits to be applied beyond the next five years. This fundamental issue must be addressed in the final Guideline. Only once a rational target has been established should the Guideline give advice on accommodating expansion in specific areas.

15. The issue of management of the Cairngorms is being progressed by the Cairngorms Partnership management strategy. This could lead to a fundamentally different approach to the operation of the skiing development at Cairn Gorm. We recommend that the final NPPG, or at the very least the Cairngorm advice, should not be published until the Partnership has completed its strategy.

16. We support the suggestion that, subject to EA, limited expansion of skiing into Coire Laogh Mor and Marquis Well would be acceptable. This limited and conditional expansion will only be consistent with environmental safeguards if appropriate protection is afforded to the mountain core and to the Northern Corries.

Comment

Scotland is the only area of the UK containing significant skiing developments. The same biogeographic circumstances which lend themselves to this, however, also mean that many of these areas contain fragile montane habitats and rare birds such as dotterel and snow bunting.

The draft NPPG discussed here will replace the extant 1984 guidelines. As such, the RSPB welcomed the draft NPPG as it promised to bring up to date a number of matters, particularly environmental issues, which had become outdated. Many existing and proposed ski areas are affected by European nature conservation designations and the draft updates planning authorities with regard to SPAs and SACs.

The issuing of this guidance was very topical in the light of the prevailing controversy over a proposed funicular railway on Cairn Gorm. This application, ostensibly a modernisation of the skiing facilities, remains of concern at the time of writing because of its potential to permit access to increased numbers of non skiers to the fragile mountain environment. The draft NPPG suggested a presumption against the use of skiing developments outside the skiing season, unless it is shown that no environmental impact will result. At the time of writing the finalised version of the guidance is still awaited.

Comments to the Department of the Environment on the *draft Circular on Section 78 planning appeal procedures*. RSPB. May 1996.

Summary

1. The RSPB is grateful for the opportunity to comment on this draft *Circular*. We welcome the Secretary of State's intention (stated in the covering letter with the draft *Circular*) to make the appeals system even more effective without compromising the quality of the decision or the underlying principles of natural justice.

2. We welcome much of the guidance contained in the draft. Our detailed comments concern the need to promote best practice and to ensure that third-parties have a full opportunity to participate in the appeal process on fair and equal terms. Whilst the revised *Circular* should help achieve this, further improvements could be made in respect of preappeal considerations, submission of appeals, costs and the general conduct of public inquiries.

3. Unsuccessful applicants should only be encouraged to re-apply for planning permission if objections can realistically be overcome. This is especially important when dealing with proposals affecting nature conservation interests.

4. The encouragement to use written representations and informal hearings is noted. However, there are occasions when a public inquiry is the only way of properly considering an appeal, especially when there are potentially harmful impacts on sites of national or international importance for wildlife.

5. Third-parties should be entitled to claim costs at planning inquiries if circumstances warrant it.

6. Emphasis on prompt appeal procedures and setting timetables (especially for public inquiries) is welcomed. All parties should also be encouraged to provide ready access and copies of all appeal documents when requested.

7. More encouragement should be given to representatives of Government Departments to answer questions directed to the merits of government policy.

8. More recognition should be given to the importance of competent assessors in the consideration of specialised issues such as nature conservation.

9. The provision for "reference back" or reopening of an inquiry should be used if new environmental information comes to light, or if there is a change in the status of a site, particularly its legal status.

10. The updated codes of practice for appeals are welcomed, as is the encouragement to parties to exchange information and identify areas of dispute prior to an appeal being heard. This advice is equally applicable prior to the submission of any application. The RSPB

also supports the intention to curb repetitious or irrelevant evidence and aggressive cross-examination.

Comment

The RSPB is a regular participant in planning appeals and public inquiries. The appeal process can often be the arena where new environmental legislation and government policy advice are most pointedly put to the test. We monitor the progress and outcomes of appeals very carefully. We do this to test the workability and strength of legislation and advice and to ensure that we have a full opportunity to take part in the process. We welcomed the draft *Circular* on planning appeals. However, our experience suggests that still more could be done to ensure that "third-parties" such as the RSPB have the opportunity to participate equally and fairly in the process. Our comments on the draft *Circular* sought to emphasise this.

Chapter 9

MINERALS AND WASTE

It is an often-repeated maxim that "minerals can only be worked where they occur" and the same might be said about conserving wildlife. This could be expected to produce some intractable conflicts and the example of superquarries covered in this Chapter has been portrayed by many in that way. Policy frameworks need to be particularly carefully crafted for this sensitive area. Involving, as they may do, large-scale landscape and habitat manipulation, minerals operations also potentially offer great scope for positive creation and enhancement of conservation interest and much imaginative after care and restoration work has produced such benefits. The item on waste management also presented here underlines the often intimate relationship between these two fields. Related items on offshore oil and gas extraction, marine oil pollution and waste disposal facilities in ports can be found in Chapter 10.

Comments to the Department of the Environment on draft *"Minerals Planning Guidance note 7: the reclamation of mineral workings"*. RSPB. February 1996.

Summary

1. This guidance note covers one of the most important areas of mineral activity, dealing as it does with the long-term implications of extraction and the resultant problems and opportunities. We welcome this draft revision as timely in view of the many policy developments since 1989. We welcome those elements of the guidance which encourage nature conservation after use. Overall, however, we do not consider that it provides the positive encouragement of such use which accords with other government objectives for the conservation of biological diversity, in particular those espoused in the UK Biodiversity Action Plan.

2. The text still deals predominantly with agricultural after uses. There is no recognition of the important amenity and nature conservation benefits of certain kinds of agriculture and forestry. We are disappointed that what information there was in the existing MPG7 is now transferred from the main text to an annex.

3. The RSPB's fundamental principle is that all mineral extraction must be located so as not to affect adversely areas of nature conservation importance. The precautionary approach must therefore be taken when considering granting permission for extraction. On sites of high wildlife value, mineral working is likely to be unacceptable, irrespective of the quality of any restoration proposals that may accompany an application. The quality of restoration should not be a material factor in deciding whether a location is suitable for mineral extraction, but should be a key element of any decision once the "in principle" acceptability of the site has been determined.

4. The restoration of worked-out mineral areas provides a major opportunity to contribute to objectives of the Biodiversity Action Plan and the targets set out in the report of the Biodiversity Steering Group. This can be achieved by creating new semi natural habitats and appropriate locations for the re-establishment of lost or threatened species. The lack of linkage to the Government's objectives for biodiversity conservation is therefore both surprising and disappointing. We seek explicit reference to these opportunities in the final text. The guidance acknowledges that nature conservation is an option, but it could give a much stronger endorsement of nature conservation after use.

5. We welcome the statement in paragraph 14 that nature conservation after uses are acceptable on even the best and most versatile agricultural land, provided that it retains its long-term potential as an agricultural resource. The guidance could help planning authorities by being more specific in identifying those habitat types which meet this criterion. Paragraph 62 still appears to assume that such "alternative standards" are only applicable to land that is not the "best and most versatile" and this should be amended.

6. Much of the detail in the draft still relates to techniques primarily for reversion to agriculture. The dearth of detail on restoration to nature conservation and other amenity uses may discourage the industry from tackling alternative proposals. The MPG should include, in a detailed discussion of nature conservation after use:

- further discussion of the opportunities to fulfil objectives in the UK Biodiversity Action Plan;

- guidance on when restoration to nature conservation is particularly appropriate, for example where there are important adjacent habitats or where soil or hydrological conditions suit a particular habitat type;

- discussion of some of the key habitats which can be created in old mineral workings such as reedbed, heathland and grassland;

- reference to other useful information sources;

- mention of the additional need for planning agreements, to ensure that management can continue beyond the five-year aftercare period; and

- a tabular summary of basic requirements for different nature conservation after uses, akin to that given in Table 5 for water-based recreational uses.

7. It is apparent that the five-year aftercare period is not always adequate to secure nature conservation interests and that longer-term management is essential on almost all sites managed for wildlife. These management proposals should be submitted as part of the application and modified in the light of the environmental assessment process and in the light of subsequent evaluation of their success. We believe serious consideration should be given to extending the aftercare period where different objectives require a longer-term perspective to be taken.

8. In some cases, natural regeneration can be a very successful method of establishing a nature conservation after-use. It will normally be preferable to intensive planting of such areas and, in the longer term, can result in more successful colonisation by locally prevalent species. Mechanisms are suggested to ensure that management and enhancement of old mineral workings which have developed wildlife interest can be resourced.

9. We refer to some guidance documents on nature conservation restoration which we recommend should be mentioned in the MPG, as valuable information sources for mineral operators.

Comment

The RSPB has substantive involvement in the management of former mineral workings and a number are managed as RSPB reserves.

In general, we believe that minerals policy should strongly emphasise the need to manage demand for aggregates and to maximise use of recycled and secondary materials. We recognise that mineral extraction will continue to occur. It should not be permitted where it will affect sites of high nature conservation value whether on land or sea. We may need to do more to ensure policy-makers are quite clear on this. A rigorous approach to environmental impact assessment and creative use of planning conditions both need to be promoted. Where extraction occurs, we seek to encourage nature conservation after uses, especially restoration to key habitats such as reedbed, heathland and wet grassland.

The comments summarised here followed comments on a number of earlier minerals guidance notes, for example MPG6 on mineral aggregate supplies and MPG3 on coal-mining and opencasting. The restoration and after use issue, of course, pertains to all types of mineral activity. The perception is that, to date, the emphasis of government guidance has continued to be on restoration to agricultural uses rather than to nature conservation uses.

At the time of writing, final guidance is still due. We have followed the matter up in meetings with DoE officials. Good practice guidance has been produced by the RSPB for mineral operators and efforts to establish links with mineral companies and secure key habitats at specific sites continue.

Comments to the Department of the Environment on the *Report of the Working Group on Peat Extraction and Related Matters*. RSPB. July 1995.

Summary

1. The RSPB believes that there is a particular need and urgency to address the conflicts between continuing peat extraction and nature conservation. Alternatives are available which render continued habitat destruction unnecessary.

2. We believe that the report overestimates both the urgency of allocating new sites for peat extraction and the area of such sites that will be necessary. We request a clear statement to the effect that the allocation of 1,000 ha suggested by the Peat Producers Association (PPA) is not government policy.

3. We consider that the report gives a pessimistic view of the future availability of and demand for peat alternatives. Their use has grown rapidly in the past decade and a number of recent initiatives should encourage supplies, for example of home-produced compost.

4. Of the area of peatland with consent for extraction, 73% is notified as SSSIs. We are therefore surprised and concerned that the Working Group has not seriously addressed the option of revocation. This may be necessary to meet the objective of achieving favourable conservation status under the EU Habitats & Species Directive.

5. There is a strong case for the application of the precautionary approach to peat extraction. Not only is direct and indirect damage continuing but the science of bog restoration is in its infancy and its success is not certain.

6. There is much in the report with which we agree. It provides a comprehensive overview of the current status of peatlands and of the conflicts over their use and deals with some of the solutions. We do not seek to question any of the factual information presented but believe that there should have been debate over some of the interpretation, forecasts and conclusions.

7. The scope of the report is not clear. It states that the remit of the Working Group covered Great Britain. However, Annex A notes that the Department's remit extends only to England and that comparable guidance may be produced in Scotland and Wales. Neither is it clear whether the report is a DoE report, based on the findings of the Group, or whether it is endorsed by the Group, either unanimously or in majority.

8. The Department will be aware of our concern that, since the Working Group included representatives of the peat producers, its membership should have been balanced both by non statutory conservation interests, for example a member of the Peat Consortium, and by representatives from industries producing alternative growing media. We believed also that the Consortium would be consulted on a draft of the report and consider that its findings should have been subject to discussion before being published. We believe that further discussion and consultation should precede the publication of the Minerals Planning Guidance on peat and alternatives.

Comment

Peatlands have been a source of major conservation concern for the RSPB and other conservation bodies for some years. Accelerating horticultural demand has placed some of Britain's most valuable habitats at risk. At present, over 70% of Britain's peat comes from land in SSSIs, and only a few thousand hectares of intact raised bog remains. The Peat Campaign Consortium has worked to highlight this conflict and to secure a growth in the market for alternative growing media. Increasing imports of peat simply destroy habitats elsewhere.

Some successes have been achieved. Some large sites have been saved by purchase of land and associated peat-cutting rights. However, a demand for peat still exists and valuable sites are still being lost, such as Thorne Moors in Yorkshire.

The RSPB commented on a report by a peatland working group and on draft planning guidance for peat in England (MPG13). The forecasting in the report, issued in August 1994, formed the basis of the guidance in the MPG. Although the working group report was not issued for consultation, earlier assurances had been given that it would be. Since we disagreed with a number of its findings, we responded to record our concerns.

The final MPG13 took on board some of our views. The guidance on permitting future extraction sites in England is now fairly strong. Unfortunately, guidance in Scotland and Northern Ireland is less satisfactory, while imports continue to cause concern. We continue to campaign for revocation of extraction consents on a few large SSSIs.

Comments to the Department of the Environment on their *draft waste strategy for England and Wales*. RSPB. April 1995.

Summary

1. The RSPB welcomes the production of this document. Improved waste management practice is an important element in achieving greater sustainability. Biodiversity conservation is a fundamental component of sustainability and there are a number of ways in which biodiversity is directly or indirectly affected by decisions made on waste management. We would like to see greater

recognition of the interactions between waste management practices and biodiversity conservation.

2. There is currently no recognition in the draft strategy of the very high nature conservation value of many areas which are currently used for or threatened by landfill proposals. These are most commonly worked-out mineral workings but they may also be sites such as peat bogs or estuarine habitats. Such value provides a constraint and an additional reason why landfill should be discouraged. It provides an opportunity to make more positive use of such sites by avoiding landfill or, in certain cases, by making use of limited landfill for habitat creation.

3. We welcome the section which promotes the expansion of composting and the links made to its potential as a substitute for peat extraction. There should be some more explicit reference as to why this is desirable, ie the high nature conservation value of peatlands and the environmental costs of extraction. We also suggest the replacement of the current target with one which measures achievement by percentage or volume of waste composted.

4. The RSPB feels that the issue of river dredgings should be added to the series of waste streams discussed in Part III. These arisings are currently viewed as a waste product and their disposal has caused a series of environmental conflicts. The extent of dredging should be minimised. Where they are generated, these materials have an important rôle to play in coastal policy where they can be used positively. The Government should support research aimed at encouraging their best use.

5. The draft strategy embraces the use of targets as a means to encourage shifts in the waste hierarchy. We applaud this, but believe that additional targets should be set, once adequate information is available. To complement these, the often excellent analysis of issues needs to be followed by some more definitive measures to achieve defined objectives.

6. Success in achieving the objectives of the strategy will ultimately fall to individual companies and citizens. However the Government clearly has a vital rôle to play in providing information, facilitating change and encouraging best practice. In respect of the latter, we welcome the commitment to set targets for the Government's own waste management practices. These must be ambitious and we would

like to see the final strategy set the targets, or at least specify the time by when they will be set.

7. It is unclear whether initiatives such as the DoE Information Task Force will also apply to Wales, or whether a parallel exercise is being undertaken within the Welsh Office. This should be clarified.

Comment

The RSPB has not campaigned actively on waste management issues in the past. However, we have supported initiatives to increase the re-use and recycling of "waste" materials as a part of good environmental practice. The RSPB itself has an active internal programme which seeks to minimise use of natural resources and the quantity of waste going to landfill.

Pressure for disposal nevertheless frequently impacts upon nature conservation sites. Current threats include those to former mineral workings which have acquired wildlife value, areas such as peatlands where land raising is proposed, and estuaries subject to disposal of dredgings.

The final England and Wales strategy was issued as a White Paper. It provides the first explicit government policy supporting the notion of a waste hierarchy, with disposal as the final option. In line with our comments, targets were set to aim to achieve reductions in waste generated and increases in waste minimisation techniques such as domestic composting. This latter should in turn assist in developing substitutes for peat compost.

"Superquarries: does Scotland need any more?" **RSPB/Association for the Protection of Rural Scotland/Friends of the Earth Scotland/The Ramblers Scotland, for the Link Quarry Group. 1996.**

Summary

1. "Superquarries" are defined as those which would extract up to 10 million tonnes of rock annually, with the material being exported by sea. Crushed rock is required for road building and other projects in the south of England and elsewhere in Europe. This demand is projected to rise but cuts in the motorway programme and a construction industry downturn mean that real need (as opposed to demand) can be met from existing sources.

2. Supplies from Scottish superquarries would be vulnerable to economic fluctuations. Competition can also be expected from Norwegian sources which will often have a price advantage. Each superquarry will provide fewer than 100 jobs, many of which will go to outside specialists and to migrant labour. Local communities have expressed fears of potential local job losses resulting from impacts of pollution, noise and scenic damage on fishing, crofting and tourism.

3. The visual impact of huge quarry workings, lit for 24-hour working, would be massive, and yet they are proposed in some of our finest landscapes. Nature conservation assets (such as rare mosses and lichens) in the areas concerned have not been fully assessed by the developers. Noise can disturb nesting sites for birds, and there are risks from oil pollution in the sea. Noise from blasting and ship loading will affect the local quality of life and the typically strong winds will carry dust into freshwater areas.

4. Colossal ships up to 120,000 tonnes will be needed to transport the rock to its destinations. At full production, each quarry would generate 400-600 shipping movements per year, and the Minch could see a 40% increase in traffic. No assessment has been made of the risks associated with this. Ballast waters from ships could cause foreign or toxic organisms to be introduced into pristine waters, with potentially disastrous results for the traditional fishing industry.

5. We need a national strategy for mineral use, allowing appropriate consideration for superquarries. National Scenic Areas (NSAs) and other designated areas must be protected from such major developments. Government commitment to sustainable development means that demand for natural resources should be regulated as well as supply. Research needs to be undertaken to improve knowledge of the environmental, economic and social impact of superquarries.

6. The Highland Council, Western Isles Council and Shetland Council should conduct any search for suitable locations strategically, and no further developments should be approved until this strategic analysis is completed. Shipping and harbour requirements are integral to coastal superquarries and should be fully considered.

Comment

This document took the form of a brochure and was produced jointly with other members of the Scottish Link Quarry Group. It formed part of a continuing campaign to raise public awareness about the issue of superquarries in Scotland. A booklet published at the same time, *"The Case against the Harris Superquarry"*, details the case made to the public inquiry into the proposed superquarry at Lingerbay, Isle of Harris, by the Link Quarry Group.

The apparent "need" for superquarries in Scotland arises from the projected increases in demand for aggregate in Southern England and Europe, along with the perceived increase in controls over local extraction. Policy guidance on superquarries in Scotland is provided in National Planning Policy Guideline 4, issued by the Scottish Office in April 1994. In response to comments from many parties, including the RSPB, this guidance is very much more cautious about possible superquarry development than both its earlier draft, and the Department of the Environment's Minerals Planning Guidance 6.

Chapter 10

THE MARINE AND COASTAL ENVIRONMENT

M arine life, and coasts and estuaries, have been the focus of
major high-profile RSPB campaigns in recent years. These
ecosystems support some of the bird communities for which the
UK is of greatest international significance. In the case of coasts
they also exhibit some of the most complex interweavings of different strands of policy and legislation and a theme of bringing about
better rational cohesion in this runs through the items presented
here. Solutions to seabird problems lie as much with fisheries and
shipping as with habitat management and the Society in recent years
has built up new policy capabilities in these areas. There are links
with the item on European marine sites in Chapter 4, and while
marine aspects of mineral extraction and waste management are
covered here, land-related aspects of these subjects appear in Chapter 9.

**Comments to Department of the Environment on Draft Policy
Guidelines for the Coast. RSPB. June 1995.**

Summary

1. The RSPB welcomes the initiative to produce policy guidelines
for the coast. However, we believe the draft is seriously flawed and
likely to confuse and mislead those it is intended to help. We recommend that it should not be published in this form.

2. The draft is a confusing mixture of policy guidance and (poor)
explanation of legal requirements. The intended status of the guidelines is not clear and there is no indication of how Government ex-
pects them to be used. There should be an overall stated aim of
achieving environmentally sustainable development.

3. The draft guidelines are very sectoral in their approach. Government has stated that they will not replace anything that already
exists; but if they are to make a significant additional contribution
to coastal zone planning we consider that they must demonstrate
how existing guidance should be integrated. The RSPB believes that
MAFF's national policy guidance, integrating flood defence and

coastal defence issues with other coastal uses and interests, provides a better model.

4. It is disappointing that a potentially useful initiative such as these guidelines is limited to England only. We consider that there are issues of inconsistency in coastal policy and planning between UK countries which need addressing urgently.

5. The complete omission of agriculture from the draft is a significant oversight, which must be corrected.

6. In several respects the draft guidelines fall short of relevant recommendations made by the House of Commons Environment Select Committee in 1992 and 1994.

Comment

As part of its response to the 1992 House of Commons Environment Select Committee inquiry into Coastal Zone Protection and Planning, the Government published two important discussion papers. *"Development below low water mark"* reviewed the mechanisms regulating all kinds of development in the marine environment, concluding that there was no evidence that the prevailing "sectoral" approach was a problem. *"Managing the coast"* reviewed the coastal management planning system and in particular the powers available to coastal planners. This concluded that there were limitations in existing powers to zone and regulate the use of the seashore and coastal waters.

In 1994, the Government was once again criticised by the Select Committee for its lack of positive action in the coastal zone. It was pointed out that many representations had been made to the Committee concerning the need for a national coastal strategy and that the Committee had recommended such a strategy to set long-term objectives and guidelines for implementation of coastal policy. Whilst acknowledging that a range of sectoral strategies had already been published, DoE agreed that there might be a case for drawing together the main elements of some of these. Subsequently, DoE announced as part of their coastal zone management initiative an intention to develop "Policy Guidelines for the Coast".

The Society commented extensively on the draft which was circulated to members of the English Coastal Forum, recommending that unless there were major changes, the guidelines should not be published. Unfortunately, many significant problems remain in the final publication. In many places, the guidelines are a confusing mix of policy, legislation and procedures. Where there appears to be little or no policy, a legislative account is given. It is often difficult to distinguish between legal requirements and other procedures. There are also notable omissions from the legislative accounts and certain sectoral interests are poorly represented.

According to DoE, the guidelines reflect the new emphasis on integrated management of the coast and improved links between sectors. However, they make no attempt to provide an integrated approach. Of particular note is the failure to inform regional coastal zone management. Perhaps the most significant omission from the guidelines is the setting of any long-term objectives. This is despite a Select Committee recommendation and an indication that DoE would do this. It is widely accepted that coastal zone management requires a national perspective with a long-term view of planning and management. It is therefore in the RSPB's view most regrettable that the Government still refuses to put in place one of the most fundamental building blocks of coastal zone management.

Comments to the Department of the Environment on their *Review of byelaw making and coastal zone management powers in the coastal zone*. RSPB. August 1995.

Summary

1. This response reviews in detail the problems associated with managing the coastal zone and proposes a model for delivery of coastal zone management, based on the approach recommended by the House of Commons Environment Select Committee and on the system developed in the USA. The model suggests that conflict resolution and the degree of regulation should be commensurate with the wildlife importance of a site and its vulnerability to disturbance or damage.

2. Our review of problems is based on an analysis of some of the key operating authorities and legislation in the coastal zone. This includes the powers of harbour authorities and sea fisheries committees, the problems of implementing Sections 3, 28 and 29 of the Wildlife and Countryside Act 1981 and problems associated with management in Marine Nature Reserves. In addition, the response

draws upon 40 detailed case histories of management problems within the coastal zone. Issues raised include: funding; the need for proactive management; the rôle of voluntary agreements; legislative constraints including local planning authority jurisdiction; problems associated with licensing and the issue of discrimination; managing the unforeseen; enforcement; and guidance.

3. We make 25 detailed recommendations in our main report and a further 22 recommendations based on its annexes.

4. In 1992, the House of Commons Environment Select Committee reported that there were over 80 Acts of Parliament dealing with the regulation of activities carried out within the coastal zone. There was a general feeling that rather than needing more legislation, there should be a review of the existing powers and their effectiveness. The RSPB therefore welcomes DoE's initiative to review the management powers of authorities with jurisdiction over the coastal zone.

5. Even at a very local level a wide range of regulatory authorities (the Environment Committee estimated 240) exercise powers within the coastal zone. Regulatory systems overlap. The RSPB supports the recommendation by the Select Committee that there should be a single coastal zone authority for the whole of the UK. The area over which any one regulator can exercise its powers for different purposes should be standardised. There is still a general divide between powers exercisable on land and those at sea. The Environment Committee believed that this was a fundamental cause of problems in the coastal zone and we urge that methods for harmonisation be sought.

6. DoE's review shows how restrictive some powers are in their application. Of key concern to the RSPB is the number of powers which cannot be exercised for the purpose of protecting the environment. Regulators must be given strong nature conservation duties.

7. Another key problem with existing powers is the inability of regulators to introduce effective activity zoning. This stems from an inability to prohibit activities and in particular navigation and from some legal ambiguities which need clearing up.

8. Government has provided a significant amount of money for the production of coastal zone plans. This is welcomed. Policing and

implementing coastal management controls is not cheap, and finding new sources of money, such as fair user charges, would be advisable. Fine collection could be made easier.

9. Many existing coastal management schemes are reactive, rather than pre-empting problems and avoiding conflicts. Numerous examples exist where regulation in one part of the country has resulted in a shift of the problems to another area. A more proactive régime should be encouraged. Even reactive controls can often take too long to bring into effect, and introducing "framework" regulations and less stringent tests of need might help with this. Voluntary agreements have a rôle to play but are in our view are relied on excessively and often fail.

10. In 1992, relevant Ministers and fisheries managers in England and Wales were given a duty to have regard to nature conservation under the Sea Fisheries (Wildlife Conservation) Act. However, it soon became apparent that this conflicted with the statutory functions of fisheries managers, constrained by the Sea Fisheries Regulation Act 1966, and was virtually worthless. The solution now advanced in the Environmental Protection Bill is most welcome. However, similar legislative problems exist for other key coastal managers such as port authorities, the statutory nature conservation agencies, the Crown Estate and local planning authorities.

11. The exercising of ancient rights, particularly non proprietary rights, is widespread around the coast of the UK and can cause significant conflict, eg between bait-digging and nature conservation. This needs addressing and new controls over third-party activities affecting SSSIs are required.

12. The limits of planning jurisdiction on the foreshore are confusing, and recent caselaw and DoE reviews of the issue still leave it unresolved. The RSPB believes that this situation needs urgent clarification in order to facilitate a consistent approach to management in the coastal zone. We consider that local authority areas should extend to cover all intertidal and sub-tidal areas within estuaries, inlets and bays, and to a standard distance offshore on the open coast.

13. Permits and licences can aid aspects of management but each has problems. The RSPB believes a combined permit/licence system which combines the benefits of both tools would make a significant

contribution to coastal zone management, provided it is overseen by the right sort of management authority.

14. The RSPB believes there is scope for enhancing the effectiveness of enforcement of certain coastal controls, by for example making more use of local action groups for monitoring.

15. The RSPB acknowledges that there are a number of DoE initiatives which go some way to providing the guidance which is necessary. However, in a number of areas we believe that more is required.

16. A section of our response proposes a framework for the provision of coastal management aimed at addressing conflicts with nature conservation interests. This embodies a hierarchical approach to strength of regulation, matching it to the significance of the interests at stake, and a similarly hierarchical system of conflict resolution.

Comment

One of the four initiatives with which the Government responded to attention on coastal zone issues from the House of Commons Environment Committee, referred to in earlier comments in this Chapter, was to review and if necessary overhaul the byelaw-making powers available to coastal managers (in particular local authorities). DoE consulted a number of statutory and non statutory groups and invited individual organisations to submit details of their concerns, drawing in particular on real examples of problems and solutions.

The RSPB, believing that the successful implementation of many coastal zone initiatives will depend not only on co-operation and co-management but also on an adequate "safety net" of regulatory and management powers, submitted the detailed report summarised here. At the time of writing DoE's review has been delayed, due to the need to complete other coastal zone management initiatives (*"Policy Guidelines for the Coast"* and *"Coastal Zone Management - Towards Best Practice"*).

Comments to Department of the Environment on draft "Best practice guide for coastal zone management planning". RSPB. September 1995.

Summary

1. The RSPB strongly supports the production of a practical guide to implementing coastal zone management. Given that this is to be published by DoE, the Society feels that the guide must make a significant contribution to the development of coastal zone management in England and beyond. Our response therefore goes beyond specific comments on the draft text and considers also the underlying aims, objectives and principles of coastal zone management.

2. Among the issues addressed by our comments are: the definition of the coastal zone; the problem of the "land-sea divide"; sustainable development in the coastal zone; scales of planning and management; conflict resolution; "top-down" versus "bottom-up" planning; and vertical and horizontal integration of policy.

3. We consider that the guide needs a clear statement of what coastal zone management is. Whilst the coastal zone and planning, etc, within it are considered, coastal zone management as a concept is not. Many of the principles of coastal zone management are explained. However, these are wrongly attributed to "coastal zone management planning". Coastal zone management is the concept which embraces all the sectoral plans and initiatives at all levels in the context of principles such as long-term forward planning. Coastal zone management planning, however, is the additional process, ideally using an overarching integrated plan, by which such coastal zone management is achieved.

4. The draft guide gives the impression that coastal zone management is a process distinct and separate from other sectoral coastal initiatives and plans. The RSPB recommends that it be made clear that the coastal zone management concept should instead drive initiatives in the various sectors.

5. The Society considers that the process for developing management plans outlined in the draft is generally sound. However, much of this is not new, and there is a good deal of repetition. The draft falls short of its own stated objectives to an extent, since the principles of coastal zone management outlined in its opening sections are not clearly identifiable in the "process" chapters.

6. It is unfortunate that the draft does not draw all the information, examples and lessons to be learnt together in the form of conclusions. In our view, it should also clearly identify the way ahead and identify the opportunities which should be taken, by changing current practice, to make significant improvements to the delivery of coastal zone management in future.

Comment

One of the four initiatives with which the Government responded to attention on coastal zone issues from the House of Commons Environment Committee, referred to in earlier comments in this Chapter, was to publish a coastal zone management guide to best practice. DoE contracted the work to a consortium of consultants and set up an advisory group made up of interested parties (including the RSPB) from the Coastal Forum.

RSPB invested much time and effort in assisting the DoE and their consultants on the key principles, objectives and approaches to coastal zone management (CZM) which should feature in the guide (written submissions were made in September 1995, November 1995, February 1996 and comments on the final draft in August 1996). In particular, it was argued that it was not possible to publish a guide to "best practice" since it is too early to assess whether any existing CZM plans deliver sustainable use. The title was therefore changed to "towards best practice". It was felt that the final draft still concentrated too much on plans (which are an important component of CZM) rather than on coastal zone management as a whole. Another significant problem which remains unresolved is how to achieve integration a cornerstone principle of CZM. The guide is due to be published in the autumn of 1996 and hopefully may be updated as practice evolves.

Comments to the Ministry of Agriculture, Fisheries & Food on *"Food & Environment Protection Act 1985 Part II: Fees for licences to deposit materials at sea and for the approval of oil dispersants".* **RSPB. October 1995.**

Summary

1. The RSPB is pleased to respond to this consultation paper, which sets out the legal basis for fees and charges for licences to deposit materials at sea, and proposes to revise the fees. We have taken this

opportunity to highlight issues relating to the Food and Environment Protection Act [FEPA] more generally with respect to the disposal of port dredgings, since the majority of licences issued relate
to this activity.

2. Our response points out the fragmented nature of the dredge
disposal decision-making process, between those who regulate
dredging activities (ports, under the General Development Order
[GDO] and local acts, and in some cases the Department of Transport) and those who regulate disposal (MAFF). Dredge disposal on
land is regulated by local planning authorities, in cases where ports
do not have a permitted development right. In addition, some forms
of dredging are not covered at all by any consenting mechanism.

3. The RSPB believes that there is a need to rationalise and integrate the legislation and policy applying to dredging activities.

4. This response also considers whether better use of port
dredgings can be made. We briefly examine examples of constructive uses of port dredgings from elsewhere in the world. These include coast protection, beach recharge, aggregate supply and, most
importantly, wildlife habitat creation. It is suggested that greater
incentives for beneficial use of dredgings be developed as part of
the review of licensing fees.

5. We have also considered MAFF's decision-making procedures.
We are concerned that consultation generally relates only to new
licence applications and not to licence renewals. Many sites of nature conservation importance are considered to have been subject
to "routine" dumping for many years. However, the Society argues
that just because an activity has been carried out does not mean
that its continuation is necessarily appropriate.

6. Related to this is concern about the level and scope of monitoring environmental impacts. Whilst an appropriate environmental
assessment is required for dredging proposals affecting Special Protection Areas and Special Areas of Conservation, and existing consents can be reviewed under the Habitats & Species Directive, these
are in the nature of "one off" assessments which cannot assess impacts over time. In addition, consenting procedures under the Coast
Protection Act 1949 do not currently require equivalent reviews.

Comment

Noting that the majority of FEPA licences now issued are related to the disposal of dredgings, the emphasis of the RSPB's response is on both dredging disposal and the activity of dredging, since these activities are inseparable. The Society has few comments on the costs of licences except with respect to the beneficial use of dredgings.

One of the yardsticks which the RSPB uses to measure progress towards achieving an integrated system of coastal zone planning and management in the UK is the recommendations of the House of Commons Environment Select Committee inquiry into Coastal Zone Protection and Planning. With respect to the disposal of dredgings, the Committee recommended that there should be better co-ordination between those authorities responsible for dredging, disposing of and utilising marine aggregates in order to avoid the unnecessary dumping of dredged material and to encourage its use elsewhere as appropriate. In addition, the Committee recommend that the environmental impact of dumping should be assessed and that DoE should issue guidance notes on the possible harmful effects of dredged material and the alternative beneficial uses to which it can be put.

The Government rejected the suggestion that dredged material disposed at sea is not controlled so as to prevent marine environmental damage. It believed that the requirement to consider alternative uses other than disposal at sea was fully respected and that guidance notes on dredge disposal were not needed. However, as part of its response to the Select Committee's report, the Government looked at the issue of co-ordinating "development" below low water. Here, MAFF undertook to carry out a number of enhancements to the licensing of dredging disposal and dumping at sea. Tangible progress on these matters has however been slow.

Another consultation paper which reviews the costs of FEPA licences was published by MAFF at the end of July 1996. There was no evidence that any of RSPB's suggestions had been considered but the Society will continue to pursue them.

A North Sea View: BirdLife International's recommendations to the 4th International Conference on Protection of the North Sea (the North Sea Conference, [NSC]). RSPB/BirdLife International 1995.

Summary

1. The 3rd International Conference on the Protection of the North Sea in 1990 took a first step towards protecting species and habitats, in calling attention to the need to identify marine sites of national or international importance. The North Sea Quality Status Report (QSR) advises that improving the quality of the North Sea requires more emphasis to be given to species and habitat protection. BirdLife International (BI) calls on participants at the forthcoming 4th Conference in Esbjerg in June 1995 to address the following particular problems for species and habitats: inadequate fisheries management; the lack of protection for marine sites; and pollution from shipping.

2. The QSR acknowledged that the harmful impact of fishing on fish populations, on benthic ecosystems and on marine mammals and seabirds is a matter for concern. BI calls on North Sea States to agree to manage fisheries in an environmentally sensitive manner: by tackling overfishing, ie reducing fishing effort to match the availability of fish resources and secure their long-term sustainability; by reducing the large quantities of fish wasted through discarding; and by stopping practices which directly damage the environment.

3. BI calls on participants at the 4th North Sea Conference to:

- control damaging fishing activity in important or vulnerable areas through the use of fisheries "boxes", and give damaged areas a chance to recover by establishing areas closed to fisheries;

- take a "precautionary approach" where the risk of damage to the marine environment is high or where the level of damage is potentially serious, for example in the case of industrial fisheries, precautionary low quotas must be agreed or an outright ban introduced; and

- introduce coastal management initiatives which integrate fisheries management with other coastal activities and planning.

4. Current species and habitat conservation effort is concentrated almost exclusively on coastal areas within national jurisdiction. The North Sea Conference is a unique opportunity to address the international problem of managing and protecting key areas in the open sea. Too frequently, lack of information causes action to be postponed. BI and many other organisations and individuals have now invested in the production of an atlas of internationally important areas for birds in the North Sea. Coastal waters are widely recognised by governments for their high ecological value but too often the importance of offshore areas is ignored. BI calls on the North Sea States to give particular consideration to these offshore areas and to use the bird data to pilot innovative measures for improving the open sea environment to benefit birds, wildlife and fisheries.

5. BI calls on participants at the 4th NSC to:

-       identify, designate and manage marine sites that qualify for protection under the EU Wild Birds and Habitats & Species Directives and under national legislation;

-       establish management zones, or Marine Protected Areas, at sites of high wildlife value beyond territorial waters, to ensure that activities are allowed to continue at levels and in ways which do not damage the value of the areas concerned; and

-       establish a collaborative North Sea habitat and species monitoring programme.

6. Depressingly, the evidence from beached bird surveys and aerial surveillance indicates that oil pollution in the North Sea continues unabated and at unacceptable levels. Much of this pollution is illegal. BI charges the North Sea States to gain the upper hand on monitoring and enforcement to benefit birds and the environment.

7. BI calls on participants at the 4th NSC to:

-       make effective use of the range of routeing measures available to protect important wildlife areas, and to monitor ships' compliance with such measures;

-       improve the adequacy and use of port reception facilities; and

- work towards zero discharge limits and the mandatory use of port reception facilities.

8. To date, the NSCs have agreed no measures for wildlife conservation beyond existing national and international legislation and agreements. Ministers in Esbjerg must integrate the environment and the conservation of species and habitats into their broader North Sea policy-making. The 1995 Conference is possibly the final opportunity to address a challenge common to the North Sea States, namely how to address the shared responsibility for protecting offshore species and habitats.

Comment

The 4th NSC held in Denmark in June 1995 presented an excellent political opportunity to lobby for progress on marine conservation, including marine protected areas, fisheries and shipping. BI used its observer status to promote its views on these policy areas for inclusion in the declaration signed by Ministers at the Conference. The declaration, while not legally binding, is a strong expression of political intent.

The degree of success in this was variable, and some achievements were undoubtedly attributable to the combined efforts of all environmental non governmental organisations with observer status. Interventions by BI assisted in obtaining Ministerial commitments to apply the precautionary principle to fisheries management and to study the effects of industrial fisheries on the sustainability of both the target fish species (such as sandeels) and their dependent predators; to commence planning processes to protect species and habitats beyond territorial waters; and to make use of routeing measures for shipping.

BI continues to be involved with the NSC process, and is involved with preparations for the Intermediate Ministerial Meeting on the Integration of Fisheries and Environmental Issues, scheduled for March 1997, and the 5th NSC, scheduled for some time between 2000 and 2002. The agreement to hold an Intermediate Ministerial Meeting arose out of the failure, tacitly recognised at the time, of the 4th NSC to make acceptable progress towards resolving the wider environmental impacts of fishing activities in the North Sea: in short, a failure to agree ways of implementing the Ministerial commitments made in Denmark.

Comments to the Ministry of Agriculture, Fisheries and Food on *"The environmental responsibilities of Sea Fisheries Committees".* **RSPB. October 1995.**

Summary

1. The RSPB welcomes the initiative by MAFF to examine this issue. We have for some time believed that detailed guidance which explains to Sea Fisheries Committees (SFCs) their environmental responsibilities is needed. A number of generic points arise from our detailed comments.

2. The draft guidance note appears very selective in the legislation which it considers. As it stands, it appears only to consider the implications which the Habitats & Species Directive, the Environment Act 1995 and the Sea Fisheries (Wildlife Conservation) Act 1992 each have for the Sea Fisheries Regulation Act 1966. Sea Fisheries Committees draw powers from a variety of statutes. Perhaps one of the more important is the Sea Fisheries (Shellfish) Act 1967. The Society has been led to believe that Regulations made under a Regulating Order may now be made for environmental purposes. We seek confirmation of this from the Ministry.

3. The draft guidance note does not seem to be completely clear about the relationship between the Sea Fisheries (Wildlife Conservation) Act 1992 and the Environment Act 1995. As we understand it, the 1995 Act does not confer any new environmental duties on Sea Fisheries Committees. What it does is to facilitate the implementation of the 1992 Act in the wider marine environment, and of the Habitats & Species Directive within European Marine Sites.

4. Finally, we feel that a short introduction to the Habitats & Species Directive is warranted. In particular, clarification about the purpose of the Directive, the rôle of Natura 2000, etc, would be useful.

Comment

The guidance drafted and subsequently published by MAFF on SFCs' environmental responsibilities represented the culmination of five years' work by the RSPB. This work was founded on the belief that local management of inshore fisheries was the best way to achieve sustainable exploitation. However, SFCs lacked the necessary legislative duties, powers, resources and guidance to achieve this. Working closely with some of the Committees, the Society drafted and promoted a Private Member's Bill which became the Sea Fisheries (Wildlife Conservation) Act 1992. This gave all fisheries managers a general duty to have regard to the marine environment and thus reflected amendments made to the Common Fisheries Policy.

However, it became apparent that whilst the new legislation allowed SFCs to "have regard", they could not make or amend byelaws for nature conservation purposes (a similar problem currently facing ports). This problem was identified in DoE's review *"Managing the Coast"*, and it was suggested that changes to legislation might be useful. With the adoption of the 1992 EU Habitats & Species Directive a solution to this problem became even more urgent.

In 1995, a legislative opportunity arose through the Environment Act to make small but significant amendments to SFC legislation, to allow committees to make and amend byelaws for marine environment purposes. The eventual changes also facilitated the inclusion of marine environment experts on the committees. With such important and welcomed changes, the logical conclusion to the process was the publication of guidance to the SFCs about their new environmental powers. RSPB welcomed the guidance, although it was imperfect and there is some disagreement concerning the interpretation of references to plans, projects and programmes in the Habitats & Species Directive.

The RSPB continues to work closely with SFCs, identifying where small but significant legislative changes could be made to legislation in order to help SFCs with better management of inshore fisheries. In March 1996, evidence was submitted to the House of Commons Welsh Affairs Select Committee concerning the need for adequate funding of SFCs. In representations in July 1996 to the Scottish Office concerning their discussion paper *"Scotland's Coast"*, the development of local inshore fisheries management which incorporates the principle of co-management was once more promoted.

RSPB's *Vision for Sustainable Fisheries:* a discussion paper. Dunn, E and Harrison, N. 1995.

Summary

1. The main thrust of this *"Vision for Sustainable Fisheries"* is to highlight chronic mismanagement of fish stocks under the European Union's

Common Fisheries Policy (CFP) and the manner in which Member States interpret and implement the CFP. That the fishermen themselves often disregard the CFP's rules compounds the problem but is further symptomatic of a deeply flawed policy. Until a sounder, more equitable policy framework emerges, fishermen will rightly regard themselves as the victims rather than the villains of the piece.

2. This document identifies the pressures that an industry under strain is putting on the wider marine environment in general, and on marine birds in particular. It outlines the RSPB's stance on these crucial issues and marks the start of a process of developing proposals for the next review of the CFP in the year 2002. Its purpose is to stimulate and further the debate between the RSPB and government departments, fisheries scientists and representatives of the fishing industry, with a view to generating better fisheries management.

3. The fishing industry is undergoing rapid and radical change on many fronts and, like agriculture, has increasingly become a victim of its own technological progress and harvesting efficiency. Attempts at management and conservation of fish stocks in the north-east Atlantic are under siege, progressively undermined by overfishing.

4. The most direct impact is on fish stocks themselves, manifested by dwindling catches and acrimony among fishermen about restrictive measures and unfair competition. But there is also disruption to the wider ecosystem. By making inroads into the base of the food chain, industrial fishing may have far-reaching implications.

5. Although marine birds have to some extent benefited from the growth of the fishing industry this century, notably as scavengers of offal and discards, research by the RSPB has demonstrated that they are not thriving uniformly throughout their range, with some species showing distinct regional declines. Sudden collapses of breeding output have apparently increased in recent years and there is growing evidence that the fishing industry can tip the balance against bird populations.

6. The future welfare of marine birds is seen by the RSPB to lie in prudent husbandry of the marine environment by policy-makers, fisheries scientists and by fishermen. The RSPB is committed to establishing a wider remit for the fishing industry which acknowledges its impact on the entire marine ecosystem. The concept of

sustainable fishing involves securing the survival of the fishing industry by ensuring that fish stocks are not over exploited. This paper addresses the means of achieving this. It is clearly not possible to rely on market forces or technical measures, and regulations (and the CFP) must play a part.

7. Crucial areas of the CFP addressed in this document (and in its 13 recommendations) include:

-   fleet capacity (the need to accelerate decommissioning of vessels);

-   Total Allowable Catches (TACs) and quotas (the need to develop more sensitive methods of effort control for conserving not just the targeted stock but the wider food-web);

-   discards (the need to eliminate discards in the interests of better of stock assessment);

-   closed areas (the need to develop these in the interests of stock protection and recovery);

-   industrial fishing (the need to manage this in the interests of the wider ecosystem);

-   monitoring and enforcement (the need for much better surveillance of fishing practices to ensure compliance); and

-   local fisheries management (the need to promote community control of fisheries management).

8. It is now widely acknowledged that the CFP in its present form has manifestly failed to safeguard fish stocks, safeguard the livelihoods of fishermen, or safeguard the wider marine ecosystem. Historical conflict between Member States on the apportionment of resources heads at least one published list of reasons for this. Member States have continually put political expediency before conservation objectives and ignored the scientific advice of their own advisors to cut fishing effort for the collective good. Against this background of vested interest it is scarcely surprising if fishermen follow suit and regard fish stocks as being "up for grabs".

9. A deep malaise afflicts the CFP in its present form and nothing short of radical surgery will save it. Clear objectives, linked with sound interpretation, sound management and sound implementation by the Member States are crucial to the CFP's future success. Above all, the CFP must reconcile its structural and conservation policies which are currently pulling in opposite directions. The overwhelming dependence on the CFP's cumbersome TAC-quota system has presented a serious obstacle to developing better husbandry of fish stocks. Acceptance of the need to control access to fishing grounds has been painfully slow. The licensing scheme proposed in this document seeks to address this problem.

10. However, licensing will not succeed on its own. It needs to be allied with a bold reduction of fleet capacity across Member States, strategic deployment of closed areas for stock conservation, and higher investment in monitoring and enforcement. In addition, the CFP must address the phasing out of discards by retention of by-catch, the regulation of industrial fishing, and the development of a much more sensitive "ecosystem" approach to stock assessment and fisheries.

Comment

The production of this document coincided with a huge upsurge of political interest in fisheries and their regulation. In January 1995, the first report of the UK Government Panel on Sustainable Development (GPSD) identified overfishing and depletion of fish stocks as a key threat to the sustainability of fisheries and called for urgent action to restore the balance between fishing effort and fish stocks. Media interest over the Canadian "cod war" in spring 1995 also raised the profile of overfishing and fuelled the contemporary debate about Spanish access to the so-called Irish Box.

In the short term, when the document summarised here was published in February 1995, it gave the Society a platform for advocacy with fishermen's organisations, with MAFF and the UK Government, the European Commission and the International Commission for the Exploration of the Sea (ICES). In the long term, this is part of the ongoing policy development necessary to achieve significant change in the next major review of the European Common Fisheries Policy in 2002. Beyond its intrinsic function as a discussion document, it also provided a framework for contributions to the *"North Sea View"* document, (see page 146), and subsequent submissions to the Intermediate Ministerial Meeting, to BirdLife International's Marine Habitats Conservation Strategy and its new initiative on global threats to seabirds, and to the RSPB's Marine Life Campaign.

In general terms, the *"Vision for Sustainable Fisheries"* established the RSPB as a player in this developing field, and it has helped to put environmental impacts on the fisheries agenda. The widening of the debate in this way has opened up a number of opportunities, notably the extension of the Society's influence in the campaign for better regulation of North Sea industrial fisheries, thus building on our previous experience with the local Shetland sandeel fishery. A conflict of major importance for the Society highlighted by the report is that successful reduction (or elimination) of discarding waste fish could have a serious detrimental effect on the status of discard-dependent seabirds.

Comments to the Department of Transport on *"Waste Reception Facilities in UK Ports"*. RSPB. May 1995.

Summary

1. The RSPB is very concerned at the potential impact of ship-sourced pollution on marine wildlife. Though we attended the "Braer" spill, we consider that the deliberate discharge of waste from shipping, rather than accidental spills, is a more pervasive threat to the marine environment. The Society gave evidence to the Donaldson Inquiry on both issues. We are therefore particularly keen that reception facilities for such wastes should be both adequate and well used.

2. We therefore welcome the chance to comment on the consultation document. We hope that as a result of responses received, the UK Government will feel able to offer some progressive initiatives at the forthcoming North Sea Conference, especially regarding waste auditing systems and financial arrangements for reception facilities.

3. The Society does not agree with the ports industry that the provision of reception facilities is adequate. The WRc survey of 35 UK ports and harbours (10% of the total) confirms that there is "considerable room for improvement". The Government should publish its survey of the remaining UK ports and harbours, to allow public scrutiny of their facilities.

4. The RSPB considers that a wider statutory duty is essential. We fully support the recommendation in the Donaldson Report that ports should have a statutory duty to ensure provision of facilities which are not only fully adequate but which are also geared to ease of use and avoid disincentives. The definition of these terms should be elaborated in more detail.

5. The two Department of Transport proposals to require ports "to have regard to the ease of use" of reception facilities, or to require ports to consult the shipping and waste industries about the adequacy of provision of facilities, are totally inadequate and do not meet the spirit of Lord Donaldson's recommendation.

6. The RSPB proposes the introduction of three duties:

(i)   Port authorities should be required to incorporate fees for use of reception facilities into harbour dues, whilst making the reception facility component explicit.

(ii)   Port authorities should be required to consult with their port users and waste contractors for the purpose of preparing, implementing and updating comprehensive waste management plans.

(iii)   Port developers should be required to place any fixed reception facilities no more than a certain distance from the main berths, the distance being such that vessels do not have to move berths in order discharge their wastes.

7. The Society considers that wider adoption of formal waste management plans would help to improve reception facilities. This would involve collaborative production by the port authority and representatives of the port users. Provisions for receiving feedback on the completed plan and updating it should be included.

8. The elements proposed by the Department of Transport are all desirable. Particular attention should also be given to: the need for port authorities to monitor the system in place and be actively involved in ensuring it is used; the pros and cons of barges versus road tankers for oily waste; coordination of waste disposal by individual port authorities for all port users; improved facilities for disposal of small quantities of oily waste from numerous small users; and the fate of received wastes.

9. There should be a system for annual certification of port waste management plans. Overall certification should be undertaken by the Marine Safety Agency (MSA), in consultation with the relevant waste regulation authorities.

10. The consultation document appears to have failed to address the Donaldson Report's recommendation (which the RSPB supports) for the establishment of a system of certification to ensure that facilities are adequate. This is distinct from certification of waste management plans.

11. Regarding funding of facilities, the ports industry has raised several points in opposition to a "free at the point of use" system. The RSPB disagrees with their assertion that German experience with such a system showed that use would not be encouraged: firstly, as the Department's consultation paper itself shows, the German exercise appears to have been a success, and secondly, those facilities were free of any charge, rather than being paid for by inclusive harbour dues. Thirdly, facilities run by private operators would need to be reimbursed by the port authority, but this would not render the system impractical, as alleged.

12. Varying the reception facilities element of port dues according to expected waste arisings from different types of vessel would be in accordance with the polluter-pays principle. Surcharges would help to prevent "tourism of waste" but must be set in such a way as to minimise illegal discharges at sea.

13. In the UK, aerial surveillance and initial port state control inspections are carried out by the Coastguard Agency (CA) and MSA respectively; and we understand that funding is provided by the taxpayer rather than by levies on the ports or shipping industries. It would therefore be incongruous to seek funding for enforcement of ports' statutory duties from the shipping industry, through harbour dues. Industry funding is by no means anathema but this potential incongruity needs more study.

14. Further policing of ports is justified and should cover the aspects covered in the new statutory duties we propose. Further policing of vessels is also justified. Aerial surveillance needs to be supplemented by higher penalties for offenders and by additional enforcement of MARPOL through waste auditing systems in ports. While the Donaldson Report advocates waste auditing for garbage

only, the Society considers it should also be carried out for oily waste and chemical residues. A receipts system may be useful.

15. Education is not explicitly addressed in the consultation document but is an important means of improving the use of reception facilities. We believe the Department should take relevant action based on recommendations in the WRc report.

Comment

The RSPB considers that illegal deliberate discharges of oily waste from shipping cause more bird deaths than accidental oil spills. Adequate and well-used waste reception facilities are essential if we are to see a decline in the number of these discharges, along with those of chemical residues and garbage. The report of the inquiry by Lord Donaldson, published in May 1994, dwelt in depth on deliberate discharges from shipping and made recommendations on this important matter. Most of these recommendations were followed up by the Department of Transport, through two consultation papers, the second building on the responses to the first. The exercise led to the publication by the Department in January 1996 of details of a package of 18 new measures to cut down on deliberate discharges from shipping.

Some of these measures were incorporated into a draft bill (the Merchant Shipping and Maritime Security Bill), which the Department of Transport circulated for consultation in June 1996. The RSPB responded to this consultation. The Society was pleased that the draft Bill included enabling powers to require waste management plans, mandatory discharge of waste and an inclusive fee system, but was disappointed that it did not go further by requiring ports and harbours to develop waste plans without the interim step of enabling powers.

Port State Control comments to the Marine Safety Agency on the draft statutory instrument to implement the EU Directive on Port State Control. RSPB. October 1995.

Summary

1. The Port State Control Directive refers to the continental shelf in its definition of "off-shore installation". We note that the draft Regulations refer to the Continental Shelf Act 1964, presumably to reflect this. However, we are concerned that this definition may be

too restrictive and we consider that port state control should apply to vessels at off shore installations anywhere in waters under UK jurisdiction.

2. The Directive refers to non mandatory guidelines for expanded inspection of certain ships. Nevertheless, we urge the UK Government to adopt these guidelines as minimum requirements and to reflect this in the Regulation.

3. We are concerned that the requirement to pay compensation under the proposed appeal provisions may operate as a serious disincentive for inspectors to detain vessels. There is no requirement for compensation under the Directive. In the interests of an EU-wide "level playing-field" it should not be more advantageous to dispute detention in one Member State than in another. The burden of proof on the owner should be put at the highest level.

4. We suggest a definition to clarify the meaning of "responsible parties".

5. We make a drafting suggestion to ensure that pilots engaged on a ship leaving a UK port and bound for a port in another EU Member State would be bound by the relevant reporting requirements, as well as those on ships bound for another UK port.

6. We are unhappy with gearing fines to the statutory scale, and consider that provision for fines (and imprisonment) should be on the same basis as for pollution under the Environmental Protection Act 1990 and the Water Resources Act 1991.

7. Amendments are recommended to overcome the problem of an offending ship moving outside waters under UK jurisdiction before it can be caught.

8. We note that the Donaldson Report makes several recommendations on port state control. We are aware that the UK Government is promoting these to other members of the Port State Control Committee but we feel that some of them could be implemented unilaterally. The draft Regulations provide an important opportunity for doing so.

Comment

In the light of inadequate enforcement of international standards of ship safety and marine pollution prevention by flag states, enforcement of these standards by certain port states is developing worldwide. An EU Directive on port state control, which among other things set minimum standards among EU Member States for the port state control of foreign-flagged ships, was adopted in June 1995. In October 1995, the Marine Safety Agency (MSA) issued draft Regulations to implement this Directive, for consultation. The MSA accepted the RSPB's suggestion concerning pilots, referred to in the summary above, and agreed to amend the Regulations accordingly.

The Donaldson Report also featured recommendations on port state control. These were not tackled by the draft Regulations. However, a consultation document issued by the Department of Transport in June 1995 on sub standard and uninsured ships specifically addressed some of Lord Donaldson's port state control recommendations. The RSPB responded, welcoming the progressive attitude of the Department in developing their proposals. We supported most of the proposals and recommended urgent and unilateral action on foreign fish-actory ships ("klondykers") in UK waters.

Comments to the Department of Trade and Industry on *Proposed changes to regulations for licensing offshore oil and gas activities*. RSPB. October 1995.

Summary

1. The RSPB agrees with the possibility of incorporating some of the licence conditions that apply to all licences into the model clauses attached to licences. Reference to interested environmental NGOs should be added.

2. We have concerns about the text of certain conditions and about the lack of application of these conditions to Exploration Licences, and to the development phase of Production Licences. Nevertheless, the concept of using conditions is itself satisfactory.

3. The RSPB believes that the proposed "environmental case" concept requires considerably more development by the Department. The concept might be acceptable if environmental cases were prepared on a block-by-block basis and were individually approved

by the statutory nature conservation agencies [SNCAs]. We would then consider this to be a type of project Environmental Impact Assessment (EIA) and would wish to see it required for both Exploration Licences and Production Licences.

4. We welcome DTI's undertaking that the Regulations necessary to implement the EU EIA Directive for oil and gas activities will be in place by April 1996. The description of the application of these, however, contains potential contradictions. We urge that it be clarified that EIAs should be undertaken at any stage where activities, including seismic survey and drilling, are likely to have significant effects, rather than limiting their application solely to the development phase. Guidance on EIA for operators is required.

5. We understand that DTI is planning to apply the new EIA Regulations to licences granted from the 16th offshore round onwards. We urge the DTI to also consider applying them to the development phase of licences granted prior to the 16th round, in cases where a development plan has not yet been submitted.

6. In addition to project EIAs, we believe there is a need for a strategic EIA of oil and gas activities in UK waters.

7. We are aware that the UK Government has yet to ratify the Espoo Convention on Environmental Impact Assessment in a Transboundary Context and we understand that part of the reason for this is inadequate Regulations regarding consultation on oil and gas activities.

8. The RSPB is currently seeking designation of Special Protection Areas (SPAs) under the EU Wild Birds Directive out as far as territorial limits. Data are available now to identify SPAs in territorial waters and even beyond. There should be a strong presumption against oil and gas activities where they could affect Special Areas of Conservation (SACs) and SPAs, or sites proposed for these designations.

Comment

The RSPB is concerned at the risk of oil pollution from oil and gas exploration and development activities. Environmental conditions on licences can help reduce these risks. The oil and gas industry is keen to move away from the prescriptive licence approach, to a more goal-setting approach. This has been termed the "environmental case" approach. The RSPB has concerns about this as the document summarised here shows. There appears to have been little further development of the concept since by the DTI.

The UK Government has in the RSPB's view failed to implement the EU Environmental Impact Assessment Directive for offshore oil and gas activities. This remains the case, although the consultation exercise by the DTI in August 1995 did address this issue. At the time of writing no action has yet been taken, although it is hoped that the DTI will issue draft Regulations. Following the publication of the "Habitats & Species" Regulations in 1994, further Regulations are awaited on implementation of the EU Habitats and Species Directive in the marine environment. The 1995 DTI consultation tried to gauge consultees' views on licensing within so-called European marine sites, ie those designated under the Directive.

Comments to the Department of Trade and Industry on *Draft Guidance Notes for Industry on abandonment of offshore installations and pipelines under the Petroleum Act 1987.* **RSPB. August 1995.**

Summary

1. The RSPB is concerned by the damage that may be caused to birds and their habitats by the land and sea disposal of decommissioned offshore installations and is therefore keen that options for disposal should be considered thoroughly and discussed in detail with environmental organisations.

2. Among the key arrangements which RSPB calls for are:

- all case-by-case assessments to take place within the framework of a Strategic Environmental Assessment (SEA) approach;

- early and full consultation with environmental NGOs on both the case-by-case assessments and on the SEA stages, by the operator and Government jointly;

- a scoping environmental impact assessment (EIA) to be produced for all disposal options considered by the operator in the comparative assessment of options, rather than an EIA merely for the best practicable environmental option;

- adequate checking by Government of the validity of any studies conducted by operators or their consultants; and

- monitoring to be considered in detail for land and sea disposal options, to be accurately costed by the operator, and results of monitoring to be allowed to inform decisions on possible modifications to the entire decommissioning programme.

3. We would view with grave concern any proposal to dispose of an installation within or adjacent to a site of importance to wildlife, particularly any site designated, or with potential for designation, under the Wildlife and Countryside Act 1981 or the EU Wild Birds or Habitats & Species Directives.

Comment

At the time of the controversy surrounding the disposal of the Brent Spar facility, the DTI issued the consultation document to which the paper summarised here was the RSPB's response. Subsequent to this document, inquiries into decommissioning were initiated by the Natural Environment Research Council and the House of Lords Science and Technology Committee, to whom the Society provided some comments in October 1995. Both of these inquiries have now reported, and the issue remains a sensitive one.

Chapter 11

WETLANDS AND WATER

L and drainage and watercourse management have at various times been centre-stage as causes of damage to bird populations and their habitats, often being more significant in this respect than the pollution and water quality concerns which perhaps receive more popular attention. More recently the RSPB has greatly increased the efforts it makes on the quantity of water which is demanded and supplied for society, showing that increasing demands are beginning to pose serious threats to wetland habitats and wildlife, and arguing for sustainable resource management measures. Examples of policy submissions on this are covered here, together with wider wetland conservation and flood defence issues. Aspects of statutory responsibilities for water and wetland management can be found in the Environment Agencies items in Chapter 3; hydrological planning in Spain features in Chapters 5 and 15; and Chapter 8 includes an item on planning and flooding in Scotland.

"Water Wise": the RSPB's proposals for using water wisely. **RSPB. 1995.**

Summary

1. Freshwater wetlands are vital to birds, other wildlife and people. These valuable habitats depend on a reliable supply of clean water to maintain their many plant and animal species. The drought and hot summers of 1988-92 have highlighted just how vulnerable wetlands are to the loss of their water source.

2. Supplies of water to wetlands are increasingly threatened by our demand for water. The drying out of important wetlands has serious consequences for our wetland birds. River beds are also adversely affected by low river flows. Biodiversity, simply the variety of life, is threatened if wetlands are allowed to dry out and river flows to drop.

3. Demands for water are predicted to continue to increase across the United Kingdom, especially in areas of low water availability. These

trends will continue to affect wetland habitats and their associated birds. For example, under medium demand scenarios the amount of water needed by the public in south and east England is expected to rise by an average of 18% over the next 30 years.

4. Alternative approaches to water resource management are required to ensure the sustainable use of water resources. Water use is only sustainable if biodiversity is conserved.

5. The RSPB seeks to:

-   ensure that important wildlife sites are not damaged further by water resource management policies and practices;

-   ensure that adequate water supplies are available to enhance important wildlife sites and to restore sites recently damaged by water resource management practices;

-   reduce the impact of water resource management policies and practices on biodiversity in the wider countryside; and

-   ensure adequate water resources to maintain biodiversity within the wider countryside and to facilitate the creation of wetland sites.

The Society believes that these objectives can be met through mechanisms addressing site protection, improved regulation, financial measures, demand management and planning guidance.

6. In respect of site protection, the statutory nature conservation agencies (SNCAs) should undertake a comprehensive review of the adverse impacts of water abstractions and impoundments on recognised important wildlife sites. Where such a review has been completed, actions must be prioritised and taken to remove these impacts.

7. In respect of improved regulation, a consistent regulatory system should be operated to control water abstraction throughout the UK. Protection of the environment should be a key consideration in such a mechanism. The system should be based on "environmentally acceptable flows"that is, flows which are able to sustain biodiversity. Proper assessments of groundwater availability are essential.

8. In respect of financial measures, greater use should be made of these in the management of water resources, to encourage the efficient long-term use of water and to ensure that the price the public pays for water reflects the environmental cost of removing that water from the environment.

9. In respect of demand management, the Government should set up initiatives immediately to encourage the efficient use of water by all sectors of society the public, commerce, industry and agriculture.

10. In respect of planning guidance, the Government should formally recognise that the detrimental impact of built development or land-use change on water resources can be a justifiable reason for limiting such development or land-use change.

Comment

It is increasingly evident that demands for water are at odds with the needs of wetland wildlife. Since the 1970s the RSPB, working with other nature conservation bodies, has fought to protect our remaining wetlands from adverse influences of land drainage, flood protection and poor water quality. This report represents the first comprehensive work by the RSPB in a further field, namely water resources policy.

Two years of research into water quantity issues preceded the publication of *"Water Wise"* in August 1995, at a timely moment when much of the country was in the grip of a serious drought. But it is not only during droughts that rivers and wetlands suffer from a lack of water, and the document highlights the year-on-year impact of sites affected by over-abstraction. In the same month that *"Water Wise"* was published, the Government published its long-awaited follow up on their 1992 consultation report *"Using Water Wisely"*. But after three years of waiting, the RSPB found the eventual proposals and the lack of commitment to action disappointing.

The *"Water Wise"* report was mailed out with a questionnaire to gauge support for our recommendations from key decision-makers. We also produced a simple leaflet to win public support and encourage wise use of water. Results included an RSPB-inspired Private Member's Bill on water conservation being put forward by Richard Burden MP. This had wide all-party support in Parliament and among trade unions and conservation groups but failed to gain government support and so did not become law. It did, however, stimulate a major water conservation debate among MPs, the press and decision-makers. An RSPB appeal mailing produced pledges of support for the Bill from 74,000 people and 3,000 letters were received by DoE.

An Environment Committee Inquiry into Water Conservation and Supply was held in the summer of 1996. The European Commission has agreed a Groundwater Action Programme which calls for Member States to introduce authorisation measures for water abstraction. This will be important in encouraging the introduction of abstraction control into Scotland and Northern Ireland. The RSPB has initiated research into tradeable permits at a pilot site, to feed into the early stages of a government consultation exercise on the use of economic instruments in relation to water abstraction. Some companies have now introduced compulsory water metering of households with sprinklers and swimming pools. Water companies have committed themselves to "demanding targets" for leakage reduction: despite being a step in the right direction, the RSPB views these as not demanding enough and is concerned at the lack of adequate enforcement procedures.

The RSPB supported a successful amendment to what became the Environment Act 1995, to include a duty on water companies to promote the efficient use of water by their customers. Government research has identified a need for new planning guidance on water resources. We have seen some improvement in the integration of Catchment Management Plans (CMPs) with local authority development plans. There will need to be continued improvement with the new Local Environment Agency Plans (LEAP).

Comments to the National Rivers Authority on their consultation report *"Saving Water"*. RSPB. January 1996.

Summary

1. The RSPB warmly welcomes the production of the National Rivers Authority's consultation report *"Saving Water"* and its consideration of the opportunities for demand management measures to be introduced into England and Wales. This report is a significant step towards promoting and taking action on the wise use of water.

2. We support the measures outlined in *"Saving Water"* as one means of ensuring that the NRA's duties to conserve, redistribute, augment and ensure the proper use of water resources and to further nature conservation can both be met without one or the other being the loser.

3. The RSPB looks forward to the Environment Agency formulating its policy on sustainable water resources management. This report provides a firm foundation for the demand management aspects of such a policy.

4. Some of the proposals for demand management in *"Saving Water"* could be met by the Water (Conservation and Consumer Choice) Bill. This Private Member's Bill is supported by the RSPB and by the Chartered Institute of Environmental Health.

5. It is disappointing that, by and large, *"Saving Water"* limits itself to assessing measures which are achievable only under current legislation and to demand management potential only in the domestic sector.

6. The document recognises the lack of any assessment of the environmental costs and benefits of demand management. The RSPB is concerned to know how and when these costs will be included. We recommend early consultation with statutory and non statutory environmental organisations on this matter.

7. The RSPB is concerned about the commitment of some organisations to the promotion of demand management measures. Now is the ideal opportunity to promote water conservation among the whole water sector. This opportunity must be grasped. As a matter of urgency, the Government must publish a national policy statement on demand management.

8. The RSPB supports the idea of a National Water Conservation Committee to be set up to develop a National Water Conservation and Demand Management Strategy. We recommend that such a committee should be chaired by a Minister or senior official of the DoE, and should:

-       provide a forum for policy review;

-       review the opportunities for implementing demand

Conservation Policy Directions

management measures outside the constraints of current legislation;

- review the opportunities for demand management in all the water user sectors (domestic, commercial, agricultural and industrial); and

- be properly represented by environmental bodies (the RSPB would be happy to make a representative available).

Comment

Water conservation and demand management are primary elements in ensuring the sustainable use of water. The UK has the technical knowledge to implement demand management measures. Yet attempts to influence demand trends and reduce the need for additional new water supplies have been and remain limited. In fact, the UK is behind many other industrialised nations in the implementation of demand management measures. With demands for water predicted to continue increasing in much of England and Wales, demand management will have to play an increasingly important rôle.

The RSPB in this document was responding to an NRA consultation report which had been produced by their Demand Management Centre. The NRA, and now the Environment Agency, see the need for demand management to play an increased rôle in water resources management. The consultation report was intended to open up debate and gain support for the NRA's recommendations. The NRA supported many of the RSPB's own demand management recommendations. In fact, some of their proposals could easily have been met by the RSPB-stimulated Water Conservation Bill. At the time of writing, the Environment Agency's conclusions are still awaited.

Efficient water use: **Comments to the Office of Water Services (Ofwat) on their consultation paper on the new duty placed on water companies to promote the efficient use of water. RSPB. January 1996.**

Summary

1. The RSPB welcomes the opportunity to present our views to Ofwat on the new duty placed on the water companies by the Environment Act

1995, to promote the efficient use of water. The RSPB actively supported this amendment to the Environment Bill in 1994. The duty provides a significant step towards promoting and taking action on the wise use of public water supplies.

2. We support the promotion of water conservation among water company customers as one means of ensuring that the water companies' duties to supply water to whoever demands it and to further nature conservation can both be met without one or the other being the loser.

3. Demand management and water conservation have a key rôle to play in ensuring water resources are managed in a sustainable way.

4. If it is implemented correctly, the new duty for water companies to promote the efficient use of water among their customers will provide a significant step towards achieving the sustainable use of water in the public water supply sector.

5. Prior to any decision being made on future schemes promoting the efficient use of water, Ofwat must review the effectiveness of the current water conservation schemes run by the water companies.

6. Ofwat should, in our submission, set an eighth "level of service indicator" for water companies. Such a new indicator, "DG8 Promotion of water efficiency", should set standards of performance for water companies for fulfilling their new duty to promote the efficient use of water to both domestic and industrial/commercial customers. Targets should be set at three levels:

-       an England and Wales water-saving target;

-       individual water company water-saving targets; and

-       a series of water company "means" targets for actions to be taken to help with the achievement of the water-saving target.

7. Water conservation action by the water companies should be targeted to areas where the greatest environmental benefit will be achieved. These areas should be identified in liaison with the Environment Agency and NSCAs.

8. Whilst the RSPB supports water metering as one way of managing demand for water, we are concerned that the sole purpose of this duty should not simply be to introduce widespread metering at the expense of other water conservation measures.

9. Current legislation should be amended to allow water companies to provide grants for the installation of water-efficient devices in the home. This will be achieved if the Water (Conservation and Consumer Choice) Bill, presented as a Private Members' Bill by Richard Burden MP, becomes law.

Comment

Demand for water in England and Wales has been predicted by the NRA to increase by between 5% and 25% under different forecast demand scenarios. If demand is not constrained through demand management and water conservation, it is likely to follow the higher scenario. Under such a scenario there would be concern over the environmental effects of the new resource developments which would be needed. However, demand can be managed to follow the lower demand scenario if management and water conservation measures are introduced.

In the UK, attempts at promoting water conservation measures to reduce the need for additional new supplies have been limited and the UK is in fact behind many other industrialised nations in this. If implemented correctly, the new duty for water companies to promote the efficient use of water among their customers (recommended and actively supported by the RSPB as an amendment to what became the Environment Act) will provide a significant step towards achieving this approach in the public water supply sector.

Ofwat has followed up the consultation exercise by requesting all water companies to prepare Water Efficiency Plans by 1st October 1996. It has been left to the companies to decide how they will meet the new duty but Ofwat has suggested that a minimum component of the plans should be optional water metering, public education and tackling customer supply pipe leakage. Ofwat will then consider the plans to ensure that they properly reflect a given company's circumstances. It is not clear what action Ofwat will take where it is not satisfied with a plan. Actions of this sort cover some of the issues on which the RSPB expressed concern but they fail to address the key issue of setting a long-term target to stabilise and then reduce the amount of water taken from the environment.

Water conservation and supply: **Submission to House of Commons Environment Select Committee inquiry. RSPB. May 1996.**

Summary

1. A number of important wetland wildlife sites are being damaged by drying out owing to over abstraction of the water source which sustains them. Our present use and management of water resources cannot, therefore, be regarded as sustainable if such major problems are occurring.

2. With demands for public water supply and spray irrigation predicted to escalate, there will be ever increasing pressures placed on wetland environments. It is essential that new approaches to water resource management are implemented to ensure the sustainable use of water for people and wildlife, now and in the future.

3. The water companies, the regulators (the Environment Agency and Ofwat) and the Government all have rôles to play in managing our demands for water. The current regulatory régime, however, means that it is entirely unclear who should lead in the development of a strategic sustainable approach to water resource use and conservation. This is a reflection of the failure of the UK Government to provide a comprehensive national policy on water resource management.

4. We recommend that each water company should undertake, with the regulators, a transparent and accountable water resource planning process which considers all the options (from demand management to new resource development) to meet demands for water in the long term. This process must be subject to a strategic environmental assessment.

5. The response to recent droughts has been one of piecemeal knee-jerk reactions. A more strategic approach to emergency water resources planning is clearly needed. This should be instituted at the national level and should give a national overview for emergency water resource planning in England and Wales. Regional Emergency Water Resource Plans, which have been assessed for their environmental impact, should then be developed for each company in liaison with the Environment Agency, Ofwat and other interested parties.

6. The Government must, as a matter of urgency, clarify its position on demand management and the sustainable use of water by publishing a national action programme for saving water. The Government and the regulators (Ofwat and the Environment Agency) should ensure that a consistent and coherent approach is adopted to leakage control.

7. An additional "level of service indicator" should be set for the water companies by Ofwat, "DG8 Promotion of water efficiency". This should set a standard of performance for water companies in respect of the new duty to promote water efficiency and should include targets for the reduction of water use. We consider that the Government should promote the setting up of a Water Savings Trust, analogous to the Energy Savings Trust.

8. Metering should be targeted to areas where water resources are stressed or could become so, and to users of nonessential water such as hose-pipes, sprinklers and swimming pools. We recommend that grants should be provided by MAFF to spray irrigators for the installation of winter storage reservoirs where this is linked to relinquishing a potentially damaging summer abstraction licence.

9. We call on the Environment Agency to implement a rolling programme to review the sustainability of water use in all catchments. The Government must provide planning guidance on the implications of new development and land-use change on water resources. Finally, we recommend that the Environment Agency, in liaison with SNCAs, should identify and then review those licences which could be potentially damaging to important wildlife sites and should take action on those sites where abstraction is shown to cause significant damage.

Comment

The unusually dry weather which the UK has experienced in recent years, especially the long hot summer of 1995, has focused public attention on water to a degree not paralleled since the drought of 1976. With the prospect of a continued increase in demand and the uncertainty of the impact of climate change on water resources, the Environment Committee's inquiry was timely. The RSPB submitted both written and oral evidence. It was keen to highlight the environmental problems, which we were already seeing as a result of water usage, and additional concerns raised by the prospect of increased demand.

The Environment Committee published an interim report to draw attention to a few specific matters which featured prominently in the evidence they received. These were water use in the garden, the use of water for agricultural irrigation and leakage. The interim report recognises the need to encourage wise use of water in gardens, and the need for a more consistent and coherent approach to leakage. The full report was due to be published in Autumn 1996.

Nature conservation matters to include in Catchment Management Plans: **Submission to the National Rivers Authority. RSPB. July 1995.**

Summary

1. This paper elaborates two subject areas which the RSPB wishes to see addressed in and to an extent delivered by catchment management plans (CMPs):

-    international nature conservation obligations on the National Rivers Authority (NRA); and

-    biodiversity conservation targets and the NRA.

2. We provide background information on the two issues and then give examples of how the NRA can use the catchment management planning process to deliver on these.

3. The UK authorities are subject to two European Union Directives on nature conservation (the Wild Birds Directive and the Habitats & Species Directive) which are just as binding on the NRA as Directives on water quality. Special Protection Areas (SPAs) and Special Areas of Conservation (SACs) under these Directives must be protected from damaging developments and/or activities such as land drainage, flood defence, water abstraction and water pollution. The Ramsar Convention on Wetlands of International Importance especially as Waterfowl Habitat also gives rise to designated Ramsar wetland sites, which should be given the same protection as SPAs and SACs in catchment management plans.

4. For catchments holding SPAs and/or SACs and/or Ramsar sites, the NRA should identify its activities management, regulatory or operational which may threaten damage or deterioration to these sites. Any damaging activity identified should have an action

identified to prevent that damage or deterioration. The NRA's obligations under the Wild Birds Directive and the Habitats & Species Directive apply across all its functions. Recognition to date of relevant sites in plans is patchy, and even where recognised, plans often fail to recognise the NRA's obligations.

5. We propose a general text which can be inserted in plans to cover these issues.

6. The Government in its document *"The UK Biodiversity Action Plan"* accepted the need for a targeted approach towards biodiversity conservation. The Action Plan makes a commitment to produce costed targets for key species and habitats by the end of 1995. Delivery of these targets will require concerted effort from all sections of government and non-government organisations and individuals.

7. *"Biodiversity Challenge"* was published by a group of six voluntary conservation bodies as a stimulus to the UK Action Plan, spelling out specific actions in a systematic way. The approach is focused on the outcomes to be achieved for individual species in terms of number and ranges, and habitats in terms of extent and quality. It can easily be applied at the local level in CMPs.

8. Local Agenda 21 is an initiative for sustainable development at the local level by local authorities and others. In parallel to this, many local authorities are also seeking a full local contribution to the UK Biodiversity Action Plan through the preparation of biodiversity action plans. As part of these processes many local authorities will be setting local targets for species and habitats and action plans for meeting these targets.

9. The NRA will also be a key organisation in helping to achieve targets relating to wetland species and habitats identified in the Biodiversity Action Plan and Local Agenda 21: for example, ensuring the appropriate water quality, water levels and water supply for particular sites to ensure the right conditions. Early NRA liaison with local authorities during the preparation of Local Agenda 21 or local Biodiversity Action Plans is clearly needed.

10. Once targets have been set as described, the NRA should identify them in the relevant CMPs. NRA actions in water quality, water resources, flood defence, conservation, fisheries, recreation and other

functions required to help deliver these targets can then be identified. This target-led philosophy should cut across all NRA work, with cross-referencing between functions as appropriate.

11. Targets and indicators are tools for helping to agree priorities and for measuring progress towards sustainability. In some catchment management plans the NRA already defines targets for water quality, water quantity and physical features. This needs to broaden to a target-led identification of areas suitable for enhancement and rehabilitation of selected habitats. Some NRA regions are beginning to identify habitat and species targets: we welcome these and hope that these ideas will be taken up across the Authority as a whole.

12. We set out some example texts which plans could incorporate on this subject.

Comment

CMPs were being prepared by the NRA for 163 of the principal river catchments in England and Wales. They are intended to provide a framework for decision-making on a catchment-wide basis, examining the interactions between the water environment and land uses. CMPs seek to reconcile conflicts and to protect and improve the water environment. They are therefore key to delivering biodiversity objectives in the freshwater environment.

As a matter of principle, the RSPB supports the idea of integrated catchment management plans. We do, however, have some concerns over what the plans deliver, how this matches external requirements and whether the actions identified are what the relevant bodies were going to do anyway. The RSPB has two key concerns regarding CMPs, namely acknowledgement of the NRA's international nature conservation obligations and setting and helping to meet biodiversity targets. As well as submitting this paper to the NRA, a presentation on the key issues was given.

The NRA proved receptive. Soon after this work they were subsumed into the Environment Agency. The Agency has taken on a wider environmental remit, also looking at air quality and waste. The old NRA's CMPs will now be replaced with wider environmental management plans called Local Environment Agency Plans [LEAPs]. The Agency will produce 10 pilot LEAPs between September 1996 and January 1997, and these will begin to indicate the extent to which in practice our thinking has been taken on board.

Comments to the Environment Agency on the agency's discussion document *"Research and Development note 381: The National Rivers Authority's rôle in wetland conservation"*. RSPB. June 1996.

Title Note: The consultation document was issued by the NRA before it evolved into the Environment Agency. The subject is therefore the Agency's rôle in wetland conservation The Agency had come into being by the time the RSPB submitted is responce.

Summary

1. The RSPB welcomes this opportunity to submit comments on the NRA's (now the Environment Agency's) rôle in wetland conservation. This response provides comments on the objectives proposed and identifies some additional issues which would benefit from being addressed as part of the strategy. We recommend actions that could be taken by the Environment Agency, with support from the UK Government and in partnership with other organisations, which would make it a leader in the wise use and conservation of wetlands.

2. Wetlands are important to people and to wildlife. UK wetlands are of global significance because they support internationally important numbers of birds. Wetland losses in terms of both quality and quantity have occurred throughout the UK due to urban growth, industrial expansion, intensive agriculture and river regulation. Numbers of wetland bird species such as bittern and some waders have declined.

3. The RSPB encourages the initiative of a wetland strategy, as it supports the wise use and conservation of wetlands which the UK Government undertook to promote when it became a signatory to the Ramsar Convention in 1973. A strategy for wetland conservation is urgently needed to promote an integrated and sustainable approach to wetlands. The Government, the regulators (the Environment Agency and Ofwat), business and industry all have a rôle to play in managing impacts upon wetland habitats. However, under the current regulatory régime it is unclear who should lead in the development of a strategic approach to wetland conservation.

4. The Environment Agency, with its range of both regulatory and op-

erational powers and duties (including water resource management, flood defence and conservation) is well placed to take on this rôle, in partnership with others.

5. The wetland strategy should identify clear goals, objectives and targets for wetland management and conservation, restoration and creation. A biodiversity audit at catchment level is needed in order to select priorities. Targets should relate to those set in the UK Biodiversity Action Plan.

6. The strategy must support the delivery of effective management for wetland areas designated as SPAs, SACs, Ramsar sites and SSSIs, as well as wetland areas in the "wider countryside".

7. The objectives of the European Commission's Communication on wise use of wetlands (no further wetland loss, no further wetland degradation, wise use of wetlands, wetland improvement and restoration, international co-operation and action) should all be central to the wetland conservation strategy.

8. Strategic environmental assessment and planning which integrate water resource management, catchment management, flood defence and coastal zone management are needed to support wetland conservation. The catchment management planning process, now in the form of Local Environment Agency Plans (LEAPs), will be crucial to this at local level. LEAPs should be used to identify opportunities for wetland habitat creation and enhancement, and to deliver on some of the national targets for wetland species and habitats identified under the Biodiversity Action Plan. An increased programme of funding and incentives for wetland management and creation has to be made available, as recommended in the Action Plan Steering Group report.

9. A comprehensive national policy on water resource management needs to be developed in conjunction with the wetland conservation strategy.

10. A programme of monitoring of wetland habitats and species must be initiated, to review their status and assess progress towards targets and the implementation of local action plans.

11. The wetland conservation strategy must address the impact of water quality on wetlands, the delivery of statutory water quality objectives and the need for stringent discharge consents.

12. We recommend that the Agency's definition of "wetland" be extended and a national wetland classification system and wetland resource inventory be developed.

13. The Agency should in our view review its operational activities and in a precautionary way identify priorities for removing significant damage to wetland sites. We recommend transferral of the functions of Internal Drainage Boards (IDBs)to the Agency. Finally, we advocate a complete national review of abstraction consents.

Comment

The NRA's statutory conservation function made it clear that they had a key rôle in conserving wetlands, through their range of regulatory and operational functions relating to inland waters. However, in the RSPB's view, the Authority suffered from the lack of a wetland strategy to guide policy and decision-making. The submission summarised here encouraged the adoption of such a strategy, stressing the particular value of wetland biodiversity targets, strategic environmental assessment, effective management for protected sites and a precautionary approach to operational decisions. We were keen that the strategy should draw on existing internationally defined principles on these matters.

The same messages are being promoted in consultation responses on draft LEAPs and Water Level Management Plans. We also continue to press more generally for better co-ordination of wetland conservation efforts between the environment agencies, agriculture departments and statutory conservation agencies.

Submission to the House of Commons Select Committee on European Legislation inquiry into the Communication from the European Commission to the Council and the European Parliament on the "*Wise Use and Conservation of Wetlands*". RSPB February 1996.

Summary

1. This memorandum of evidence provides some additional material to supplement the Commission's examples on the importance of wetlands and wetland loss. It provides comments on the policies proposed and indicates some additional issues which would benefit from being addressed in the Communication on the wise use

and conservation of wetlands. We also identify actions which could be taken by the UK Government to make it a leader in Europe on wetland wise use and conservation.

2. Wetlands are of importance to people and to wildlife. UK wetlands are of global significance because they support internationally important numbers of birds. This importance is recognised by the listing of sites for waterfowl populations under the Ramsar Convention and the conservation action requirements of the EU Wild Birds Directive. Certain wetland habitats and the species dependent upon them are of European significance and are identified for conservation action by the EU Habitats and Species Directive.

3. Wetland losses in the UK have been as significant as elsewhere in the EU and across the world. Losses have occurred both in the area of wetlands in the UK and in the quality, as measured by bird populations, of the remaining wetlands. The UK Government already has a programme for the conservation and wise use of wetlands. This programme constitutes significant progress toward sustainable and wise use of wetlands. Additional actions, particularly for wetland management and creation, have been identified in the report of the UK Biodiversity Action Plan Steering Group (UKBAPSG).

4. The Communication from the Commission contains a sound analysis of the state of wetlands in the EU and issues which have affected this. It has a series of well-justified and valid conclusions. As a consequence, the RSPB supports the proposals in the Communication.

5. The Communication could be further improved by fine-tuning to give greater clarity and focus on the effects of global warming and climate change; the proposed decision rules on wetland loss; the setting of targets for wetland improvements and restoration; and by making links to EU proposals on the quality and quantity of water and on spatial planning.

6. The RSPB would ask the House of Commons Select Committee on European Legislation to endorse the proposals from the Commission and to urge the UK Government to do likewise.

7. The Society would ask the UK Government to endorse the proposals from the Commission and to restate the commitment to the

wise use and conservation of wetlands which it made by virtue of becoming a signatory to the Ramsar Convention in 1973.

8. The RSPB would ask the UK Government to increase the programme of funding for wetland management and creation, in accordance with the recommendations of the UKBAPSG.

Comment

The European Commission initiative which led to this inquiry took its cue from the Ramsar Convention on wetlands of international importance. The RSPB was very supportive of the Commission Communication and pointed out to the Select Committee the opportunity it provided to define the way forward in delivering relevant aspects of the UKBAPSG and the UK's obligations under the Convention. Perhaps not surprisingly, the Government's attitude has tended to be that by comparison with other European Member States it performs well on wetland conservation and does not need to alter existing policies or processes. The RSPB continues to assert that, on deeper analysis, there are many improvements that should be made if the UK is to live up to the standards that have been defined.

Comments to The Scottish Office Agriculture, Environment and Fisheries Department on their *proposed revision of flooding legislation*. RSPB. March 1996.

Summary

1. Inappropriate flood defence measures and lack of regard to development in areas prone to flooding can adversely affect sites of nature conservation importance.

2. There is no compelling case for the creation of a flood defence body in Scotland and no persuasive case for changing local authorities' rôle from the current one they have in exercising permissive powers.

3. Any person carrying out flood defence works should be given a duty to further nature conservation. The Scottish Environment Protection Agency (SEPA) should be given a duty to regulate such works and a duty to further nature conservation when carrying out its functions in relation to flood defence. The Scottish Office/Secre-

tary of State should also be given a strong duty towards nature conservation when exercising their functions in relation to flood defence.

4. The RSPB recommends that the relevance of the Land Drainage Acts should be reviewed and the opportunity of legislative reform should be taken to repeal or amend these Acts where appropriate to prevent conflict with conservation of the natural heritage.

5. The RSPB advocates the development of a system of integrated catchment management to achieve strategic co-ordination of the work of the unitary authorities and other bodies with responsibilities within catchments. The Society has recommended that SEPA should have a key rôle in this but clearly any such system would have to be very closely tied in to the development plan process.

6. Operations outside planning control such as agriculture and forestry can have significant impacts on flood risk and this should be reflected in the approach taken to flood defence of both urban and non urban land. This must in our view be reflected in any proposed legislative changes.

7. In many cases there may be opportunities to prevent flooding of built development by utilising agricultural land, in the form of washland. This could be provided through agri-environment measures and would provide opportunities for the creation of floodplain habitats such as wet grassland and reedbed.

8. The RSPB supports the concept of managed retreat from existing coastal defences where appropriate. The Scottish Office should investigate how this principle will be incorporated into flood defence measures, and should develop a co-ordinated approach to this issue.

Comment

The proposals for change on which this paper commented came as a response to flooding of urban areas in recent winters. Responses to the consultation were, generally, rather negative. In general, local authorities do not wish to have a new duty unless it is accompanied by assurances of increased funding. The Secretary of State, however, appeared to remain keen to progress the proposed changes. There remains a lack of will to link flood protection of urban areas with land management and flood management of rural areas. This is reflected in Scotland's recent National Planning Policy Guideline on planning and flooding (see Chapter 8). The RSPB is continuing to advocate a catchment management approach which can use "soft engineering" solutions to cope with flood water. Flood water can be used to enhance flood plain habitats and to assist the conservation of wetland species, while at the same time reducing impacts downstream.

Comments to the Ministry of Agriculture, Fisheries and Food on their *draft Code of good environmental practice for flood defence operating authorities*. RSPB. July 1996.

Summary

1. The RSPB welcomes MAFF's initiative to integrate and consolidate existing "good practice" guides for flood defence and land drainage authorities and to extend the guidance to include strategic planning issues. However, the Society feels that the draft Code is not as the title might suggest a practical guide, in the sense of MAFF's existing *"Coast Defence and the Environment: a guide to good practice"*. The draft Code is instead a procedural guide aimed at replacing existing procedural guides.

2. The draft code outlines the existing components of both coastal and inland flood defence planning and management. However, it is far from clear how these different components are meant to fit together. For example, steps 1 and 2 identified under the procedural framework for individual schemes would already have been considered within a strategic flood defence plan. The RSPB believes that this confusion arises as a consequence of not having the whole flood defence framework in place as yet. The Society believes that the missing elements of this framework can be summarised as:

- strategic river valley or catchment flood defence plans, analogous to Shoreline Management Plans;

- guidance on the production of these strategic river/catchment flood defence plans;

- a procedural guide for the production of coastal Scheme Strategy Plans, analogous to Water Level Management Plans; and

- a good practice guide for inland flood defence works, analogous to *"Coastal Defence and the Environment - a guide to good practice"*.

3. This framework should facilitate the integration of coastal and inland flood defence planning and management, and in particular the creation of freshwater habitats away from the coastal flood risk zone, contributing to more sustainable coastal flood defence management.

4. The code needs to consider in detail the implementation of flood defence strategies. In particular, the rôle of incentive schemes and agri-environment measures in facilitating strategic flood defence planning needs to be assessed. Finally, as with some other government "good practice" guides, for example the Coastal Zone Management guide, the draft code fails to make the necessary links between the "good practice" text and the legislative requirements outlined at the back of the document.

Comment

The RSPB has a long history of involvement with MAFF and flood and coastal defence issues. In the past, this has tended to concentrate on major lowland wet grassland capital drainage schemes. More recently, coast protection and sea defence issues have also been a priority in the face of significant habitat loss and degradation due to sea-level rise. Over the past five years, and partly in response to the House of Commons Environment Select Committee inquiry into Coastal Zone Protection and Planning, and the National Audit Office (NAO) report *"Coastal Defences in England"*, MAFF have been developing a flood defence and land drainage planning framework.

Whilst the development of this framework has been an iterative process, RSPB has been involved at all stages of its development. At the level of individual works, conservation guidelines and an environmental good practice guide have been developed. Strategic procedural guides have been produced to aid decision-making, and prescriptive water level management plans are now being developed for wetland SSSIs. Perhaps most significant is the development of strategic planning in the form of Shoreline Management Plans; although there is currently no equivalent or parallel approach for inland flood defence management.

With the passage of the Environment Act in 1995, the opportunity was presented for MAFF to publish statutory codes of practice for flood defence operating authorities. For the first time, MAFF is trying to fit the various pieces of flood defence guidance and advice into one integrated guide. Most important will be the linking of coastal and inland flood defence strategic planning and the identification of habitat creation and enhancement opportunities, as coastal habitats (both freshwater and saltwater) are lost in the face of sea-level rise. However, the current absence of a strategic forward planning framework for inland flood defence works is a major obstacle. The code is due to be published in autumn 1996.

Chapter 12

AGRICULTURE POLICY

It has long been appreciated that despite specific instances of damage to important sites perhaps most easily being the cause of public outcry about the fate of our birdlife, what is equally important in determining its fortunes are policies shaping the way the wider countryside as a whole is managed. Central to those policies is agriculture policy (CAP). This is so dominated by the European Common Agricultural Policy that to a large extent the "domestic" policy arena for these affairs lies in Brussels rather than Whitehall. As the items here show, agricultural policy now includes a number of schemes aimed at producing environmental benefits. However, the RSPB has for some years been seeking to build a more fundamental environmental objective into the CAP, to better reflect where the true public interest lies - that is not in distorted income support which destablises markets and harms the environment. Alarming new data on declines in once-common farmland birds across the whole of Europe has emerged. The facts are drawn on in these papers to reinforce the case the Society puts forward.

The Future of the Common Agricultural Policy. RSPB. 1995.

Summary

1. The RSPB has been working for over 10 years towards reform of the CAP, not only as part of our international partnership, BirdLife International [BI], but also with other alliances of farmers, consumers and political groups. Agriculture dominates land use in the UK and Europe and so policies for it have a profound influence over wildlife, their habitats and the environment. Farming is both the greatest threat to Europe's biodiversity and the industry which can contribute most to its conservation.

2. The first half of 1995 is a particularly opportune time to take stock of recent changes to the CAP and to plan for the future. We believe that the particular needs of wildlife, together with its public appeal (especially the appeal of birds), mean that biodiversity conservation should be a part of any proposed reforms to the CAP.

3. In this submission, we outline objectives and ideas for reform, considering some of the institutional and tactical blockages to change. In particular, we propose a strategy for handling the future enlargement of the EU which, we believe, is likely to be the next major force for changing the CAP, much as the Uruguay Round of the GATT was in the past. Our interest in Central and East Europe is not, however, simply as an external influence over the CAP; we are also concerned with land use and nature conservation policies in those countries.

4. With BI, we recently published the results of an exhaustive review of the status of all of Europe's birds, covering 46 countries across the whole continent. They show that farmland habitats support the largest number of species facing conservation threats and, of these, much the greater proportion of their populations are found in Central and East Europe. The catastrophic decline in populations of once-common farmland birds witnessed in the UK is matched across much of the European countryside. Most of Europe's key ornithological interest lies in countries subject to change in the context of EU enlargement.

5. The disappearance of birds from our farmland is symptomatic of much wider ecological change that results from changing farm structures, technology and practice.

6. CAP reform is, therefore, of the utmost priority and urgency for the conservation of wildlife in the UK, EU and indeed the whole of Europe.

7. The CAP so dominates the way land is used in the UK and EU that it influences every farm business and almost the whole of the rural environment of Europe. Historically, in the UK the rationalisation and development of farm structures and technologies caused considerable losses to wildlife and the countryside. Whilst this destruction is now less obvious, problems still exist in the farmed landscape. The difficulties birds and other wildlife face in the UK are matched across the whole of Europe. Moreover, the CAP is not yet helping to redress this damage, despite small-scale moves to promote environmentally sensitive farming.

8. Decision-making in agriculture policy lies more centrally in the institutions of the EU than with almost any other policy and so it is essential that, in framing a UK view, a European perspective is

taken. We believe that in the short term (probably until the end of the current Uruguay Round agreement in 2001), a number of relatively minor reforms will be necessary both to meet Uruguay Round commitments and to maintain control over EU budgets. These provide significant opportunities to reduce the environmental impact of the CAP, by:

-   fully implementing the Agri-environment Regulation;

-   giving set-aside a much clearer environmental rôle;

-   applying environmental conditions to all other policies, particularly arable and livestock; and

-   sending a signal to the agricultural policy community that the CAP must have the environment as an objective by amending the Treaty of Rome during the 1996 intergovernmental conference.

9. In the longer term (beyond the year 2000), the next multilateral trade round will force more substantial change on the CAP. More significantly, the EU will have to make a difficult strategic choice about bringing the economies of Central and East Europe into the EU, particularly into the single market for agriculture.

10. Strategic options suggested so far have been polarised. On the one hand it has been proposed that the CAP should be maintained and extended to the enlarged EU. An alternative option is that the CAP should be abolished by bringing prices down to world levels and removing border protection, export subsidies and supply controls. We reject the former outright, believing that its costs to the UK and European environment will be too great. However, we also believe the latter to be flawed because, to date, its advocates have failed to consider environmental and social consequences and political constraints. Because key issues have not been addressed, the resistance to this option will prevent its general acceptance. We believe there is a feasible way of reforming the CAP which, because it addresses social, environmental and political constraints to reform, will be more likely to succeed.

11. Specifically, we suggest:

-   A selective and gradual reduction of overall protection and subsidies (price support, direct subsidies, border protection, export subsidies and supply controls) in the EU by 2010. The target for this should be to achieve a level equivalent to the OECD Producer Subsidy Equivalent as a percentage of the value of total agricultural production of 25% (from the current of about 50%). This should aim to remove the damaging distortions in land use and farming practices that subsidies cause.

- The retention of a level of protection and subsidies (preferably in the form of area payments) only for defined farming systems, products and regions which contribute to the protection of Europe's countryside and biodiversity; some farming (which currently enjoy high levels of support) should receive little or none.

- That whenever payments are made direct to producers, in whatever form (whether generally available, degressive over time, capped according to farm size, or in other ways "conditional"), all payments should be conditional on recipients protecting the environment.

- An increasing reliance on environmentally-led payments and incentives to achieve the new objectives of the CAP; by the year 2010, 30% of the EU agricultural land surface should be targeted by specific environmental payment schemes, based on the existing Agri-environment Regulation. 5% of UK farmland should be removed from production so as to create habitats such as woodland, heathland and wetland.

- All reforms (including reduction in subsidy levels) must be made with the specific intention of achieving environmental goals and extensifying farming overall: this should be monitored, using environmental targets and indicators.

- Support for rural development, forestry and other diversification of the rural economy should not be as "compensation" for changes in agricultural policies but should only be on the basis of specific social or economic need or to pay for specific environmental "services". All rural economic development policies should be at least environmentally neutral.

12. In order that the institutional resistance to reform is overcome, decision-making in the CAP should be made more accountable and must represent the interests of a wider spectrum of the public than just producers. Greater dynamism and innovation in rural policy-making is needed, with more strategic policy being made outside departments of government and the EU which implement (and therefore have vested interests in) the status quo. The UK Government should have a key rôle to play in advocating reform and supporting innovative, strategic research on land use policy in Europe. UK statutory nature and landscape protection agencies also have a rôle in providing technical support to agri-environment policy across the EU.

13. The UK Government could act alone on many issues: indeed the development of the Agri-environment Regulation and application of conditions to Arable Area Aids (AAAs) would require minimal involvement from the Commission.

Comment

European agriculture policy has a very important influence over markets, subsidies, uptake of technology by farmers and landuse. UK decision-making on agriculture policy is largely within the framework of the EUs CAP. Environmental issues have become more important within the CAP over the past 15 years. For 10 years the RSPB has been working towards reform of the CAP and the integration of environmental concerns within it. Several policy analyses, position papers and other inputs have been prepared by RSPB staff. The one described here was submitted to a working group convened by the UK Government in December 1994. The group reported in the summer of 1995. The RSPB submission was the basis of more focused lobbying of UK and EU institutions, including a meeting with EU Commissioner Franz Fischler in May 1995.

Increasingly, the RSPB works as part of a wider coalition consisting of the EU partners within BI and other environmental interests. Through these alliances the RSPB has been influential in promoting an environmental element within the 1992 "MacSharry" reforms, in promoting the environmental incentive element of the CAP the Agri-environment Regulation and also in making specific comments on, for example, EU cereals, livestock and structural policies. More recently, effort has been directed at the next round of CAP reform, which is likely to be forced on the EU by GATT commitments, enlargement eastwards and because of the 1996 beef crisis.

In the immediate period after the 1992 reforms, the RSPB embarked on a series of case studies designed to illustrate the relationship between farming systems and birds. These include arable farming in France (May 1994), transhumance pastoralism in Spain (May 1994), rice farming in Italy (July 1994), olive farming in Portugal (May 1994) and lowland wet grasslands in the Netherlands and Germany (March 1994).

Submission to the House of Lords European Communities Committee Sub-Committee D (agriculture, fisheries and consumer protection) inquiry into *European Union enlargement and Common Agricultural Policy reform*. RSPB. February 1996.

Summary

1. The RSPB welcomes the opportunity to comment on the European Commission's strategy for CAP reform and enlargement. As the Sub-Committee has itself concluded, the future accession of the countries of Central and Eastern Europe challenges the CAP. As we have argued in other submissions to the Sub-Committee, the CAP is one of the greatest influences on farming and on the countryside and its wildlife. Therefore, in seeking to foster stewardship and environmental protection amongst farmers, it is essential that the CAP is reformed to support sustainable practices and not to promote environmentally damaging ones.

2. This submission concentrates on the strategic options for the CAP outlined by the Commission and their consequences for the UK countryside and farming industry. However, we also summarise our work in the remainder of the EU and the Central and East European countries (CEECs).

3. Land use and farming practices in CEECs have changed dramatically in response to a collapsed agricultural market. For both the CEECs and the EU, agriculture poses exceptional difficulties for enlargement negotiations. The environmental consequences have rarely featured in analyses of future enlargement to date.

4. Relevant environmental issues include the environmental legacy of former CEEC policies, the consequences of the recent agricultural crisis and the environmental aspects of future policies for

both the EU and CEECs. This has been the subject of a major pro-gramme of work undertaken jointly in Europe by BirdLife Interna-tional [BI] with the World Wide Fund For Nature (WWF) and the World Conservation Union (IUCN) which has been funded and sup-ported by the RSPB. A recent outcome of this is the *"Action Plan to 2010 for Central and Eastern Europe"* which has the support of all of Europe's major environmental organisations.

5. The Commission's paper is the first Commission policy paper (as opposed to a theoretical analysis) on the agricultural situation in Central and Eastern Europe and the impacts on the CAP of hav-ing the agricultural markets and systems of these countries become part of it. It does not, however, contain specific proposals for legis-lative change, which we see as a priority need. It is weak in its analysis of the environmental situation of the CEECs, and draws conclusions about the 1992 CAP reforms in the EU which we be-lieve may be premature.

6. Arable Area Payments Scheme payments to English arable farmers have increased to £1,081 million per year. They have little social, agricultural, economic or environmental justification and, unlike all UK livestock subsidies, no environmental conditions ap-ply. It is indefensible that the industry and MAFF have resisted applying even the most basic environmental conditions to these payments.

7. The Commission paper considers the production and consump-tion patterns of an enlarged EU in 2010, concluding that increases in production (largely from the existing EU) would result, beyond levels allowed under GATT. We strongly agree with the Commis-sion's rejection of the status quo as an option for the future and its view that reforms based on the 1992 changes are the most likely way forward. We suggest that the Sub-Committee should set its own guidelines for the development of the Commission's view of this, steering it towards a more radical approach in the detail, rather than selecting an option billed overall as "radical".

8. Commissioner Fischler has offered the Council European Coun-cil of Ministers a choice of a high cost CAP (based on high levels of direct, area-based aid to all farmers) or a lower cost CAP (where payments are only made to certain groups). We prefer the latter. The question now is on what basis these payments should be made. We strongly support the intention to develop an environmentally-de-

termined system of support to the CEECs. Indeed, we believe that the Agri-environment Regulation provides a strong basis on which such a system of support can expand. We do not believe it necessary for a support system to equate to any current or future levels of support to farming in the EU or CEECs. Rather, it should be objective-led. These payments must not serve as production subsidies "through the back door".

9. Preaccession policy will be less about market access (which the CEEC governments want) or market price support (which the Commission rejects) and more about improving technical assistance programmes. The Commission paper proposes a preaccession structural adjustment programme concentrating on processing industries, rural development and accompanying environmental measures. The latter accords with our proposals in the "Action Plan" referred to above.

10. We recommend that there should be a more ordered and regular timetable for CAP reform. The annual price-fixing should be subsumed within a five-year "omnibus" reform to which democratic institutions, professional organisations and nongovernment organisations can make an input.

Comment

In autumn 1995, the European Commission began a process of reviewing its policies on agriculture and rural development, prior to enlargement of the EU towards the end of the century. The RSPB was instrumental in preparing an "Action Plan" for Central and Eastern Europe and leading a coalition of non governmental organisations to influence the development of CAP policies. The Commission published its outline proposals for future reforms for discussion at the Madrid Council of the EU in December 1995. These proposals were the basis of the House of Lords inquiry to which the RSPB submitted the evidence summarised here. At the time of writing, the EU is working on further papers which will include more specific proposals for reforms to the CAP later in the decade.

Comments to the Ministry of Agriculture, Fisheries and Food on the *review of Environmental Land Management Schemes in England*. RSPB. June 1995.

Summary

1. This review of environmental land management schemes (ELMS) is a major opportunity for Government to ensure that it meets its commitments to a range of UK environmental objectives and targets for priority habitats and species.

2. The present range of schemes, with Countryside Stewardship (CS) and Environmentally Sensitive Areas (ESAs) as core schemes, are well placed to begin to meet these objectives. However, new priorities demand the continued development of schemes, which will require funding.

3. This review is a major opportunity to take action for conservation by:

-    streamlining the operation of all incentive schemes to produce the best strategic programme for the countryside;

-    retaining and expanding the existing CS options;

-    introducing new (or much expanded) CS options for arable areas and for acid and neutral grasslands;

-    continuing development and expansion of options in CS and other schemes for creation of priority habitats, such as reedbeds, lowland heath, chalk downland, woodland and lowland wet grassland; and

-    retaining and in the long term developing the ESA programme.

4. In this response we attempt to define, according to current knowledge, the range of conservation problems on farmland in the UK. We establish the rôle of financial incentives and their relationship to other policy measures and the importance of using a suite of different policy measures to respond to different conservation problems. More specifically, we offer comments on the development of CS and ESAs as core incentive schemes, the opportunities for

rationalisation of other schemes in future, the need to set clear objectives and targets (especially the need for a National Agri-Environment Steering Group), and the rôle of advice in meeting environmental objectives.

5. Greater resources are required to achieve higher uptake of target habitats under existing CS options. There is a growing body of empirical knowledge of some of the causes of declines of farmland birds. This has been applied to show that arable land can be managed for the benefit of birds and other wildlife by encouraging extensification (reduction of inputs, outputs and "intensity" of management operations) and diversion (creation of noncultivated or even nonfarmed habitats on part or all of land previously under cultivation in a given area). In particular, changes to the way in which cropped land is managed and provisions for the protection, creation and maintenance of field margins and boundaries and other "microhabitats" such as ponds adjacent to cropped land need to be introduced.

6. The Government faces a critical decision as to how to change the signals given to UK arable farmers. We understand that Ministers would favour payments to farmers for more onerous prescriptions. To be effective, these would need to be available to a large number of farmers managing a high proportion of UK farmland rather than simply the ESAs. Payment rates would have to compete with the profits of arable farming (including subsidies) and be additional to arable subsidies.

7. Whatever the overall approach, an important step will be developing an experiment to test prescriptions. We outline some proposals for this and estimate that funding of £1 million per year over 3-5 years would be required.

8. It is essential that remaining areas of grasslands are not only protected but managed. "Abandonment" can be as damaging for permanent pasture as direct destruction. The availability of grassland management CS options should be extended to this habitat throughout England. We estimate that a further £7-10 million per year would be required to bring all neutral and acid grasslands that have retained their conservation interest into management.

9. Only small proportions of vulnerable habitats such as moorland, heathland and reedbeds can be covered by current levels of

CS resourcing. We detail as an example the action required for reedbeds if conservation targets, such as those being developed by the Biodiversity Steering Group, are to be met.

10. Overall we estimate an additional £60 million is required between now and the end of the century to fund the core schemes of CS and ESAs.

11. Regulation and statutory protection must continue to underpin the Government's conservation strategy. The RSPB also supports the imposition of environmental standards on all farming enterprises in receipt of subsidies, as a form of cross-compliance. We believe it is important that Government seeks to address conservation problems in the context of a UK-wide conservation strategy.

12. We also consider that a scheme such as CS could equally apply to Scotland, Wales and Northern Ireland. We discuss in this response factors which influence uptake, quality and effectiveness of the scheme, and argue that greater emphasis should be placed on ends objectives rather than means objectives.

13. The adoption of CS by MAFF provides an opportunity to extend ESAs and link the two schemes more closely. Our experience indicates the need for some specific changes within current ESAs in the short term, including prescription changes and extensions to existing boundaries and, in the longer term, designation of a number of new ESAs. We outline some specific proposals.

14. We agree with the review Working Group that now is a good time to review the scope for consolidation and the strategic development of schemes. ESAs and CS are well placed to develop as core schemes for the future, together with advice and regulation. We consider it is imperative that ELMSs are developed to focus on arable areas. We recommend that MAFF conducts an arable pilot project with a view to adding an arable option to CS at a future date and we have set out a detailed project proposal for this.

15. We support the Working Group recommendation that the Farm and Conservation Grant Scheme (F&CGS) should not continue as a separate scheme in England but that capital grants for conservation purposes should be integrated into MAFF's other schemes. We believe capital grants for pollution control should continue to be available to all farmers and not just within proposed

Nitrate Vulnerable Zones and we urge Government to reconsider this issue.

16. We agree that CS is sufficiently broad and flexible to have the potential to absorb other schemes and consider that the Habitat Scheme, Moorland Scheme, Nitrate Sensitive Areas Scheme, Organic Scheme and Countryside Access Scheme would all be potential candidates.

17. Agri-environment spending in the UK is still very small compared to other agricultural subsidies and is less than comparable expenditures in other EU Member States. The UK must not be left behind.

Comment

ELMSs such as those discussed here are among the main ways of meeting conservation objectives on farmland. The announcement by MAFF in early-1995 of a review of such schemes was a major opportunity for the RSPB to ensure that such objectives were indeed being met. With increasing knowledge about the declines in biodiversity, especially farmland birds, the RSPB and other conservation organisations were taking steps to find solutions to the causes of this. The Government strongly favoured an incentive-led approach, as opposed to regulation (eg "cross-compliance" measures), and the review of schemes was therefore seen as a positive step in finding new solutions to problems affecting farmland birds.

This exercise began a process, which has continued through 1996, of promoting the introduction of some new incentive measures for farmland birds such as skylark and corn bunting. We had submitted some earlier comments to MAFF on the overall direction being taken by agri-environment schemes but the submission summarised here contained our first call for the development of an arable pilot project. We were also at the time undertaking a project with BirdLife International, funded by the European Commission, looking at the benefits of the EU Agri-environment Regulation.

The RSPB was not successful in persuading MAFF to fund an arable pilot project but we did succeed in raising the profile of the farmland birds issue. This contributed to MAFF's inclusion, in subsequent consultation proposals on the CS scheme, of field margin options (one of the elements of our suggested arable pilot project). A neutral and arid grassland option, and a National Agri-Environment Steering Group, both of which we had supported, were later introduced.

Comments to the Ministry of Agriculture, Fisheries and Food on the *Countryside Stewardship Scheme*. RSPB. January 1996.

Summary

1. This response concentrates on the issue of arable farming and the plight of the birds dependent on it and reiterates previous arguments put to MAFF in favour of an arable pilot project. We ask that MAFF reconsiders its decision not to proceed with a more broadly-based arable scheme. We also offer comments on the other proposals set out in the consultation paper (including arable field margins, acid and neutral grasslands and field boundaries) and on the overall administration of Countryside Stewardship (CS).

2. The RSPB welcomes the MAFF consultation paper. We support the transfer of CS from the Countryside Commission to MAFF in April this year and its continuation as one of the core environmental land management schemes (ELMSs) alongside Environmentally Sensitive Areas (ESAs). The RSPB has supported the development of UK and EU agri-environment incentives since their inception in the early-1980s because we believe that they play a significant rôle in the conservation of wildlife and the countryside.

3. We agree with the recent draft EU Regulation on the implementation of Regulation 2078/92 that its objective should be to achieve specific environmental objectives above and beyond those which are expected of good agricultural practice or which are better achieved as a condition of an agricultural payment. We therefore believe that it is important to judge MAFF's proposals alongside what might be expected from future proposals for environmental conditions to apply to Arable Area Payments (AAPs). We wish to see the limited funds available for CS directed at issues which cannot realistically be addressed other than by an incentive payment.

4. A proportion of the new CS funds should be allocated to an arable pilot scheme in response to declines in farmland birds which are now a conservation priority. An arable pilot scheme would have significant advantages over MAFF's proposed arable field margins scheme, in that it would benefit a wider range of bird species by

targeting the arable habitat (rather than just one component of it). It would therefore follow the current CS habitat based approach.

5. A pilot such as that proposed would also have significant advantages over set-aside (even if improved), namely that prescriptions would be more tightly focused, the scheme would be less constrained by EU decision-making and would lead to extensification of production. An arable pilot scheme would allow new prescriptions to be trialled and tested for their environmental benefits and would allow a determination of how practicable they are for farmers and the economic environment in which they must operate.

6. If MAFF does not respond to the impoverished nature of biodiversity in arable areas with an arable pilot, then it must take steps to introduce environmental conditions on AAPs. This is the least that could be expected in return for payments of £1.08 billion which are being made during a period of unprecedented high returns in arable farming.

7. If MAFF only proceeds with an arable field margins option, it is extremely important that this is well targeted to make best use of limited resources. This option would also be of greater environmental benefit if it was freestanding, rather than linked to boundary restoration, and if grass margins and conservation headlands were separate items rather than being linked together.

8. Targeting is also important for the new old meadows and pastures and the field boundaries options. We have indicated target areas in our regional responses to the Countryside Commission's County Targeting exercise.

9. We look forward to seeing the National Agri-Environment Steering Group and the National Forum determining conservation priorities as their main tasks and we welcome the arrangements made to transfer staff from Countryside Commission to MAFF.

Comment

Countryside Stewardship was introduced in 1990 as a five-year pilot project by the Countryside Commission. In 1995 the Government announced that at the end of the five years (March 1996) the scheme would transfer to MAFF, to join existing schemes administered by them under the EU Agri-environment Regulation, such as ESAs and the Habitat Scheme. This was significant, in that it confirmed the value of the CS scheme and secured a longer-term future for it, while moving it to a part of Government with more significant resources. The RSPB saw this as an opportunity to press again our proposals for an arable pilot project and to call for an expansion of the CS with extra funding.

We recast our pilot project proposals in the knowledge that regulatory cross-compliance measures were not likely to be supported by the Agriculture Minister. We also emphasised that set-aside, while providing some form of lifeline for farmland birds, had an uncertain future and in any event was not an environmental measure.

MAFF duly took over CS and increased its funding by £10 million over the succeeding two years. The arable field margins option was introduced but MAFF did not act on our pilot project proposals. A National Agri-Environment Steering Group and a wider consultative National Forum, both of which we supported, were introduced, with the membership of the latter including RSPB and other environmental NGOs. We have continued to press the pilot project idea, and through the Forum have secured the setting up of an Arable Working Group (AWG) which has asked for a paper on possible solutions to the problems of arable farming to be prepared by RSPB, English Nature (EN) and the Game Conservancy Trust (GCT).

Submission to the House of Commons Agriculture Select Committee inquiry into *Environmentally Sensitive Areas and other schemes under the Agri-environment Regulation*. RSPB. May 1996.

Summary

1. The RSPB welcomes the opportunity to submit comments to this inquiry into the various schemes run by the Ministry of Agriculture, Fisheries and Food (MAFF), which operate under the provisions of Council Regulation 2078/92 (the "Agri-environment Regulation").

2. We comment on: the rôle of agri-environment schemes, such as ESAs, in responding to conservation priorities; the development of the Agri-environment regulation; the development of agri-environment schemes and the suite of schemes currently in operation in the UK; the environmental performance of the agri-environment programme; the relationship between agri-environment schemes

and wider agricultural policies; and the future development of agri-environment schemes.

3. Twelve RSPB reserves are wholly or partly within areas designated as ESAs and 2,448 ha of RSPB land is currently under ESA agreements. We are also directly involved in a number of ESA bird monitoring programmes and have organised training days for ESA Project Officers.

4. Agri-environment schemes such as ESAs are at present the main way of ensuring that conservation objectives are met on farmland. They achieve this by protecting vulnerable systems of farming which, by their nature, support important biodiversity; and by helping to provide an alternative to the incentives to intensify output and specialise production. In effect, agri-environment schemes provide a support system for environmental "products" from farming, and they have become extremely important to UK environmental policy. Without them, the future for our biodiversity across large swathes of the countryside would look bleak.

5. The main omission from the current suite of schemes is incentives targeted at the cropped area of arable farmland. Birds such as skylark and other wildlife in arable fields have suffered catastrophic declines over the past 25 years. Some of these species are recognised as conservation priorities in the UK Biodiversity Action Plan. No measures currently exist to enhance their populations.

6. By integrating agricultural and environmental objectives, agri-environment schemes send an important signal to farmers about the future of agriculture policy. The balance between funding for agri-environment schemes such as ESAs and for agricultural production must shift significantly towards the former.

7. These schemes should be seen as part of a package of measures needed to achieve environmental objectives. Environmental conditions attached to agricultural payments (conditionality or cross-compliance) and advice and training for farmers are also important.

8. The agri-environment programme should continue to develop and expand, and greater emphasis needs to be given to restoration and enhancement of habitats and species populations as well as maintenance of the status quo.

9. Birds are an important indicator of biodiversity as a whole. They are probably better monitored than any other wildlife group. Farmland birds have suffered population declines and range contractions to a greater extent than bird species associated with other habitats. It is highly probable that it is the fundamental changes in agricultural practice which have had the biggest impact. These include the move from spring to autumn sown cereals, a simplification of crop rotations, increased use of chemical pesticides and inorganic fertilisers and more intensive grassland management.

10. The UK must therefore continue to take an innovative and experimental approach to the development of agri-environment schemes, in order to find practical solutions to serious conservation problems.

Comment

Following various reviews of agri-environment schemes, and the transfer of the CS scheme from the Countryside Commission to MAFF, the House of Commons Agriculture Committee decided to conduct the inquiry described here. This coincided with a major MAFF policy review of the individual ESAs, begun in 1996 and due to continue until 2000. RSPB's evidence drew on previous submissions to MAFF, evidence to a 1995 Scottish Affairs Committee inquiry on agriculture, and on the results of a project undertaken with BirdLife International, funded by the European Commission, looking at the benefits of the EU agri-environment Regulation. We saw this as an opportunity to encourage a more wide-ranging debate about agri-environment schemes, highlighting their importance in meeting conservation objectives. At the time of writing (August 1996) the inquiry was still underway, and the RSPB was expecting to be called to give oral evidence later in the year.

A review of the 1992 CAP arable reforms. **RSPB. 1995.**

Summary

1. This is the first in a series of papers on arable policy produced by the RSPB. It reviews the effects of the 1992 reforms of the Common Agricultural Policy (CAP) arable régime, based on information available in August 1995.

2. The RSPB is very concerned about recent declines in lowland farmland birds in the UK and Europe. Survey work has revealed

that no fewer than ten species have declined by more than 50% in the UK in the past 25 years. While individual species are affected by different factors influencing feeding and nesting habitat, the intensification of arable farming under the CAP provides the principal explanation.

3. Changes associated with this process of intensification have included the shift from spring sown to autumn sown crops, which has led to loss of winter stubbles and changes in ground nesting habitat; the loss of hedgerows and other small features; the increased use of chemical pesticides and inorganic fertilisers; the simplification of crop rotations; and the specialisation of farming, with a decline in mixed farming systems. These changes were stimulated by the CAP arable régime which, by supporting agricultural commodity prices, has encouraged farmers to strive for ever higher yields.

4. In order to reverse these declines, major changes in agricultural practice on arable land are likely to be required. This paper attempts to assess the extent to which the 1992 CAP arable reforms have influenced the management of arable land, in order to gain some idea of the likely impact on biodiversity. In addition, it considers other key issues such as production levels, farm incomes, budgetary effects, world market conditions and potential future influences on the CAP, in order to consider the overall impact of the reforms, the degree to which they have met their objectives, and the extent to which further reform is likely to be required in future.

5. The 1992 reforms of the EU cereals, oilseeds and proteins (COP) régime were introduced in an attempt to curb increasing surplus production and budgetary costs, and to move the EU closer to world markets to comply with commitments made in the GATT Uruguay round. The reforms introduced price cuts compensated by direct area payments, the latter conditional on farmers setting aside a fixed proportion of their land.

6. Opinions as to the effects of the 1992 arable reforms are divided. Some commentators maintain that it is still too early to judge whether the reforms are working, because during the limited period since their adoption there have been abnormal weather conditions and unusually buoyant world markets. In contrast, the European Commission has claimed that the reforms have been successful, citing increased prices and falling surpluses as evidence of this.

7. The reforms have had the effect of fixing the area of land used for arable farming, as Arable Area Payments (AAPs) are available

only for land which was in arable use in 1991. While total arable area has remained unchanged, the area devoted to crops has declined, as land formerly used to grow COP crops has been set aside. This fall in cropping area has been greater in the UK than in Europe, principally because of the different structure of arable farming and the exemption from set-aside for small farms. Fluctuations in area devoted to different crops have made the effect of the reforms difficult to discern, although the greatest cut in area sown in the UK has occurred for cereals, and particularly for barley. The area devoted to wheat suffered a sharp initial decline following the reforms but has since recovered to approach preform levels. A decline has occurred in sowings of potatoes, which are not eligible for AAPs.

8. Rules enabling production on set-aside land of crops for industrial uses have led to a massive expansion in industrial oilseeds production which threatens to exceed limits agreed by the EU under GATT. Recent relaxations in set-aside requirements, reducing set-aside rates and allowing transfers between farms, are expected to result in increased production in 1995, particularly of wheat.

9. There has been little change in cereals yields but a marked decline in yields of oilseed rape and linseed since 1992 suggests a possible reduction in intensity of production following cuts in prices to world levels. Prices for COP crops have been buoyant since the reforms, with cereals prices rising above intervention levels, enabling intervention stocks to be cut substantially, and world oilseeds prices exceeding forecasts and enabling cuts in area payments. Potato prices soared in 1994, as cuts in area were accompanied by a poor harvest. The reforms have coincided with a period of rising world cereals demand and low harvests, which have helped to increase world cereals prices. As a result, benefits to the consumer have been less than envisaged.

10. The effect of the reforms on use of agricultural chemicals is not yet clear, with different studies producing conflicting figures. However, it appears that any decline which may have occurred is likely to be a result of a reduction in area treated rather than a decline in intensity of use, although there is some evidence of a reduction in use of fertilisers by growers of oilseeds. The reforms have had a more significant effect on the UK land market. Demand for arable land has been strong as a result of increased farm incomes, and this, together with the fixed supply of land eligible for AAPs, exacerbated by a decline in effective supply as a result of set-aside,

has resulted in a significant rise in land prices. There is evidence that the introduction of set-aside has reduced employment.

11. The reforms have significantly increased the administrative burden of the CAP arable régime, and some commentators have suggested that the administrative cost of the system is unacceptable. However, the introduction of the Integrated Administration and Control System (IACS), while it represented a substantial effort to both farmers and to MAFF, appears to have been achieved without major difficulty in the UK, although it has created some problems for growers of spring crops.

12. By shifting the cost of the CAP arable régime from the consumer to the tax payer, the reforms have substantially increased expenditure under the CAP arable budget which, by 1996, will have almost doubled compared to prereform levels. This increase results from the introduction of direct payments for arable farmers, while the budgetary cost of storing and disposing of surplus production has declined.

13. The overall effect on incomes of EU arable farmers appears to have been positive, although variations in exchange rates have resulted in differences in income effects between Member States. UK farm incomes have been buoyant since the reforms, boosted by favourable exchange rates. There has also been some redistribution of incomes between farms. Small farms have benefited from exemption from set-aside, while the shift away from price support and towards direct payments has favoured farms with lower crop yields.

14. The principal impact of the reforms on agricultural habitats has been the large increase in the area of set-aside, which has been shown to provide winter feeding and nesting habitat for farmland birds. These benefits have, however, been eroded by the recent cuts in set-aside rates and the introduction of industrial crops to set-aside land. The future of set-aside is also uncertain given the potential of external influences to effect further reform of arable policy.

15. The reforms do not appear to have led to any significant environmental improvement over the remaining cropped area, at least in the short term. There is no evidence of a reversal of the trends believed to have reduced farmland bird populations: intensive chemical use; the shift to winter cereals; the loss of hedgerows and other small features; and the specialisation of arable farming. Indeed, the reforms are likely to discourage a reversion to mixed farming systems.

16. Higher land prices have meant that the cost of alternative use of arable land has risen substantially, although the potential for diversification of land use will improve following the recent decision to allow habitat creation and forestry on set-aside land.

17. The substantial increase in agricultural budgets, brought about by the switch away from market support to direct payments, increases the opportunity for introducing subsidies to farmers to encourage good environmental management. Price support itself offers little opportunity for rewarding good environmental practice, whereas direct payments have more potential in this respect, through development of cross-compliance measures. The increase in the size of the agricultural budget may also enhance opportunities to increase funding for environmental schemes in future, particularly if further reforms are introduced, focusing the CAP on meeting environmental and social objectives.

18. It is too soon at present to assess the effect which the reforms have had on farmland birds and biodiversity, and whether the introduction of set-aside has been sufficient to halt the declines of the past 25 years. However, apart from set-aside, the 1992 CAP reforms have offered little to encourage us that these declines will be reversed. Set-aside may offer some respite to farmland birds but considerable uncertainty surrounds its future.

19. The recovery of farmland bird populations is likely to depend on further fundamental reform of the system to encourage the extensification of arable farming, unless further food surpluses lead to greatly increased rates of set-aside. In the shorter term, development of environmental cross-compliance for arable area payments, enhanced management of set-aside land for wildlife, and the introduction of environmental schemes designed to enhance arable biodiversity, would help to prevent further declines occurring.

20. The 1992 reforms have therefore had some success in bringing the CAP arable régime closer to world markets, albeit at substantial cost to the tax payer. In spite of this achievement, there is a broad consensus outside the Commission that continued increases in cereals yields will eventually make the system in its current form unsustainable, while external influences such as the next GATT round and the expansion of the EU to take on board the Central and East European countries will ensure that further reform is required early in the next century.

21. The 1992 CAP reforms have had some success in reducing surplus production of arable crops, although this has been achieved at considerable budgetary expense and with limited benefit to birds and biodiversity.

Comment

The RSPB is deeply concerned about the drastic declines in several species of formerly common birds of lowland farmland which have taken place over the past 25 years. These declines are the result of a variety of changes in farming systems which have occurred in recent decades. The CAP arable régime, which has encouraged the development of intensive crop production systems, has been a major factor in promoting these changes. The RSPB has for many years recognised the importance of arable policy in affecting farmland habitats and has pressed for reform of agricultural policy to encourage farming practices less destructive to wildlife.

The 1992 MacSharry reforms introduced substantial changes to the CAP arable régime, reducing price support and compensating farmers with direct payments, linked to set-aside. The review summarised here was undertaken in order to improve the RSPB's understanding of the changes which had taken place following the 1992 reforms, the effects on arable land use and the likely impact on wildlife. By considering the environmental and broader implications of the 1992 reforms, the review has helped the RSPB to develop its thinking regarding the future of arable policy. As well as being used internally, the report has been distributed to a wide range of policy-makers, academics and NGOs, in order to inform the debate about the future of the CAP.

The world grain market. **RSPB. 1996.**

Summary

1. It is often said that businesses and governments are increasingly operating within a global marketplace. This is very much the case for the grain trade which is a business based on perhaps the most basic of all commodities. Changes in agricultural land use, in particular, have been shown to be one of the greatest influences on birds.

2. With the development of a "single market" in agricultural products under the Common Agricultural Policy (CAP) the "home market" has expanded to include all the 15 Member States of the European

Union. The CAP impacts greatly on global trade. It analyses the likely impacts of changing market conditions in a key economic sector in a key UK and European wildlife habitat.

3. Future policy development will have to address questions such as what the environmental consequences will be of further increased demand for grain which is driven by population growth, changing diets and changing economic circumstances throughout much of the developing world, and how this demand can be met sustainably.

4. Grain production accounts for large areas of land world wide and changes in production have significant environmental consequences. The production methods employed have significant implications for the value of arable land as a habitat. World production of grain is dominated by a few countries and regions. The area devoted to grain crops has actually fallen in the past decade, due to intensification which has had adverse effects on biodiversity.

5. The bulk of wheat production is consumed directly by humans, while coarse grains are more important as animal food, and as a result, their consumption depends on the demand for livestock products. Demand for coarse grains is consequently more income elastic than wheat demand. Demand for grain is much more stable than supply, with less variation from year to year, since grain stocks absorb the effects of production volatility, enabling consumption to exceed output in years when the latter is low. Demand for grain is growing fastest in developing countries, in response to rising incomes and populations. In the developed world, where malnutrition is less of a problem, grain consumption has been fairly static in recent years. World demand for wheat is rising more quickly than demand for coarse grains, as changing tastes are causing developing countries to consume more bread.

6. Marketing structures show various levels of state involvement. Futures markets play an important rôle in reducing the risk caused to farmers and traders by fluctuations in prices. The majority of grain is produced for domestic markets. Most exports are driven by the need to dispose of surplus domestic production. The US is the world's leading exporter. The EU has emerged only recently as a grain exporter, and, by subsidising the disposal of surplus production onto world markets, triggered off a subsidy war which depressed world grain prices in the 1980s, imposed significant budgetary costs on both the EU and US and raised agriculture on the

agenda in the GATT Uruguay round. Importers of grain include the former Soviet Union, and many parts of Asia, Latin America, North Africa and the Middle East. The UK, while a significant producer and exporter of grain, regularly imports specific varieties for specific uses.

7. The price of grain has important implications for farmland wildlife, as it determines the incentive which farmers have to vary the area and intensity of arable production. The Food and Agriculture Organisation (FAO) estimates that stocks are now below the levels required to maintain security of supply and has called for an increase in area planted in 1996. The Worldwatch Institute has called for cuts in EU set-aside and the US Conservation Reserve Programme in order to rebuild grain stocks.

8. European arable policy has had a substantial impact on the world grain markets, keeping grain prices in Europe above world prices and subsidising disposal of surplus production on world markets. This has had the effect of suppressing prices on international markets.

9. The GATT Uruguay round produced an agreement between the EU and US to liberalise grain markets by limiting subsidised exports, reducing import levies, limiting aggregate domestic support measures with potential distorting effects and introducing minimum access requirements for imports as a proportion of domestic consumption. The GATT agreement has helped to raise the world grain price.

10. The Central and East European countries (CEECs), whose arable production has declined since the collapse of communism, have the potential to become substantial net exporters of grain. Their accession to the EU could make it difficult for Europe to meet its GATT commitments to limit subsidised grain exports.

11. When finally passed, the US Farm Bill will cut the cost of US farm support policies and increase the US share of the world grain market, reducing world prices and positioning the US to argue for further trade liberalisation in the next GATT round. This presents a challenge to the EU to adapt its arable policies to maintain its competitive position.

12. In the longer term, world grain demand is likely to rise substantially as a result of population and income growth. Most forecasters expect

that world production will keep pace with demand but that further intensification of production and replacement of areas growing other crops will be necessary.

13. The state of the world grain market also determines the need for set-aside and the area that the EU can devote to crop production. Changes in market conditions have implications for other EU policies including rural development policies.

14. The European Commission has acknowledged the need for the CAP to move further away from price support and towards direct income support, to enable European farm prices to move closer to world market prices and to allow farmers to export to growing world markets without subsidy. However, large differences remain between US and EU positions on arable policy. The Commission remains cautious about the need to control production to limit subsidised exports, while US policy-makers are bullish about global market prospects and are already implementing market-orientated policies to position US agriculture to respond to world food needs.

15. In the longer term, grain prices can be expected to fall, and a move towards world prices might offer possibilities for arable extensification. It seems that the EU is unlikely to abolish set-aside in the short term; but further cuts in percentage set-aside rates may be expected while grain stocks remain low and prices high.

16. Many species of European farmland birds have suffered drastic population declines as a result of intensification of arable farming under the CAP. In the past, the RSPB has called for cuts in support prices for grain in order to encourage arable extensification. The 1992 MacSharry reforms brought some hope for farmland birds, principally through the introduction of set-aside and reductions in cereals support prices. Clearly, however, we cannot rely on set-aside in its current form to safeguard the future of farmland birds. A new set-aside scheme, designed to meet environmental as well as supply control objectives, and with a secure long-term future, would help to improve the prospects for the wildlife which depends on Europe's lowland farmland.

17. Since the development of arable farming is a cause of biodiversity loss in all regions of the world, global policies which affect the patterns of production and trade are only likely to shift conservation problems from one region to another. However, some

measures could be taken at a regional level to mitigate these impacts. Policies to limit world population growth are necessary for conserving biodiversity as well as reducing human suffering. Research and development policy should aim to promote technology which increases agricultural yields without adversely affecting wildlife. Agricultural strategies should, where possible, be designed to limit the adverse environmental effects of developing production, through a combination of careful land use planning, targeted yield growth, agri-environment schemes to improve arable biodiversity and measures to secure the protection of wildlife sites such as forests, wetlands and grassland.

Comment

Changes in world grain markets have important implications for wildlife in Europe and the rest of the world. Market conditions affect decisions by farmers and drive changes in arable policy which in turn affect the methods used to manage arable land and hence the habitats on which farmland birds and wildlife depend. At a global level, rising world population and food demand is bringing pressure to convert other habitats to farmland and to intensify agricultural production.

This report has helped to inform RSPB arable policy work, as well as the Society's thinking in relation to global trade and land use. Its release in 1996 coincided with an upsurge in grain prices which brought calls for the abolition of set-aside and new reforms of the CAP arable régime. The RSPB was able to participate in this debate and used the findings of the report to call for new agri-environment schemes for arable areas.

Chapter 13

FORESTRY POLICY

Several species of endangered birds depend on the way our forests and woodlands are managed. Many more species can be unfavourably affected by the establishment of new forests on important open habitats such as bogs, heathlands and wet grasslands. To enhance the contribution of forestry to bird conservation in the UK, the RSPB works to improve Government's forestry policies and delivery mechanisms. This Chapter illustrates three examples of this work which are aimed at securing improved application of international agreements on sustainable forestry in UK policies, in subnational strategic plans and in the structure and objectives of the national Forestry Authority.

"Forestry Plan Scan '96": A review of Indicative Forestry Strategies. **Marshall, N. 1996.**

Summary

1. This report reviews the background, development, methodology and current status of Indicative Forestry Strategies (IFSs) in the UK. It analyses the key policies in Scottish IFSs and suggests some alternative wordings. We also set out the RSPB's position in relation to key components and issues in IFSs.

2. Indicative Forestry Strategies (IFSs) have been produced by nine regional or county councils in Great Britain (eight in Scotland, one in England). At least three other counties have draft IFSs.

3. IFSs have a key rôle to play in delivering government policies and international commitments, including the European Union (EU) Wild Birds and Habitats & Species Directives. Evidence shows that afforestation of important areas of open ground for birds continues and that currently IFSs (as well as the current consultation procedures) do not provide adequate protection for habitats and species.

4. IFSs are not alone in giving locational guidance for forest expansion. The significance of much of the wide range of other guidance is understated or ignored in many IFSs. The absence of a National

Forestry Strategy is a major problem limiting the effectiveness of IFSs. Some IFSs have included wider issues and introduced improvements not covered in the Government guidance notes.

5. The approach taken in Scotland, where there is great pressure for large-scale commercial non native conifer afforestation, is very different from that needed for England and Wales where much existing woodland is neglected and economic factors discourage woodland expansion.

6. The procedure for drawing up IFSs understates both the importance and extent of conservation interests which can be adversely affected by commercial afforestation. The "sensitive" category fails to provide adequate protection of key conservation resources from adverse effects of afforestation.

7. The "unsuitable" category should be extended to provide additional protection for land with multiple constraints or one overriding constraint for instance, key habitats which would be damaged by any forest expansion which would effectively exclude such areas from further planting.

8. Some basic information necessary for sensitivity assessment is not comprehensively available, leading to serious inadequacies in some IFS zonation maps. Monitoring of IFSs is inadequate. It is thus impossible to determine whether IFSs are delivering their aims.

9. Improved policy wording and consistency of coverage of all key conservation-related issues is needed. This is one of many benefits which could be gained from a more co-ordinated approach from the statutory bodies (in particular the Forestry Commission [FC] and environment agencies) to assist drafting of IFSs.

10. We present some recommended wordings for IFS policies on environmental assessment, expansion of native woodlands, management of existing woodlands, identifying and protecting key non-woodland habitats, linking IFS priorities to incentives, promoting marketing of timber from broadleaved and native woodlands and promoting local woodland initiatives.

11. With the advent of IFSs, improvements in consultation procedures and changes to the Woodland Grant Scheme (WGS), much of the unproductive confrontation has left the debate between forest-

ers and conservationists. Increasingly, the common ground between the two sides is being recognised and extensive consensus on the future development of forestry is becoming a possibility.

12. Since the first IFSs, international commitments have clarified the duties of forestry and other land-based industries towards the environment. Such commitments and policies and the grants, guidance and regulation introduced to deliver them mean that the policy framework within which IFSs fit has changed completely since their introduction. IFSs will certainly have to change to reflect this.

Comment

Since 1990 most Regional Councils in Scotland have prepared IFSs under guidance from the Scottish Office. IFSs allocate land to zones which reflect the land's sensitivity to commercial afforestation. Similar guidance from Government Departments to local authorities in England and Wales was provided in 1992 but, with less new woodland planting taking place outside Scotland, fewer of these authorities have seen the need to produce such strategies.

The RSPB has contributed to the development of government guidance and to the production of most IFSs in Great Britain. Our experience of their content and implementation identified some areas for improvement. In 1995-96 we undertook the review which is summarised here, to capitalise on several opportunities for the improvement of IFSs: local authority functions and structures in GB were being revised; the Scottish Office/Forestry Authority had commissioned a review of the guidance on IFSs to local authorities in Scotland; and in England the Government announced plans to identify the next steps in regional strategies by the end of 1996.

The study was the basis of the RSPB's input into the Scottish Office review, the output from which is due to be the subject of consultation in late 1996. *"Forestry Plan Scan '96"* was published in June 1996 and is being promoted to central and local government throughout GB. If its conclusions are followed there will be greater support for widespread adoption of improved IFSs which will more effectively support woodland expansion in areas where it will enhance biodiversity, reduce the planting of unsuitable sites of high conservation value and further encourage the diversification of existing plantations.

The report was drafted before local government reorganisation in April 1996. Pre-1996 local authorities are used in the analysis and will remain directly relevant until future strategic plans replace existing Structure Plans. However, the analysis and recommendations will also be relevant to any future IFSs or other regional strategies for forestry.

The implementation in the United Kingdom of the Helsinki Guidelines for sustainable forest management. **Cosgrove, P and Turner, R. 1995.**

Summary

1. This document follows the Government's 1994 statement of UK forestry policies and plans, *"Sustainable Forestry: The UK Programme"*, and its March 1995 report on the application in the UK of the Helsinki Guidelines. We have compared the Helsinki Guidelines with the UK Sustainable Forestry Programme, to identify the extent to which current UK policies and mechanisms deliver the Helsinki Guidelines and whether any changes are needed to implement them more fully.

2. A matrix for relating key policy and action statements to elements of the guidelines was drawn up and we then identified corresponding delivery mechanisms for each of these. We have also reviewed information available to decision-makers and managers to inform their practices and information about actions being taken by other government departments and agencies.

3. All of the Helsinki Guidelines and many of the accompanying Future Actions have some comparable policies and mechanisms to ensure their delivery in the UK, though the closeness of fit varies. In relation to some Guidelines the UK policies appear weak, mainly because our view of forests is different from that in other parts of Europe. For some others, the UK Government's response is to undertake research which might ultimately lead to guidelines and actions, or to rely upon information available in Research Information Notes which are not accessible to everyone. Much has therefore been achieved or addressed, but more work is still needed. We set out an analysis of the recognisable gaps.

4. Several of the Helsinki Guidelines and Actions address both positive and constraining locations for forestry. New areas for afforestation, are

suggested, such as protective forests for flood control. Constraints upon afforestation such as the need to avoid planting ecologically fragile sites, are recognised as an essential component of sustainable forest management. UK forestry policies do not fully address these. Whilst forests receive varying degrees of protection, there does not appear to be a cross-government process for establishing a coherent network of priority forests. Some locations where new forests will maximise public recreational or landscape benefits have been identified but strategic identification of locations where afforestation will harm non forest biodiversity, and explicit policies to prevent planting in such areas, operate in only limited areas, eg Northern Ireland.

5. Very few UK policies are designed to prevent harmful impacts of forestry on soil, air, and non forest ecosystems and their values, as required by the Helsinki Guidelines. Even where they do exist they are stated in broad and general language, in contrast to policies for other benefits from forestry, and few guidelines are provided to forest managers or regional decision-makers to inform their judgement.

6. This analysis illustrates that *"Sustainable Forestry: the UK Programme"* falls short of a coherent strategy, indicating few balances or priorities between the objectives, policies and actions. This is true of those policies within the lead remit of the Forestry Commission (FC), but is an equally significant failing at the UK Government level, as many aspects of other department/agency policies and actions contribute to delivery of sustainable forest management.

7. In UK forestry policies the issues of genetic conservation and the use of native species appear to be separated from the approach to economically productive forestry. The Helsinki Guidelines focus upon extensive use of native species and local provenances, and use of non-native species and provenances is seen as acceptable only in situations where harm to indigenous biodiversity would not result, and efforts are made to conserve native flora and fauna. The effects upon the whole ecosystem including the ground layer are therefore addressed. Current work by the FC to prepare a policy on genetic conservation could address these issues.

8. Above the local level there are no regional or national forest management plans. *"Sustainable Forestry: the UK Programme"* provides a programme of actions and policies but no quantified or re-

gionalised objectives. Regional IFSs provide frameworks for afforestation but few supporting mechanisms and no targets for actions, while the Forest Enterprise Corporate Strategy provides a national programme for a proportion of the forest estate. These need pulling together and developing further.

9. UK forestry policies contain no explicit statement that practices running counter to sustainable forest management are unacceptable, or will be actively discouraged.

10. No strategic approach to conserving and enhancing biodiversity in the UK in this context has yet emerged. For instance, UK policy and practice currently exhibit no strategies with targets for rare and endangered species or representative forest types with target-based actions. We would hope that these emerge from the government-appointed Biodiversity Action Plan Steering Group (BAPSG), the Forestry Authority's Forest and Biodiversity Initiative (FABI), and the Forest Enterprise's Framework Document and Corporate Plans.

11. Whilst the Helsinki Guidelines require adequate appraisal and monitoring arrangements to inform the conservation and enhancement of biodiversity, these appear to be lacking in UK forestry policies and practice.

12. *"Sustainable Forestry: the UK Programme"* provides no explicit policies and mechanisms for pan-European collaboration on plans and programmes for biodiversity, or afforestation, or reforestation, as required by the Helsinki Guidelines.

13. The Helsinki Guidelines were signed on behalf of the UK Government, not just the FC. Several departments and agencies work on parts of Government's forestry policies and all should be aware of, and operate to, the Guidelines for sustainable forest management. Unlike the follow-up to the Sustainable Development Strategy and Biodiversity Action Plan, the *Sustainable Forestry* document has not spawned a co-ordinating/development process, and there are many examples of unco-ordinated action. All parts of Government including the FC need explicitly to adopt the requirement that "practices contrary to sustainable management will be actively discouraged".

Comment

In June 1993, the Scottish Forestry Minister Sir Hector Monro attended the Ministerial Conference on the Protection of Forests in Europe in Helsinki. The UK Government endorsed the *General Guidelines for the Sustainable Management of Forests in Europe (H1)* and the *General Guidelines for the Conservation of Biodiversity of European Forests (H2)*. These Guidelines in turn develop the Statement of Forest Principles agreed at the Earth Summit in Rio de Janeiro in 1992.

In January 1994 the Government published a comprehensive statement of UK forestry policies and initiatives, "*Sustainable Forestry: The UK Programme*". Although it reported on the UK's application of the Helsinki Guidelines in March 1995, this was not based on a formal and open analysis. Accordingly, at the beginning of 1995 the RSPB undertook the objective analysis summarised here in close consultation with the Forestry Authority. Its conclusions have been offered to inform the development of UK forestry policies, guidelines and processes.

The report establishes that the Helsinki Guidelines are matched by some comparable policies and mechanisms in the UK but also confirms that several improvements in the UK are needed. For example, one theme of the Guidelines which is weakly developed in UK policies concerns suitable and unsuitable locations for afforestation. Upon receipt of the completed RSPB report, the FC asked their Home Grown Timber Advisory Committee for advice. The Committee agreed with the analysis and advised the FC that many of the required improvements could be made if a UK Forestry Strategy was developed, and that other major gaps should be addressed in a FC Research Strategy. The RSPB has promoted the idea of a UK Forestry Strategy for many years, to steer future expansion, reduce conflict and improve the allocation of resources.

Comments to the Forestry Authority *The future structure of the Forestry Authority.* **RSPB. March 1995.**

Summary

1. The mission of the Forestry Authority (FA) should be the promotion of multiple-purpose forestry, which is ecologically and economically sustainable, and at the heart of this should be the conservation of biodiversity. The FA has made a substantial commitment to this

objective in recent years. Any changes to the structure and purpose of the FA should aim to strengthen this commitment.

2. The FA faces several serious challenges to its commitment to this objective. These will require a flexible structure which is responsive to these demands and which will maintain the environmental and other public benefits at the heart of UK forestry policy.

3. The development of the FA since the reorganisation of the Forestry Commission in 1992 has been welcome and has introduced greater clarity and a degree of necessary devolution to the policy-making and delivery functions. Nevertheless, we believe that in some areas this structure can be improved.

4. Policy-making responsibilities appear to us to rest in two main locations but parts are scattered widely throughout the current FA structure and this causes confusion. We believe that increased clarity of the structures for and parameters of policy development should be introduced, to bring gains in effectiveness.

5. In recent years, forestry policy interpretation and delivery have become increasingly regionalised. With this growth in regionalisation, lack of clarity between levels of the FA with responsibilities for policy development could retard the development of valuable and appropriate diversity. Present arrangements for control and accountability are neither completely centralised nor sufficiently decentralised.

6. We believe that it is necessary that the FA negotiate public expenditure at a Great Britain (GB) level and remain accountable for its allocation and the deployment of FA staff time at all levels.

7. A framework for determining the priorities for future forestry, and the level of inputs/outputs expected of and by the FA is required. Such a framework could attract national and local credibility, assist proper allocation of resources and ensure that the efficiency or effectiveness of delivery can be monitored and adjusted where necessary.

8. We have recommended the development of a hierarchy of frameworks/strategies for forestry more fully elsewhere. We would further recommend that the FA should establish an overt policy development function at international, GB, country and Conservancy

level. It should introduce a structure which allows extensive and transparent interchange between the four tiers of policy development from international to regional. The parameters for policy development at these four levels should be established after consultation and should be embodied in a national framework for forestry.

9. Current FA policy activity at the GB level displays one serious inadequacy, namely the inability to integrate forestry policies with those relating to other land uses and sectors. This has resulted in loss of opportunity for the environment on a number of occasions.

10. We therefore recommend as a minimum that the Policy Development Divisions of the FC should be expanded to include staff from related land-use, ecological and economic disciplines. Integration could be further strengthened by seconding a senior forestry member to several departments/agencies to help identify and promote forestry opportunities and to understand impacts upon forestry from the development and delivery of other policies. The FA could appoint staff to liaise with the Government's Integrated Regional Offices in England to identify areas in other policies which impact upon or are impacted by forestry.

11. While maintaining separate departments for the distinct functions of government can produce a healthy balance between functions, it can also promote unnecessary and wasteful competition in policies and resources and reduce valuable practical integration. As forestry seeks to relate to diverse land-use and enterprise policies, there is merit in considering more formal integration of the forestry department with other government functions. Throughout Europe, forestry forms part of government departments responsible for forestry and agriculture, or other matters. We believe that such a model might secure better integration.

12. Enhanced integration will also benefit the FC in its international negotiations. In taking the lead for the UK Government in negotiating international forestry policies and practices, the FC International Relations Division needs to reflect and contribute to policies concerned with trade, international biodiversity, rural development and other issues.

13. Moreover, to remain an influential contributor to the global forestry debates, the UK needs to take seriously the implementation of international agreements and provide adequate links between

international policy negotiators and those responsible for decisions about forestry schemes.

14. FA Conservancy offices are the principal focus for the delivery of forestry policy. However, just as the development of forestry policy is a responsibility of a number of FA divisions and levels, so also is its implementation.

15. One essential function to be retained at GB or country level is the monitoring of implementation of guidelines, schemes and grant decisions to ensure that adequate standards and consistent approaches are maintained.

16. Some of the policy delivery functions are the subject of forestry legislation or Ministerial direction and could only be altered following legislative changes. However, some grant administration tasks are little different from jobs presently performed by many private forestry agents and consultancy companies. There are policy delivery tasks which could be contracted out, provided that the FA remains accountable and responsible for decision-making. In the absence of frameworks for such responsibility we believe that the decision-making aspects of grant administration must remain with the FA.

17. The relationship between the FA and the Forest Enterprise Agency (FE)] should be an important influence on any changes intended for the FA.

18. The rôle of the FA is to regulate and encourage all forms of multi purpose forestry, whoever undertakes it and for whatever objective. However, the principal strength of the Forest Enterprise is that it leads the private forestry sector, for example in the creation of new Community Forests and restructuring of uniform plantations.

19. The establishment of the Forest Enterprise as a Next Steps Agency (NSA) raises an important challenge to the FAs ability to regulate forestry to maintain this differential. As we understand it the FA's relationship with the new FE Agency will not allow a disaggregated FA to set the environmental objectives of the FEA. The performance of the FEA will be informed, changed and monitored by the Forestry Commissioners and forestry Ministers.

20. One route to maintaining this differential will be to require the Policy and Corporate Strategy Division to support the Forestry Commissioners in this rôle. That Division should also inform and co-ordinate the FAs policy delivery functions.

21. The establishment of the FA as a NSA would compound the difficulties of maintaining these differentials of practice between private forestry and those of the FEA. Moreover, unless greater separation of policy development and delivery functions is introduced to the FA at all levels, the creation of a Forestry Authority agency would be contrary to past government practice. We thus recommend against this structure being adopted.

Comment

Since 1988 the UK Government has reformed the structure and functions of many departments, introducing more commercial management practices and structures particularly to their policy delivery functions. Under its Next Steps reforms, executive agencies have been established to manage such functions.

From 1993 the Government's forestry departments came under scrutiny with a review of the management and ownership of Forestry Commission forests, ie Forest Enterprise's functions. In April 1996 the Forest Enterprise became an executive agency and its structure and objectives are now transparently recorded in a framework document and business plans. Assisted by a thorough study of the Next Steps Reform Programme and the environmental focus of other agencies, RSPB has successfully pressed for the FEA to be set strong biodiversity objectives and targets.

All other functions of the FC and its Northern Ireland equivalent, the Northern Ireland Forest Service (NIFS), have subsequently been reviewed. The RSPB has made written submissions on these reviews, such as the one summarised here, and has reinforced them by meetings with civil servants and politicians. Converting the FA and NIFS into executive agencies seems to be the favoured option of Government. Decisions about their future are still awaited at the time of writing. The RSPB has questioned the appropriateness of this structure for the FA, as it is both a regulator of private forestry and a developer of policies and delivery mechanisms.

Chapter 14

TRANSPORT AND ENERGY

The environmental aspects of transport and energy policy range widely over issues including human health, landscape aesthetics and resource use. In a measured enhancement of its attention to these two fields in recent years, the RSPB has been careful to concentrate on the aspects which can be shown to have implications for bird conservation. This has in some cases required new research, analysis and discussion to define exactly those areas in which the Society should make its particular contribution. The items included here set out or refer back to the key outcomes of this process and show some strongly focused policy views which, in respect of transport, have been well timed to respond to increased European policy-making on the subject and to the UK Government's call for a "Great Debate". More general perspectives on the environmental appraisal issues covered here can be found in Chapter 5.

"Braking Point": the RSPB's policy on transport and biodiversity. **RSPB. 1995.**

Summary

1. The RSPB recognises the need for transport in all its varying forms but the transport sector has very damaging environmental impacts. Roads across sensitive habitats, port development in estuaries and emissions from all forms of transport threaten biodiversity. Changes to the ways in which transport is planned, infrastructure is built and vehicles are used are urgently needed to protect biodiversity.

2. This document presents the RSPB's views on transport policy. It addresses some of the biodiversity issues raised in the Royal Commission on Environmental Pollution's (RCEP) report *"Transport and the Environment"* and follows on from our own document about energy, *"The Vital Spark"*. It is based on the following principles:

-    The Government should set environmental objectives and targets for transport which take account of biodiversity conservation.

- The precautionary principle should be applied to transport policy-making. Action should be taken to prevent environmental damage, even before conclusive scientific evidence of that damage is available.

- Environmental costs should be built into transport prices.

- Environmental assessment of policies, plans and programmes is needed in the transport sector, as well as environmental assessment of individual schemes.

3. Objectives we define for the transport sector are to:

- protect important sites for wildlife;

- reduce the threat to wildlife and habitats from pollution by reducing carbon dioxide (CO_2) emissions from transport;

- reduce marine pollution by routeing ships away from sensitive areas and eliminating deliberate discharges from shipping;

- achieve standards of air quality which prevent damage to human health and to the environment;

- assess and monitor the indirect effects of atmospheric pollution on sensitive sites, species and habitats, and take action to conserve biodiversity in the light of such assessments; and

- reduce substantially the demands which transport infrastructure places on non renewable resources.

4. The RSPB believes that transport policy needs a strong policy framework set by the Government. This framework needs to be formulated via a Green Paper and White Paper process. It should set out clear objectives, including the conservation and enhancement of biodiversity, and should set out the means to achieve those objectives.

5. The RSPB believes that no transport infrastructure should be built on the few thousand hectares of remaining key UK habitats, such as lowland heath, Caledonian pine and chalk grassland. The

Government should not sponsor or permit any such development, as a part of its commitment to the Convention on Biological Diversity: we need a moratorium for wildlife.

6. We set out 23 recommendations for the way forward in relation to: demand management; changing transport modes; cleaner and more efficient vehicles; safer ships for cleaner seas; site protection; and instruments, appraisal and institutions.

7. This document is the RSPB's contribution to the transport debate. It shows the need for a transport policy which recognises the importance of sustainable development not least the need to sustain and enhance biodiversity including the protection of important sites for wildlife, the effects of climate change on wildlife, the impacts of acid rain on sites and species and the impacts of the construction and use of transport infrastructure.

8. The 110 recommendations made by the RCEP will only work if all or at least the majority of measures to achieve the objectives are implemented at the same time. Only then will these measures actually start to reduce the overall environmental impact of the transport sector. In the meantime, the damage to important wildlife habitats continues apace.

9. The RSPB recognises that government policy can only provide part of the answer. Ultimately, it is the attitudes and decisions of millions of individuals and businesses which will determine whether these objectives can be met. This document focuses on what the Government can do to lead the way and influence attitudes and decisions.

Comment

After various episodes viewed by many as debacles, including protests at Twyford Down and on the M11 (and at Oxleas Wood where there was a dramatic change of position), the Government called for a "Great Debate" to reduce the political heat of the transport debate. Brian Mawhinney, the then Secretary of State, gave several speeches which were published with a request for comments. *"Braking Point"* was our contribution to this "Great Debate". While the general public regard damage to wildlife and countryside as an important feature of the transport sector, this was not and is not reflected in Government policy. More than 80 SSSIs are at the time of writing still threatened by road proposals at various stages of planning and that is even after deep cuts in the roads programme.

The rhetoric of the so-called "Great Debate" on transport, as set out in the Transport Green Paper (discussed elsewhere in this Chapter), has started to reflect the need to address the impacts of transport on the environment in the widest sense. This, however, does not yet include progress on better protection for biodiversity.

The impact of Trans-European Networks on nature conservation. RSPB/BirdLife International and World Conservation Monitoring Centre. 1995.

Summary

1. Trans-European (transport) Networks (TENs) are a major European Union (EU) programme creating transport links which include 140 road schemes, 11 rail links, 57 combined transport projects and 26 inland waterway links. The current impacts of the TENs on the environment and biodiversity in particular are significant and potentially very serious in the future. This pilot project is an attempt to quantify these impacts on Important Bird Areas (IBAs) and nationally designated sites.

2. Many planned roads and railways are close to IBAs:

-   More than 12% (309) of EU IBAs are within 10km of planned road and rail developments.

-   More than 2% (57) of EU IBAs are within 2km of planned road and rail developments.

-   Mearly 20% (9,335km^2) of the area of French IBAs is within 10km of planned road and rail developments.

-   More than 4% (1,932km^2) of the area of French IBAs is within 2km of planned road and rail developments.

-   More than 33% (26,000km^2) of the area of nationally designated sites in the EU is within 10km of planned road and rail developments.

-      More than 8% (4,900km^2) of the area of nationally designated sites in the EU is within 2km of planned road and rail developments.

3. What this means for nature conservation is not exactly clear. A road or rail development going close to, or even through, an IBA or protected area does not necessarily damage the nature conservation interest of the site. However, enough concern has been raised about transport infrastructure and biodiversity that questions need to be asked.

4. Particular issues must be addressed in EU policy, including:

-      the effect of transport infrastructure on sensitive habitats;

-      habitat fragmentation;

-      local pollution from salt or ozone;

-      more widespread pollution, such as in watercourses above wetlands; and

-      wider issues such as nitrate pollution from vehicles and carbon dioxide emissions.

5. In preparing these figures, a GIS (Geographical Information System)-based approach was followed, in order to illustrate the possibilities for Strategic Environmental Assessment (SEA). SEA is an extension of Environmental Impact Assessment from projects to the policies, plans and programmes which are their context. Such an approach both illustrates the environmental problems clearly and offers a powerful planning tool.

6. IBAs have been used as an example because the data set for them is comprehensive and in part digitised. IBAs are the basis for the selection of Special Protection Areas under the EU Wild Birds Directive. Nationally designated areas also serve as a fairly completely documented example of the data required. Many other environmental indicators are not as well documented and much effort is required to build up comprehensive databases.

7. In order to implement the provisions set out in Chapter XII of the Maastricht Treaty on Trans-European Networks, the European

Commission produced guidelines for the transport sector in 1993. The guidelines define "network schemes for the various transport modes, which illustrate the present status and how the network should develop progressively up to the year 2010". They are aimed at the completion of a single trans-European transport market, by identifying the way to achieve adequate infrastructures, which promotes efficient and safe transport services under the best possible environmental and social conditions. They also seek to pave the way to sustainable mobility for persons and goods across Europe and to improve accessibility and strengthening of economic and social cohesion.

8. This report attempts to quantify BirdLife International's concerns, while also contributing to the debate on the means to assess and reduce the environmental effects of the transport sector. In particular, we believe that methodologies and information exist which should be used to reduce the impact the TENs could have on nature conservation. It is with this in mind that we have focused narrowly on the potential effects on bird habitats as just one example of what could be done to obtain an overview of the TENs' environmental impact.

9. The report is presented at a time when the guidelines for TENs are being proposed for a European Parliament and Council Decision. It is hoped that its suggestions and findings will contribute to the debate.

10. We recognise the limits of the approach we have taken to SEA in this project. The significance for populations of birds of the effects of TENs passing through or near IBAs is not clear. It is harder still to assess the cumulative effects across Europe. While we have selected birds as indicators of environmental damage, they may not be the best ecological indicators. However, the data on bird population trends is better than for most other taxa, with priority species identified. In addition, areas of habitat identified under the Wild Birds Directive and the Habitats & Species Directive should be safeguarded from any effects of the TENs, and land take may itself be a useful indicator in some situations.

11. From the early-1970s onwards there has been an increasing awareness of the wide-ranging nature of transport's impact on the environment, going well beyond problems of air pollution and noise. However, failure to produce clear objectives and targets in order to

pursue the integration of environmental concerns in the transport sector raises doubts as to how the EU Community will balance these concerns against the strong impetus of the Single European Market. The many documents produced by Community institutions on the subject of transport since 1992 seem to have at least one thing in common: they all eventually state that transport should contribute to the attainment of environmental, social, and economic objectives. Persistent reference to such diverse and perhaps conflicting tasks could be interpreted as a sign of the Community's struggle to reconcile its original objective of economic prosperity with more recent objectives, related to social and environmental interests.

12. Several references have been made in EU policy documents to the importance of considering the environmental as well as the socio economic aspects of the networks. Virtually nothing has been done in practice.

13. The European Parliament and the Council of Ministers are to discuss the adoption of two crucial documents: the Commission's proposals for a Regulation on the financing of TENs and the guidelines for the development of TENs. These will dictate the character and pace of development of TENs. These discussions must address the absence of a clear commitment to ensure integration of environmental protection requirements, as requested in the Treaty on European Union.

14. As a testing ground for the Commission's success in introducing integration within the Community's decision-making process, the TENs and the Common Transport Policy (CTP) offer little hope. These plans are likely to produce contradictory effects which are contrary to the concept of sustainable development as espoused in the Fifth Environmental Action Programme.

15. There is a need for an SEA of the TENs as the best opportunity to put into practice the frequently-stated aim of integrating environmental issues into transport. In the meantime, pressing economic interests seem to be dictating the pace, as seen from the approval of 11 priority schemes at the Corfu Summit.

16. While many of the conclusions of this report must be based on assumption, two key points can be made:

(i)   The potential environmental impacts of the TENs are serious, as illustrated by the fact that so many IBAs and nationally designated sites are close to road and rail developments.

(ii)   SEA could provide a powerful planning tool with which to take account of these impacts and a methodology with which to integrate environmental objectives into the CTP.

17. The approach used here could be applied to other datasets, such as land cover, or habitat maps. Further work on the approach set out in this report, and particularly on building effective and useful databases, is urgently needed to create an SEA methodology that would cover a wider range of environmental issues.

Comment

Until the end of 1995, TENs were essentially the most important element of the CTP's and involved proposals for massive development of new infrastructure throughout all Member States by the year 2010. In 1994 the Commission presented a proposal for TENs guidelines to the Parliament and the Council.

Given the very weak consideration for environmental objectives in the Commission's document, BI decided to carry out its pilot project in order to highlight the potential implications of such a wide infrastructure development programme for nature conservation. We also intended to influence the debate on the opportunity and feasibility of a Strategic Environmental Assessment for an EU-wide programme and ensure that the final text of the guidelines would include environmental protection mechanisms.

Work on this project allowed BI to contribute to the general debate on transport and the environment, which has tended to focus essentially on air and noise pollution, congestion and health issues, paying very little attention to impacts on nature conservation. It also allowed us to be further involved in the development and use of SEA methodologies, adding to our experience on this topic. This enabled BI to make constructive recommendations to the European Commission on its draft Directive for SEA.

Strategic environmental assessment and corridor analysis of Trans-European Networks: a position paper. **RSPB/BirdLife International, European Federation for Transport & Environment and Greenpeace. 1996.**

Summary

1. This document stresses the difference between two assessment levels, Strategic Environmental Assessment (SEA) and corridor

analysis, and explains why SEA of the Trans-European (transport) Networks (TENs) must be carried out urgently by the European Commission. We suggest some elements of a network-level SEA, and make recommendations to the Commission in relation to its possible intention to carry out a few corridor analyses in the coming year.

2. TENs are a major European Union programme creating transport links which include 140 road schemes, 11 rail links, 57 combined transport projects and 26 inland waterway links.

3. TENs represent an obsolete approach to transport policy, focusing heavily on infrastructure building, which is at odds with the widely accepted need to focus efforts on demand management.

4. An SEA of the network is essential to ensure that the commitments to sustainable development set out in the Maastricht Treaty and the Fifth Environmental Action Programme are integrated with transport planning in Europe. Corridor analyses of every single TENs scheme should be carried out once SEA has identified the best options. Elements of TENs are posing major risks of irreversible damage to Special Protection Areas designated under the Wild Birds Directive.

5. We also recommend that corridor analysis should be a condition of funding for TENs projects and that far greater resources than at present should be urgently directed to the collection and harmonisation of environmental data. The European Environment Agency should be involved in this process, and non governmental and other environmental organisations should be consulted.

6. We urge the Commission and the Member States to explore the widest range of strategic options during the SEA process to meet overall strategic environmental and sustainable transport objectives. Options should include alternatives other than infrastructure building, such as road pricing, fuel taxation, supporting public transport, the substitute potential of telecommunications, traffic calming, etc.

7. TENs definition has not been adjusted to meet changing objectives. Indeed, networks resemble a combination of national plans, as opposed to a coherent programme directed towards the attainment of a complex set of Community objectives. We believe that there is great confusion and superficiality in the current debate about

TENs and what they are supposed to achieve. For convenient political reasons, the Community and Member States have encouraged the debate to focus on the more recent employment and cohesion arguments, but they have been unable to produce any evidence to prove the link between transport infrastructure and these objectives.

Comment

Following talks with Directorate General XI of the European Commission on the need for SEA of TENs in December 1995, it became clear that the Commission was still unconvinced of the urgency of such assessment. Indeed, it was considering an alternative solution which involved carrying out a few corridor analyses of single TENs projects, whilst continuing to explore and review existing SEA methodologies.

BI joined forces with the European Federation for Transport and the Environment (EFTE) and Greenpeace International to produce a joint position paper on these issues. This had two main objectives. Firstly, we wanted to influence the Commission's approach by stressing the difference between an SEA of the whole network, which would allow questioning of the sustainability of the TENs, and individual corridor analyses, which would only question the impacts of single projects. Secondly, we wanted to use the document to influence the debate and voting on TENs guidelines which was taking place in the European Parliament and Council.

The document was used to lobby MEPs to secure their support for an Article in the guidelines which would have requested an SEA of TENs. NGO involvement has meant that for almost a year, the issue of environmental integration in the TENs guidelines triggered heated discussions between Parliament and Council. TENs guidelines were finally approved in July 1996 and they included an Article which requests the Commission to develop a methodology for both SEA and corridor analysis. Considering the content of the initial proposal for TENs guidelines, and given the strong opposition to any environmental Article in Council, this was a reasonable success. However, the ultimate outcome will depend heavily on the interpretation of the guidelines by the Commission and Member States in the coming years.

Comments to the Department of Transport on the Green Paper
"Transport: the way forward". **RSPB. April 1996.**

Summary

1. The RSPB welcomes this first Green Paper on transport for nearly 20 years. The paper acknowledges most of the problems caused by our dependence on the car, and sets out some policies that will help. It is a very useful summary of the arguments within the transport "Great Debate".

2. However, the Green Paper seriously fails to address biodiversity conservation, ignores the Government's international and national commitments in this regard and does not acknowledge that the transport sector is one of the most serious threats to the natural environment. It does not re-state existing government commitments to protect biodiversity, nor outline any new measures.

3. Present transport planning frameworks fail to protect biodiversity. In our view, therefore, the first response to the problem, and to the UK Biodiversity Plan, should be to declare a policy of improved protection for endangered species and special sites. In the second place, and because wildlife does not all occur on a few sites, a suite of changes is needed - to the ways in which transport is planned, infrastructure is built and vehicles are used to protect biodiversity.

4. The Green Paper does not address the difficult issue of traffic growth, and does not answer the Royal Commission on Environmental Pollution's 110 recommendations set out in their report on *"Transport and the Environment"*.

5. The main proposal put forward is to integrate more closely trunk road and land-use planning. This proposal offers a welcome opportunity to solve transport problems by thinking strategically and recognising the importance of issues such as biodiversity early on in the planning process.

6. The integration of trunk road and land-use planning must be set against some wider issues with significant impacts on the transport debate, such as targets, economic instruments, transport and the economy and Trans-European Networks in particular. Unless changes are made in these areas, changing the planning system will not be enough.

Comment

The RSPB, along with all the other main biodiversity groups, requested further protection from transport developments for important wildlife sites in our response to the "Great Debate" on transport. However, the Green Paper was actually less strong on site protection than previous government statements. Co-ordinated work from the NGO and quango communities is now seen as necessary to push better protection for biodiversity higher up the agenda for the Department of Transport and the Highways Agency.

***The economic impact of motorways in the peripheral regions of the European Union: a literature survey.* EURES for RSPB/BirdLife International. 1996.**

Summary

1. As part of its work for the BI Transport Group, the RSPB commissioned this study from the Institute for Regional Studies in Europe (EURES). This examines the relationship between transport infrastructure development and regional economic growth, especially in Objective 1 regions.

2. The report reviews the literature, criticises the main theoretical arguments used to support road building as a key to regional development (a case study in Spain is used to support EURES's arguments) and suggests alternative assessment tools and indicators for a better evaluation of infrastructure's contribution to economic growth.

3. The key message is that governments and the European Union are locked into a pattern of thinking which sees motorway building as the solution to many problems. The result of such major investments (a kilometre of motorway costs around 8 million ECU) is, all too often, serious and irreversible damage to nature conservation sites and uncertain economic benefits.

4. A sad current example is the development of the A20 motorway in Germany which threatens at least two Important Bird Areas/Special Protection Areas and so requires an Opinion by the European Commission, according to the EU Habitats & Species Directive. The Commission has given its go-ahead to the motorway on the basis that it crosses the Objective 1 area of Mecklenburg-

Vorpommern which will, as a result of improved infrastructure, receive "a boost to the economy". The Commission also points out that the A20 is a section of the Trans-European Networks (TENs).

5. Key findings of the work include:

-   Development theories which favour improved transport links fail to ask the question of what kind of development it is that the peripheral region needs most (eg perhaps training, rather than new roads).

-   There is evidence that new roads can have negative economic impacts, contributing to emigration and economic decline.

-   There is an urgent need to promote a more local approach to constraints to development ("bottlenecks") and a region's potential for growth (for example, its natural assets).

-   Cost-benefit analysis lacks the necessary comprehensiveness to assess the contribution of transport to regional development.

-   More comprehensive analytical tools are suggested, which would be needed to show what a region really needs, and what the real contribution of motorways is to employment.

6. Finally, the report identifies a series of indicators to assess the impacts of roads on less developed regions. These should be helpful to staff of RSPB and other BI Partner Organisations involved in transport-related casework.

Comment

In the UK, the debate about the economic benefits of building new roads has become more intense as a result of the poor state of the public purse. The economic case for building new roads has been increasingly questioned by the Treasury. Our literature review, case studies and recommendations are intended to help apply this kind of stringent thinking to more peripheral parts of Europe. In these areas, not only is there some of the most important remaining biodiversity but there is also some rather loose thinking about the benefits that high-speed links such as motorways and railways can bring.

Birds and wind turbines: RSPB policy and practice. **Briggs, B. 1996.**

Summary

1. The energy sector has adverse impacts on birds and their environment. These must be reduced. The use of renewable forms of energy, such as wind power, can help to make a significant reduction in such impacts. However, the local effects of wind power can be such that they could outweigh the benefits. Wind power developments can lead to habitat loss, disturbance and bird mortality, through collisions with turbines or wires.

2. The RSPB believes that any renewables scheme proposed in or near an area of national or international importance for wildlife should not be given planning permission where it is likely to have adverse environmental impacts on the site.

3. Bureaucratic problems with the administration of the Renewables Orders, the severe lack of information on the impacts of wind farms on bird populations in the UK and the inconsistent approach to monitoring all serve to lessen the potential that wind power offers to reduce some of the problems caused by the energy sector.

4. The conventional energy sector is responsible for various adverse environmental impacts. These include direct site damage when plant is constructed on sites of nature conservation importance, and acid deposition. In addition, the risk of indirect damage to biodiversity is increased as a result of the emission of gases which could lead to climate change.

5. The alternative energy sector can also have adverse environmental impacts. One example is the drowning of estuaries by tidal barrages, another is the possible flooding of important wildlife sites for hydroelectric schemes.

6. The Government signed the Framework Convention on Climate Change, the Convention on Biological Diversity and Agenda 21 at Rio in June 1992. International commitments made under these conventions, such as reducing carbon dioxide (CO_2) emissions and conserving biodiversity, must be compatible with energy policy decisions, such as the promotion of renewable energy technologies.

7. Shifts in energy policy and operations are needed to reduce adverse environmental impacts. Such shifts should not in themselves have accidental by-products which cause further environmental degradation. The management of demand and in particular increasing energy efficiencies offers the most cost-effective method of reducing environmental impacts without side-effects. However, renewable energy technologies can play an important rôle in reducing adverse environmental impacts of energy supply.

8. For this reason the RSPB supports the shift towards renewable energy technologies. However, it is clear that the biodiversity impacts of some renewables schemes outweigh their environmental benefits, particularly in relation to tidal power.

9. Wind power has detrimental impacts on biodiversity which can include habitat loss, disturbance and bird mortality. Habitat loss could occur as a result of opening up an area to development that had not previously been accessible. Disturbance includes human presence and the noise of the turbines themselves during construction, operation and maintenance of the wind farm. Bird mortality can involve the turbines, their support towers and any power lines included in the development. This paper summarises evidence of each of these effects.

10. These impacts can be minimised by sensitive siting and design, and we make a number of recommendations in this regard.

11. Hundreds of sites across the UK have been proposed for wind farm development. Many of these sites are unsuitable for a number of reasons, ecological and otherwise. The guidelines to developers, and the funding mechanisms that promote so many schemes are not weeding out the most obvious problem schemes at an early enough stage.

12. In many cases, the simple availability of environmental sensitivity information would be enough. In addition, some form of strategic assessment which could point out the relationship between different proposals in the same area and their potential cumulative effects is urgently needed.

13. Individual wind farm proposals should be accompanied by a comprehensive environmental statement and an environmental monitoring system should be designed for each project.

Comment

The energy sector has many environmental impacts, many of which pose serious threats to biodiversity. The RSPB has set out an overview of these impacts and the policies that could reduce them in *"The Vital Spark: the RSPB's policy on energy and biodiversity"* (1994). A particular threat is that of climate change, addressed in a paper prepared for the RSPB in 1994 on the implications of global climate change for biodiversity.

The intense debate on wind farms across the UK has largely focused on the landscape impacts of such developments. The RSPB has had to maintain a very clear line in the arguments, based on scientific research. The paper summarised here was given as a presentation to the Institute of Terrestrial Ecology Conference on "Birds and wind turbines: can they co-exist?" on 26 March 1996, and it enabled the RSPB to position itself very clearly on the specific issue of the impacts of wind farms on birds. It has made our views clear to developers and ensures that all RSPB staff working on these issues are able to find relevant literature and appropriate recommendations in a single document.

Chapter 15

TRADE, EMPLOYMENT AND STRUCTURAL FUNDS

Probably no environmental policy can be divorced from some aspect of economics and the RSPB's staff includes full time economists. Items in Chapter 12, among others, show the significance of world markets as ultimate determinants of much that drives landuse affecting conservation. This is developed further in the contribution here on world trade. Conservation objectives are often portrayed as conflicting with economic development and employment objectives: other items here show instead, in one case, that what is good for conservation can be good for employment, and in another, that bad environmental management can be a result of bad economics. The item on economic appraisal of Spanish water management in this Chapter links with the item on environmental appraisal of hydrological planning in Spain in Chapter 5.

World trade and environment: **submission to the House of Commons Environment Select Committee inquiry into world trade and the environment. RSPB. February 1996.**

Summary

1. Changes in land-use patterns and practices are identified as the major cause of losses in wildlife richness around the world. Equally, certain land-use patterns and practices are necessary to conserve biodiversity. This is particularly well documented for birds. Implementation of trade agreements is certain to have effects on landuse in many countries.

2. In this context, this paper outlines some causes of serious concern for biodiversity conservation arising from the implementation of the GATT agreement in 1994 and the activities of the World Trade Organisation (WTO).

3. As the largest trade bloc, the European Union, and therefore the UK, has a special rôle to ensure that international trade and environment policies are mutually supportive. To date, EU trade policies have done little to address environmental concerns. EU

and global level changes are needed to ensure that trade agreements support biodiversity conservation and sustainable development.

4. The UK Government should in our view take a leading rôle on these matters, urging the EU to promote the changes we recommend in this submission. The report which the WTO Committee on Trade and Environment (WTO/CTE) submits to the Singapore Conference (late 1996) will be crucially important.

5. At present the WTO/CTE, the United Nations Conference on Trade and Development (UNCTAD) and the UNited Nations Environmental Programme (UNEP) seem to be underestimating the importance of land use changes, and their impact on biodiversity, in the trade and environment debate. We recommend that these institutions should examine how trade in certain commodities will affect patterns of land use and the species and habitats that depend on them.

6. The UN institutions should also consider mechanisms to maintain the viability of land-use practices which benefit biodiversity where such practices are under threat as a result of trade policies. They should complement their current work on timber and fisheries by examining the possible linking of agricultural commodity agreements to environmental funding under the Global Environment Facility (GEF) and to aid policies.

7. GATT '94 allows environmental issues to impinge on trade considerations to only a limited degree. The UK and EU should put forward an amendment to create a presumption of compatibility with Multilateral Environmental Agreements (MEAs). Such a measure already exists in the North American Free Trade Agreement (NAFTA) which specifically allows that, in most cases where conflicts arise between its own provisions and those of the Convention on Biological Diversity, the latter shall prevail.

8. On subsidies, while we believe all direct and indirect subsidies which cause environmental degradation or threaten biodiversity should eventually be removed, care is needed in doing so to avoid perverse effects. Where subsidies are retained, they should serve environmental objectives, cross-compliance being used to ensure this.

9. The environmental impacts of trade liberalisation are said (by WTO and others) to be dealt with by a combination of legislation

and environmental costs being "internalised" in product prices. We believe that there is a need to demonstrate that this can work, particularly for agricultural commodities which are important to conservation. Studies of the mechanisms by which internalisation can happen (regulation, taxes, incentives, subsidies, etc) are needed to demonstrate the feasibility of the approach. Until this is satisfactorily concluded, there is no reason to believe that the adverse effects of trade changes can be dealt with by internalisation.

10. The working methods of the WTO need improvement. For example, it should clarify non governmental organisation involvement and transparency.

11. European trade agreements are also extremely important. The land-use consequences of changing trade arrangements in Central and Eastern Europe and their effects on biodiversity need careful study. The EU should integrate the Environmental Programme for Europe, the Environmental Action Programme for Central and Eastern Europe and the Pan-European Biological and Landscape Diversity Strategy into the Association and Accession Agreements with countries in Central and Eastern Europe.

12. An environmental clause should be added in to the revised EU General System of Preferences (GSP) for agriculture products, expected to be approved in 1996. The clause should include additional preferential conditions for countries which implement the Convention on Biological Diversity, as well as withdrawal of preferences from countries whose production of agricultural commodities in the GSP cause biodiversity losses.

13. Procedures are needed to assess the environmental impact of EU trade agreements with third countries or groups of countries. An environment clause should be included in all such agreements, the details depending on assessed impacts.

14. Finally, we believe that the trade in wildlife, including wild birds, continues to be a serious conservation problem, for which EU and global controls are not working adequately. New approaches to promote sustainable resource exploitation whilst penalising trade which is not sustainable should be considered.

Comment

This submission was used and cited by various policy-makers in the UK, EU and farther afield, in preparation for the WTO conference in

Singapore in autumn 1996. At the time of writing, it is regarded as one of the few clear statements in existence on the links between trade policy and land-use changes affecting biodiversity.

Nature conservation, employment and local economies: a literature review. **Rayment, M. 1995.**

Summary

1. Growing concern about the conservation of species and habitats, at a time of high rural unemployment, has focused attention on the employment potential and local economic impact of nature conservation policies. The RSPB has a leading rôle to play in this debate. RSPB reserves make a substantial contribution to local economies, by providing income and employment for people, and by attracting visitors to rural areas. In addition, the RSPB is concerned with the employment impacts of policies which it advocates in the wider countryside, including agricultural reform, environmentally sensitive farming, woodland management and protection and restoration of habitats.

2. This report presents the findings of the first stage of a study examining the employment and local economic impacts of nature conservation. It reviews the available literature regarding the impact of nature conservation on local economies, including work completed by the RSPB and other organisations. It also examines the local economic impact of forestry and agriculture and the impact of nature conservation policies on employment in these sectors. This enables some preliminary conclusions to be drawn about the rôle of nature conservation in the rural economy.

3. Nature conservation is a significant and growing sector of the economy. Its exact size depends on how it is defined, but it has been estimated that nature and landscape conservation provided direct employment amounting to 8,700 full-time equivalent jobs in England and Wales in 1991-92. However, it is clear that direct employment and expenditure represent only a small proportion of the overall economic impact of nature conservation, with typical estimates being that conservation supports four to six times as many jobs by attracting visitors to rural areas than it employs directly. In addition, further employment is supported in peripheral activities such as museums, zoos, manufacture of optical goods and publishing.

4. At a local level, the importance of nature conservation is even more marked. Areas such as the Highlands and Islands of Scotland, and "kite country" in mid-Wales, receive considerable economic benefits through the management of land for wildlife and the visitors which this attracts. In the Highland region, nature conservation now provides more jobs than skiing or sawmilling, and nearly as many as fish farming. However, conservation work often requires specialist skills and experience which are not always available among local people. There is therefore scope to increase the local employment impact of conservation measures through enhanced training.

5. Expenditures by visitors to nature conservation sites account for a large proportion of the impact of nature conservation on the local economy, particularly in areas where visitor rates are high. Expenditure by visitors to RSPB reserves alone was estimated to total £7.7 million as long ago as 1989, while a more recent study has estimated that expenditures by non Scottish visitors to Scottish wildlife sites support 1,200 jobs. At a local level, wildlife is often responsible for generating a significant proportion of tourist revenues. Visits to nature reserves are less concentrated in the summer months than are other types of tourism and they can therefore play a valuable rôle in extending the tourist season.

6. Expenditures by holidaymakers are significantly higher than those by day-trippers. Spending per visit is highest for more remote sites where difficulty of access makes average stays longer and raises transport costs. There is a strong case for promoting the use of nature conservation sites as part of longer visits to an area rather than day-trips, in order to maximise the local economic benefits while reducing the environmental impact of travelling to sites.

7. The local economic impact of wildlife tourism depends on the number of visitors, the size and pattern of their expenditure and the extent to which the local economy is able to provide the goods and services which they require. Enhanced visitor management has the potential to promote this externality further, and improved provision of goods and services matched to visitor needs may increase the proportion of trip expenditures spent locally.

8. The extent to which injections of expenditure are retained in the local economy, and hence the multiplier effect, depends to a large degree on the size of the economy being considered. The more narrowly

the local economy is defined, the higher the leakages and the lower the multiplier. For instance, the total employment effect resulting from expenditures by visitors to Orkney will be greater in the Scottish economy as a whole than in the Orcadian economy itself.

9. Smaller accommodation establishments tend to generate higher multipliers than hotels, because a greater proportion of expenditure is on locally sourced goods and services. Rural locations tend to have a higher multiplier effect, as poorer communications reduce leakages from the local economy. Green tourism is often more embedded in the local economy, respecting local traditions, using local produce and employing local people and therefore often produces a large local multiplier effect.

10. Rural employment is often difficult to quantify for a number of reasons: the prevalence of self-employment (particularly in agriculture), the importance of part-time, seasonal, casual and contracted labour, the upstream and downstream employment impacts and the fluctuations in labour requirements over time (especially for forestry). This is why rural employment estimates are usually standardised and expressed in terms of fulltime equivalent (FTE) jobs.

11. Though declining, agriculture remains the dominant source of rural employment in many parts of the UK, supporting close to 500,000 FTE jobs, compared to 20,000 direct forestry jobs and perhaps 10,000-20,000 jobs in nature conservation, the latter figure being dependent on how the nature conservation sector is defined. The substantial decline in the agricultural labour force has created a need to identify alternative rural employment opportunities.

12. The intensity of use of labour varies considerably in different parts of the UK, with Scotland using less labour per hectare of land than England and Wales, in each of forestry, agriculture and nature conservation. Nature conservation, while a significant employer, is less labour intensive in terms of direct employment than most forms of lowland agriculture and productive forestry, being comparable in employment intensity to upland agriculture, sporting estates and immature forestry.

13. However, direct employment effects represent only a proportion of the total employment impact in each case. Forestry and agriculture support significant timber and food processing industries, while the principal indirect impact of nature conservation is

through expenditures by visitors to nature conservation sites. When the indirect effects of visitors on rural economies are considered, the local employment benefits of devoting land to nature conservation increase significantly.

14. Several studies have noted the long-term cycle involved in the creation of forestry employment. While planting creates some jobs, the bulk of forestry employment is generated in the harvesting phase. Jobs in timber processing are also concentrated at the end of the rotation. Therefore examination of existing forestry employment levels, which are increasing as the UK forestry stock matures, does not give an accurate picture of the employment effects of new afforestation projects. In contrast to agriculture, these increases in employment are sufficient to offset gains in productivity. Both agriculture and sporting estates have suffered continuing long-term declines in employment since the Second World War.

15. The figures in the report indicate the considerable variation in the intensity of management of different agricultural systems. This is also true for nature conservation, with some habitats being managed more intensively and requiring higher levels of employment and expenditure than others.

16. The level of expenditure per hectare tends to be much higher in agriculture than in nature conservation, although much of this expenditure relates to inputs which are not sourced locally, such as machinery and chemicals, so there is a large leakage from the local economy. Considerable variation in levels of input expenditure are also apparent, depending on the type of farm.

17. Comparison of expenditures on RSPB forestry reserves with those of the Forestry Commission on its estate reveal that expenditures per hectare tend to be slightly higher in managing woodland for nature conservation.

18. Studies have shown that the "greening" of agriculture has potential to generate rural employment. Organic farming is recognised to be more labour intensive than conventional agricultural systems and there is some evidence that processing of organic produce also offers employment benefits. In contrast, set-aside, which has some benefits for wildlife, has reduced labour requirements in arable areas.

19. ESA schemes have been shown to create employment in several areas. The scale of employment benefits depends on the design of the scheme and particularly the extent to which payments are made for conservation tasks rather than compensating farmers for not damaging habitats. These conservation tasks often require traditional skills such as hedging, dry-stone walling, shepherding and heather burning, which are often undertaken by contracted labour. The local employment benefit can be enhanced by provision of training to the local workforce in appropriate conservation skills. Although evidence is more limited, it appears that Countryside Stewardship, Tir Cymen and National Park farm schemes have also created employment, particularly by supporting capital expenditures.

20. As the debate about the future of the Common Agricultural Policy focuses on the objectives of agricultural support, and the need for subsidies to be justified on the basis of social and environmental benefits, the conservation and employment impacts of agricultural policies will come under increasing scrutiny.

21. Afforestation has also been identified by several studies as a means of diversifying rural employment opportunities. However, since most employment is associated with the harvesting of timber, new planting takes a long time to generate significant and sustainable levels of employment. There is evidence that planting broadleaved woodland requires significantly greater labour inputs than coniferous afforestation.

22. This literature review has demonstrated that nature conservation supports significant levels of income and employment. Many of these jobs are located in rural areas where rising agricultural productivity has led to increasing levels of unemployment and where alternative employment opportunities are scarce. Nature conservation and its ability to attract visitors to rural areas has an important rôle to play in aiding the diversification of rural economies which itself is necessary to reverse the adverse effects resulting from over reliance on traditional, declining industries such as agriculture.

23. Despite this evidence, conservation is often seen as a constraint to rural development, by taking land out of alternative uses such as agriculture or commercial forestry, or by reducing the productive potential of these activities. One of the reasons for this misconception has been the failure of conservation organisations to

publicise the benefits which conservation can bring to local economies as well as publicising the intrinsic benefits of biodiversity.
Highlighting the economic impact of nature conservation should
help to increase its popularity and to overcome resistance to further
conservation measures. In North America, the economic importance of wildlife-related recreation is more widely recognised and
has been used to support arguments for furthering conservation
policy.

Comment

Nature conservation is often seen as a constraint to economic
development and job creation and this argument is often used in
opposition to conservation policies and projects. However, the RSPB
has recognised for some time that conservation activities can, directly and indirectly, bring significant economic and employment
benefits. A series of RSPB studies in recent years has examined the
contribution which conservation and related tourism bring to economies in areas including Orkney, Islay and Jura, Speyside and mid-
Wales. The literature review brought together evidence on this subject resulting from research by the RSPB and others.

This has enabled the RSPB to position itself in the growing debate on environment and employment. As well as raising awareness of these issues among policy-makers and the public, studies
such as this help us to develop economic arguments in support of
conservation policies and provide evidence in support of applications for funding for conservation projects from economic development budgets. The literature review represented the first stage of a
three-year study examining the impacts of conservation policies and
activities on local economies. It is being followed up by a series of
case studies examining the rôle of conservation in individual local
economies and drawing lessons from this for policy.

The Structural Funds and biodiversity conservation. **RSPB/ BirdLife International. 1995.**

Summary

1. This document examines the implications for biodiversity (ie
the diversity of wildlife habitats and species) of the European Union (EU) Structural Funds in the period up to 1999. It focuses on
Objective 1 regions in Spain, Greece and Italy. Together, these receive

39% of total Structural Fund expenditure and have some of the most outstanding wildlife and habitats in the EU. The report also looks critically at whether certain Fund projects genuinely yield economic benefits and represent wise use of taxpayers' money. This report does not deal with the Cohesion Fund, except in passing.

2. At present the Funds tend to reinforce prevailing development models, underpinning Member States' existing approaches and magnifying their environmental impacts. The Funds' influence on the nature of development, as opposed to the "amount" of such development, is limited. But biodiversity conservation, meaningful local economic development and efficient use of EU budget resources, require that these models and approaches change.

3. Some of the policy changes needed to influence these models cannot be brought about through the Funds e.g. the introduction of a CO_2/energy tax. The strategy proposed in this document takes three approaches to encourage change in those areas over which the Funds do have an influence:

(i)   establishing the right institutional mechanism at all levels (EU, national, regional), including a review of the Fund Regulations;

(ii)   maximising the potential of the existing Fund system by promoting more thorough environmental assessment, disseminating "best practice", developing the capacity of local environmental authorities and ensuring that environmental provisions in the current Fund Regulations work effectively; and

(iii)   improving economic appraisal and exploring the replacement of some grants with loans.

4. BirdLife International's main proposals are to:

-     ensure rigorous enforcement of EU environmental legislation;

-     establish a Commission Task Force on Regional/Rural Development and Biodiversity to co-ordinate a new strategic approach;

- develop creative new ways of integrating rural development and biodiversity conservation;

- revise the Structural Fund Regulations to allow explicitly
  for nature conservation;

- investigate whether the Funds are generating real economic
  benefits and encourage a much more rigorous approach to
  economic appraisal in the Funds; and

- consider introducing loans instead of grants for certain
  development projects.

5. The 1993 Structural Fund Regulations include new environmental protection provisions. In the negotiations on the new Community Support Frameworks (CSFs) and Operational Programmes
(OPs), the Commission was able to use these provisions to seek more
environmental information and assessment from Member States
than was possible in the last round of negotiations in 1988-89.

6. Nevertheless, BI's analysis suggests that less importance was
attached to nature conservation than to issues such as water and
waste treatment. The CSFs and OPs studied in this report do not
demonstrate a thorough understanding of the relationships between
nature conservation and key sectors of the regional/rural economy
such as agriculture and tourism.

7. The CSFs and OPs studied here include proposals for many
programmes and projects which could damage important nature
conservation sites and cause wider environmental damage.

8. Recent decisions in the cases of the A20 motorway in Germany
and the Tejo bridge in Portugal give cause for serious concern about
the willingness of the EU Commission and Member States to up-
hold EU environmental law firmly throughout the EU.

9. EU governments are looking to the Structural Funds to provide resources to help implement the Habitats Directive. Opportunities to co-ordinate the use of the Funds to benefit both conservation and regional/rural economies have already been missed. If
remaining opportunities are to be exploited, a much more dynamic,
co-ordinated approach is required at all levels: Commission/Coun-
cil, national and regional/local.

10. The Fund Regulations and operational criteria should be reviewed to maximise their ability to contribute to biodiversity conservation and environmentally sustainable development more generally. We make some specific recommendations in this regard.

11. National and regional environmental authorities bear the brunt of responsibility for ensuring that the implementation of EU-funded programmes is environmentally sensitive. These authorities need substantial support and guidance in this task. We make further detailed recommendations on this aspect.

12. The Structural Fund Regulations require that Fund-supported investment should achieve "economic and social benefits commensurate with the resources deployed". There are serious grounds for doubting whether certain Fund projects satisfy this requirement. For example, public subsidies are included in economic appraisal calculations for irrigation in Spain, which is inconsistent with the Commission's "best practice" guidance. The Commission does not examine Member States' project appraisal procedures. It has never evaluated the economic performance of past EU-funded irrigation. We make further recommendations on assuring the achievement of economic and social benefits.

13. Replacing certain EU grants with loans would create stronger incentives for realistic economic appraisal of projects which are capable of generating revenue to cover their costs. This could also help to internalise environmental costs and reduce consumption of resources such as water and energy. If EU enlargement continues, budget pressures are likely to make this option attractive to "donor" Member States.

14. Overall, there are serious doubts as to whether the Structural Funds can fulfil their own environmental and economic objectives consistently throughout the EU. It is time for a new approach. Authorities and institutions at all levels must be involved. "Greening" the Structural Funds must be at the top of the political agenda.

Comment

Between 1994 and 1999 the EU Structural Funds will have spent over 140 billion ECU (£120 billion) promoting economic development in the EU's least prosperous regions. Many of these regions also retain outstanding wildlife and habitats. Experience of the previous round of Fund spending (1988-1994) showed that the pressure to absorb large volumes of funds, sometimes in countries with weak environmental safeguards, can lead to environmental damage. This paper presents the findings of analysis by BI of the plans for spending EU funds between 1994-1999. These plans were prepared according to EU legislation passed in 1993 which included new environmental provisions advocated by BI and other environmental NGOs. The paper therefore examines the effectiveness of these provisions.

It was known that while this paper was being drafted the European Commission was preparing a Communication (policy paper) on the Structural Funds and the environment. The draft BI paper was given to and discussed with key Commission officials involved in this process. Leaflets containing the summary and recommendations were produced in French, German, Spanish, Italian and Greek. The final Commission Communication on Cohesion Policy and the Environment, issued by Commissioners Monika Wulf-Mathies (Regional Policy) and Ritt Bjerregaard (Environment) in November 1995, reflected many of the points made in the BI paper.

Economic appraisal and European Union funds: a study of water management and irrigation in Spain. **RSPB/SEO BirdLife España. 1995.**

Summary

1. Analysis by the Sociedad Española de Ornitología (SEO/ BirdLife España) has shown that irrigation and water management constitute one of the greatest threats to nature conservation in Spain. The introduction of irrigation to dry farming areas transforms ecosystems which are some of the most important in the whole of Europe for nature conservation. The direct environmental impacts of the projects needed to supply water for irrigation, as well as the indirect impacts on wetlands, are substantial.

2. Moreover, serious doubts have been raised concerning the economic viability of some of the proposed irrigation schemes. The rising cost of the construction works needed, and changes in European Union (EU) agricultural policy and global agricultural markets, necessitate a review of irrigation plans, which in some cases date from the early part of the century.

3. Against this background, BI commissioned this study of the economic viability of two specific irrigation projects in Spain and of irrigation policy more generally. The study, by a team of agricultural economists from the Universitat Autónoma de Barcelona, examines two proposed irrigation projects in Spain Monegros II in Aragón and La Sagra-Torrijos in Castilla-La Mancha analysing the economic appraisal processes used and the likely private economic benefits of the schemes. Conclusions are drawn for economic appraisal both for these schemes and others in Spain. We make 12 main recommendations for further action at Spanish and European levels.

4. This report combines a summary of the consultants' report with a discussion of the issues arising. This discussion is set in the context of EU regional and rural development policy. Both the schemes studied are receiving EU funding. The Community Support Framework for regional development funds agreed between the European Commission and the Spanish authorities in 1994 allocates 2 billion ECU of public funds to water management and 3.1 billion ECU to agriculture and rural development. If the strategies outlined in the Community Support Framework and the Plan Hidrológico Nacional are followed, a significant proportion of these sums will be spent on irrigation and the related water supply. It is therefore important to ensure that the EU Regulations' requirement for "medium-term economic and social benefits commensurate with the resources deployed" is met.

5. A further section of the report contains recommendations by BI on irrigation in Spain (incorporating the consultants' recommendations) and the European Commission's approach to it. Part II consists of the consultants' report in full.

6. The process of planning irrigation in Spain assumes that the introduction of irrigation will be "in the national interest". The planning system is lengthy, complex and time-consuming. Many years can elapse between the initial declaration that a scheme is "in the national interest" and the actual start of irrigated farming. These delays make it extremely difficult to respond to rapidly changing agricultural markets and to incorporate realistic economic appraisal. The system is also highly authoritarian, allowing farmers themselves little involvement or influence.

7. The objective of the planning process is to create farms that will be financially viable. The introduction of irrigation is heavily subsidised by

public funds (EU and Spanish). Farmers repay only a small proportion of the construction and operating costs of the various works needed, on very favourable terms. The precise level of charges to farmers is adjusted to ensure that farms are profitable. Cost recovery terms (water pricing levels, etc) are decided for each scheme individually. There is no standard method. The 1985 Water Law introduces the possibility of realistic cost recovery for water. At present, however, neither methods for calculating and imposing appropriate charges nor the necessary political will are available.

8. Overall, it is estimated that Spanish farmers on average pay only 10-20% of the real cost of irrigation and that most irrigated farms would be unprofitable if they had to pay the full cost. This is contrary to the European Commission's guidance on economic appraisal for "major projects" under the Structural Funds.

9. The calculation of farmers' incomes from new crops includes current CAP subsidies. This gives a false impression of future income, since it is likely that subsidy levels will decline. It is also inconsistent with the Commission's economic appraisal guidance, referred to above. Thus two levels of public subsidy on both the cost and benefit sides are built into the Spanish calculations. The "new" plans also fail to take account of the failure of similar irrigation schemes in the past in areas with similar characteristics.

10. The consultants' report investigates three scenarios for the two irrigation schemes studied, under different water-pricing and cost-recovery terms. The results show that gross margins for the crops proposed for the schemes are highly sensitive to increases in water-related costs. If farmers had to pay the full cost of irrigation even at low interest rates and over long repayment periods gross margins for many crops would be negative.

11. For crops which may appear to have better margins, other factors nevertheless seriously limit the scope for them. These include soil quality; climate; farmers' lack of skills in irrigated farming and water management and the failure to include appropriate training in irrigation plans; the high average age of farmers in the areas concerned; and the nature of the local economy (such as the existence of a food-processing industry and closeness to markets).

12. Appraisal of irrigation in Spain concentrates on financial benefits to the individual farmer, manipulating the financial régime of

the farm until profitability is achieved. Even under these circumstances our research shows that there is no guarantee of success. The Spanish irrigation planning system does not consider with any rigour the broader concept of economic, or social benefit. Experience shows that irrigation has not succeeded in arresting rural depopulation.

13. Crucially, there is no appraisal in Spain of whether alternative ways of investing the large sums of public funds involved would yield greater benefits for society as a whole. This is again contrary to the European Commission's economic appraisal guidance. Option analysis is a central concept in the Commission's recommended approach.

14. Under the subsidiarity and "partnership" principles of the Structural Fund system, economic appraisal of projects within Operational Programmes is the responsibility of the Member State. The Commission does not scrutinise these projects individually, or "approve" them. The Commission has confirmed that it has not investigated the appraisal methods applied to irrigation projects.

15. The Commission's efforts to coordinate economic evaluation techniques and to disseminate "best practice" focus on programmes rather than projects. Yet it is obvious that if project-level techniques are flawed, programme-level evaluations derived from them will be seriously misleading. To compound this, the Commission has never conducted an evaluation of the economic benefits of past EU-funded irrigation programmes. It therefore has little basis for judgements on the appropriateness of future schemes.

16. There must therefore be serious doubts as to the ability of either the Commission or the Spanish Government to guarantee that EU funds will be used in ways that generate the greatest socio-economic benefits for the minimum public investment. This is unavoidably a source of serious concern to the EU taxpayer, and should constitute grounds for an investigation by the Court of Auditors.

17. Claimed water demand figures should be interpreted with extreme caution. The heavily subsidised water pricing policies create powerful incentives for profligate use of water. Water demand forecasts in irrigation plans are frequently far in excess of actual water consumption levels in comparable schemes. Moreover, water demand forecasts in Spain assume that water losses from the distribution network will be 40%.

18. These and other factors call into question the economic efficiency of building dams associated with irrigation schemes and a water transfer policy aimed at meeting claimed water demands. Water policy in general and irrigation policy in particular are continuing to pursue the "developmentalist" path of the 1970s. There is a need to abandon the current commitment to irrigation as the primary instrument of rural development in Spain and to find alternative ways of maintaining and creating jobs and prosperity in rural areas.

19. A response to this challenge should include:

- transferring regional/rural development resources from irrigation and water supply schemes to support for low-intensity, environmentally-sensitive farming systems such as those of the Spanish steppes;

- limited new irrigation where real benefits can be shown;

- local training, marketing and processing initiatives to support both traditional and "new" agriculture;

- appropriate afforestation;

- sustainably managed rural and "nature" tourism; and

- enhanced efforts to stimulate other local employment.

Far greater socio economic research and demonstration is needed in these areas.

Comment

This report prompted considerable reaction both in Spain and within the European Commission. Despite severe criticism of its findings from some quarters, the Spanish Ministry of Agriculture drew on the report to underpin its opposition to large-scale irrigation plans by the Ministry of Public Works. At a European level, new conditions on EU funding for irrigation have since been introduced, partly on the strength of this report.

Chapter 16

LICENSED BIRD KILLING

M uch of what has been covered in preceding chapters deals with laws, policies and decisions which affect the use of land, habitats and natural resources. The selection of topics from the period in question possibly underplays the importance of complementary fields of policy which are more to do with the management of species populations and protection of individuals of those populations from exploitation or persecution. This final Chapter looks at some of these latter aspects. In doing so, it also sheds light on two issues of principle which can affect any part of the conservation agenda: access to information, and access to justice.

Wildlife and Countryside Act 1981: **Comments to the Department of the Environment on proposed amendments to Sections 4 and 16 of the Wildlife and Countryside Act 1981. RSPB. September 1995.**

Summary

1. In general the RSPB welcomes the Government's proposals on these provisions for amending the licensing régime, and the draft statutory instrument, as a positive attempt to rectify deficiencies in the transposition of the EU Wild Birds Directive into the Wildlife and Countryside Act 1981.

2. The use of the phrase "inland waters", with definitions which then include waters which are not inland, is at best inelegant. We suggest referring instead to "relevant waters" and then giving a full set of definitions of what is relevant.

3. Addition of "waters" raises a question of who would be the most appropriate licensing authority. As the amendment is currently drafted, licensing responsibilities would fall to the Agriculture Minister. However, where the potential damage relates to potable waters or to wetland SSSIs, the relevant authority might instead be the Environment Minister, or the Environment Agency, or the relevant statutory conservation agency, depending on the case. This needs to be clarified.

4. We propose an amendment to underline the fact that the processes of demonstrating the necessity of action and demonstrating the absence of other satisfactory solutions are separate.

5. We strongly support the wording which does not allow the specified defence if it had or should have become apparent that action was necessary. Technically, the Directive does not allow such a defence at all but we accept that genuinely unforeseen circumstances may require a more pragmatic approach.

6. We argue that use of the word "protect" instead of "conserve" may be more likely to lead to pressure for licensed control of predators because of effects on individual animals, rather than providing for maintenance of populations at favourable conservation status.

7. Some of the requirements of Article 9 of the Directive in respect of conditions to be met in relation to licences are incorporated in the draft instrument, but reference to "under strictly supervised conditions" and reference to specification of the limits on the numbers of birds which may be killed have both been omitted. These aspects should be added in.

Comment

The consultation document on amendments to the Wildlife and Countryside Act 1981 was issued by Government, following the securing of leave by the RSPB to take a decision by the Minister for Agriculture, Fisheries and Food to Judicial Review. The decision in question was the granting of licences under the Act to shoot goosanders and cormorants on the River Wye, Herefordshire. The RSPB's case was based on claims that the consultation arrangements between MAFF and English Nature (EN) were inadequate; that the Act did not adequately transpose the requirements of the EU Wild Birds Directive into UK law; and that MAFF's failure to supply certain information regarding these licences was contrary to the Environmental Information Regulations 1992.

The consultation document was issued to address the second of these issues. The first was addressed by MAFF revising their arrangements with EN. The third issue on environmental information was not resolved and was the subject of an RSPB submission to a House of Lords inquiry, covered elsewhere in this Chapter.

The Judicial Review arose out of concerns that MAFF were relaxing their policy on the licensed shooting of fish-eating birds. It was also pursued as a positive move to clarify the transposition of European law generally in the UK. The Wildlife and Countryside Act 1981 (Amendment) Regulations came into force on 30 November 1995. RSPB's most significant concern about the use of the word "conserve" rather than "protect" (point 6 above) was catered for in the final Regulations, which RSPB welcomed. This enabled the Wye Judicial Review, which had been put on hold pending the amendment of the Act, to be settled without going to Court.

***Freedom of access to information on the environment:* submission to House of Lords European Communities Committee Sub-Committee C (environment, public health and education) inquiry into freedom of access to information on the environment. RSPB. February 1996.**

Summary

1. The RSPB supports the principles behind the EU Directive on the Freedom of Access to Information on the Environment, and the Regulations which give effect to it in the UK. In view of public interest in the environment and the benefits to environmental protection that can be gained from public access to environmental information, there should be a presumption in favour of open access to information. Exemptions to this should be limited and properly justified. This we believe to be important if the principles of open government are to be upheld and if the general public are to have faith in the decision-making process.

2. The RSPB considers, from recent experience, that the approach to freedom of access to information on the environment of the Ministry of Agriculture, Fisheries and Food has broken both the spirit and letter of the EU Directive and runs counter to the Department of the Environment's published guidance.

3. Subsequent legal guidance to Government has resulted in a much more restrictive interpretation of the Directive and Regulations than we believe was intended by the legislation. Our reasons for this view are set out in this evidence, which describes our work in relation to a specific case relating to release of information regarding licensed killing of fish-eating birds on the River Wye, Herefordshire. Failure to obtain information resulted in the RSPB obtaining leave to apply for Judicial Review. Thus this case has wider implications for the release of environmental information in the UK.

4. Under the Wild Birds Directive Member States may derogate from its species protection requirements, where there is no other satisfactory solution, for a number of reasons including prevention of "serious damage to crops, livestock, forests, fisheries and water". Licences to kill birds for the purpose of preventing damage can be granted by the relevant agriculture Minister under the Wildlife and Countryside Act 1981.

5. In 1993 MAFF introduced streamlined application procedures to deliver Citizens Charter standards. Subsequently, an increased number of licences were issued to kill cormorants and goosanders, in the supposed interests of fisheries. The RSPB was concerned that this reflected a relaxation of licensing policy and that licences may have been issued without proper evidence of lack of other solutions or evidence of damage.

6. Our evidence details the sequence of events when RSPB staff attempted to obtain details of licences issued by MAFF to kill protected birds on the River Wye in 1993. Despite RSPB's citing the access to information Regulations, information on the justification for the licences was withheld on the grounds of commercial sensitivity.

7. The RSPB were then given leave in the High Court to take the decision of the Minister for Agriculture to issue the licences to Judicial Review, on the basis that:

-    consultations between MAFF and EN had been inadequate;

-    the Minister did not have power to issue licences as parts of Section 4 and the licensing provisions of Section 16 of the 1981 Act did not transpose the EU Directive adequately; and

-    information about the licences had been withheld, contrary to the Environmental Information Regulations.

8. The RSPB took this case as a positive move to try to clarify some areas of uncertainty and what we believed to be inadequate transposition of the Wild Birds Directive into UK law. Following the obtaining of leave, MAFF and the Department of the Environment indicated they were prepared to recognise the points of principle raised by the case and to address these as part of a voluntary settlement.

9. MAFF announced new consultation arrangements with EN and the DoE brought forward Regulations amending the Act in 1995. With two of the three strands of the original case addressed, the RSPB agreed to withdraw Judicial Review proceedings. The issue of freedom of access to environmental information, however, was not resolved.

10. It was apparent in the Wye case that MAFF had not given any consideration to the implications of the Regulations for release of the class of environmental information at issue. They have subsequently set out what we consider to be a very restrictive position, which appears to be contrary to both the spirit and the letter of the Regulations, in ways detailed in our evidence.

11. The RSPB's difficulties in obtaining evidence of alleged serious damage to fisheries from MAFF has been mirrored by similar difficulties in obtaining specific information in Scotland and Wales.

12. The RSPB believes that it is inappropriate to attempt to invoke the "volunteered information" exception as an excuse for not providing information in support of licence applications, when the information is in reality far from volunteered. The DoE Guidance specifically supports the RSPB's position on this point.

13. It is counter to the Regulations and DoE Guidance for MAFF to indicate (by use of tick-boxes) that it is up to the applicant to decide whether information should be released. We would suggest that the correct approach would be to give the applicant the opportunity to make out a case for confidentiality but even in these circumstances the ultimate decision on information disclosure should rest with MAFF.

14. The RSPB believes that the use of the exemption relating to "commercial confidentiality" requires clarification. We believe commercial information should be withheld only where there is clear evidence that release would be prejudicial to the individual or company concerned.

15. The scope of the "legal proceedings" exception needs to be clarified. Our experience has exposed particular difficulties regarding time limits and we are not satisfied that the Regulations faithfully reflect the requirements of the Directive.

16. Similarly the circumstances under which the use of the "internal communications" exception is appropriate need to be clarified. The RSPB's view is that current interpretation is masking relevant environmental information held by separate agencies that should be disclosable under the Directive.

17. In conclusion, the RSPB considers, from its experience, with MAFF in particular, that the Government's practice is to interpret the rules in a highly restrictive way which produces less openness than the Directive (both in letter and spirit) and the Regulations require and conflicts with the way the Government itself has interpreted those requirements in its own policy guidance.

Comment

The significance of the case detailed here is as a test of the Government's commitment to freedom of information. It is the RSPB's view that they are currently failing in this. At present it would appear that a most restrictive interpretation of the Regulations is being used which is obscuring the basis of licensing decisions from public scrutiny. A supplementary RSPB memorandum of evidence, submitted in April 1996 (the Society did not give oral evidence to this inquiry), rehearsed our experience of attempting to obtain information from European committee processes in relation to proposed amendments of the Wild Birds Directive provisions on bird shooting. We also emphasised points concerning the applicability of the Access to Information Directive to the EU's own institutions, and made comments on moves towards prescribing openness procedures in Codes of Conduct. At the time of writing, the Committee has not yet issued its report.

Killing and taking bullfinches: **Comments to the Ministry of Agriculture, Fisheries and Food on their review of procedures for licensing the killing and taking of bullfinches. RSPB. April 1996.**

Summary

1. The RSPB welcomes this review and considers it most timely. The Society has recently been involved in revising the Red Data List for birds in Britain. There is great concern about the long-term decline in once-familiar farmland birds. The bullfinch has been added to the list of high priority species, because of the severity of the decline in its breeding population.

2. In collaboration with statutory conservation organisations, the RSPB is producing Action Plans for all of the species regarded as of high or medium priority for conservation action and we have recently completed the plan for the bullfinch. Policies are detailed for halting and reversing its decline, involving among other things promotion of bullfinch habitat, alternative crop protection methods, and appropriate approaches to licensing.

3. We feel that the issuing of general licences is no longer appropriate for the bullfinch, both because of the documented large-scale decline in its numbers and the recent grant-aided destruction of orchards. The latter factor indicates that the economic argument for treating bullfinches as "pests" no longer applies.

4. The effect of trapping on bullfinch populations is unknown. Licence returns show only very small numbers of birds being trapped and we cannot believe that the species poses a serious and continuing problem for orchard owners. There is no monitoring of damage or trapping by MAFF.

5. It appears to the RSPB that replacing the general licensing provision with the normal procedures for individual licences, as for other species, should provide sufficient flexibility for fruit producers to kill or take birds when serious damage can be shown. This should not place an undue burden on MAFF/ADAS, now that both the area of orchards and the number of bullfinches is so reduced. It would also send a signal that MAFF/ADAS will be seeking the use of alternative solutions more rigorously than in the past.

Comment

The bullfinch is the only species where a General Licence applies in individual counties and parishes, based on the former presence of orchards. The RSPB considers that this is now anachronistic. The results of the MAFF review are not known at the time of writing.

INDEX

The Royal Society for the Protection of Birds is the charity that takes action for wild birds and the environment. It has joined with bird and habitat conservation organisations worldwide to form the BirdLife International global partnership. The Society's conservation mission is based on the belief that birds and nature enrich people's lives and that nature conservation is fundamental to a healthy environment on which the survival of the human race depends.

The RSPB is Europe's largest wildlife conservation charity, with over 925,000 members. In addition to its UK Headquarters in Bedfordshire, the Society has a Scottish Headquarters in Edinburgh and 11 regional and country offices throughout the UK. It achieves its objectives through the conservation of habitats and species, either by owning and managing land (the Society currently has over 140 nature reserves), or by influencing land-use practices and government policies in order to benefit wildlife and the wider countryside. The RSPB employs over 900 full-time staff, including chartered planners and other specialist staff to advise central government, local authorities and others on nature conservation matters.

UK Headquarters: The Lodge, Sandy, Bedfordshire SG19 2DL.
Scottish Headquarters: 17 Regent Terrace, Edinburgh EH7 5BN.
Northern Ireland Office: Belvoir Park Forest, Belfast BT8 4QT.

Dave Pritchard is a graduate of Durham and London Universities. He began his RSPB career in 1981, doing research for two years before joining the Conservation Planning Department in 1983. Since that time he has been responsible for developing the Society's UK activities on town and country planning policy, site safeguard policy and specific casework. He now manages the RSPB Planning and Local Government Unit which covers these three functions. Publications include the key reference works *Important Bird Areas in the UK* and *Strategic Environmental Assessment*. Dave sits on a wide variety of national steering committees and working groups, and pursues environmental law interests on the international stage, including representing BirdLife International in the Ramsar Convention.

Support Europe's largest charity for wildlife and conservation

Join the RSPB today

Keep in touch on what's happening with one of the UK's key environmental charities and give it your backing.

The RSPB relies almost entirely on voluntary contributions for its support. The contents of this book show that the backing of 925,000 members has enabled it to achieve a great deal, but the problems still facing wildlife mean that there is still a huge amount to do. Please join in the knowledge that you will be helping conservation.

New members receive -

- the quarterly award-winning *Birds* members' magazine, packed with fascinating facts and stunning photography.

- free entrance to more than 100 nature reserves throughout the country.

- a membership pack crammed with information.

Membership Application

Single membership	£22 a year
Joint membership	£27 a year
Family membership	£32 a year (includes two adults and all children under 16 at the same address)

BLOCK CAPITALS PLEASE (and dates of birth where indicated)

Title .... Initials................ Surname(s)...

Title .... Initials................ Surname(s)...

Address...

....

.... Post code ....

Family members (names of children under 16):

.... D.O.B ....

.... D.O.B ....

I enclose a cheque/PO (made payable to RSPB) or debit my ACCESS/VISA account for £ ....

Credit card no. | | | | | | | | | | | | | | | | |

Expiry date............./.............

Cardholder's signature...

Cardholder's name..

Cardholder's address (if different from above):

Address...

....

.... Post code ....

Please return to RSPB, The Lodge, Sandy, Beds SG19 2DL